Rhetoric, Politics and Society

Rhetoric lies at the intersection of a variety of disciplinary approaches and methods, drawing upon the study of language, history, culture and philosophy to understand the persuasive aspects of communication in all its modes: spoken, written, argued, depicted and performed. This series presents the best international research in rhetoric that develops and exemplifies the multifaceted and cross-disciplinary exploration of practices of persuasion and communication. It seeks to publish texts that openly explore and expand rhetorical knowledge and enquiry, be it in the form of historical scholarship, theoretical analysis or contemporary cultural and political critique. The editors welcome proposals for monographs that explore contemporary rhetorical forms, rhetorical theories and thinkers, and rhetorical themes inside and across disciplinary boundaries. For informal enquiries, questions, as well as submitting proposals, please contact the editors: Alan Finlayson: a.finlayson@uea.ac.uk James Martin: j.martin@gold.ac.uk Kendall Phillips: kphillip@syr.edu

Francisco J. Bellido

Constitutional Debates, Rhetoric, and Political Philosophy in Spain's Parliamentary History

palgrave
macmillan

Francisco J. Bellido
Universidade Nova de Lisboa
Málaga, Spain

ISSN 2947-5147 ISSN 2947-5155 (electronic)
Rhetoric, Politics and Society
ISBN 978-3-031-56893-0 ISBN 978-3-031-56894-7 (eBook)
https://doi.org/10.1007/978-3-031-56894-7

Cover illustration: Stefano Politi Markovina/Alamy Stock Photo

This Palgrave Macmillan imprint is published by the registered company Springer Nature Switzerland AG
The registered company address is: Gewerbestrasse 11, 6330 Cham, Switzerland

Paper in this product is recyclable.

Acknowledgments

This book relies, for the 1977–1978 chapters, on my doctoral dissertation 'Democracy in Constituent Moments: A Political-Philosophical Exploration of the 1977–1978 Constitutional Debate in Spain', defended in January 2022 at the University of Málaga, Spain. Upon acceptance by Palgrave Macmillan to include it in its series Rhetoric, Politics and Society, they have been thoroughly revised, and three new chapters have been prepared to cover the nineteenth-century and the other twentieth-century constitutional debates.

I appreciate very much the recommendations by the reviewers and the decision of the editorial board of the book series Rhetoric, Politics and Society. I am especially indebted to Ambra Finotello, who welcomed my book proposal and encouraged me to deliver a revised manuscript suggesting its current title: *Constitutional Debates, Rhetoric, and Political Philosophy in Spain's Parliamentary History*.

My supervisor, José María Rosales, has helped me during the entire process. His careful revision of the draft chapters of this book has been determining. I had not written this book were it not for his continuous support and critical scrutiny. However, I am solely responsible for any mistake that the reader can find.

I am also thankful to the evaluation committee members Manuel Toscano, Maria Marczewska-Rytko and Elena García Guitián; and the substitute committee members, Jussi Kurunmäki, Ana Matan and Marta Postigo, for their acceptance and comments. Likewise, to the external reviewers, Kari Palonen, Gabriella Silvestrini and Emilia Salvanou. Thanks to the PhD scholarship funded by the Spanish Ministry of Education (*Beca de Formación de Profesorado Universitario*, FPU) I was able to pursue my doctoral studies at the University of Málaga.

Besides, my stay at the University of Jyväskylä and the Short-Term Scientific Mission funded by COST Action CA 16211 RECAST allowed me to focus exclusively on research tasks during 2019. I will always be indebted to the doctoral programme of Political Science at the University of Jyväskylä, where I defended a previous doctoral dissertation in 2020, later on published in a revised form (endorsed by Prof. Sir Paul Preston and funded by the research project Civic Constellation III: *Democracy, Constitutionalism, and Anti-Liberalism*) as *Democracy and Sovereignty in Spain: Conceptual Innovation in the Spanish Constituent Assembly of 1931* by Routledge in the series Cañada Blanch Studies on Contemporary Spain.

Both dissertations have been developed in the framework of two research projects, Civic Constellation II: *Debating Democracy and Rights* (FFI2014-52703-P), from 2015 to 2018, and Civic Constellation III: *Democracy, Constitutionalism, and Anti-Liberalism* (PGC2018-093573-BI00), between 2019 and 2022, and of COST Action 16211 *Reappraising Intellectual Debates on Civic Rights and Democracy in Europe* (RECAST), running from 2017 to 2021. Their many research activities, at the intersection of the humanities and the social sciences, have provided a rich and encouraging training environment.

I am also grateful to the postdoctoral fellowship I am enjoying at the Instituto de Filosofia da NOVA (IFILNOVA). Especially, I would like to acknowledge the lively discussions created by the members of the Laboratory of Ethics and Political Philosophy of the NOVA University Lisbon. Thanks to the permission of my supervisor at IFILNOVA, Prof. Susana Cadilha, I could take the time needed to write the successive versions of this book.

Likewise, I am grateful for their suggestions and support to Rosario López, Marta Postigo, Manuel Toscano, Tomás Pacheco, Mabel Holgado, Hanna-Mari Kivistö, Taru Haapala, Sia Spiliopoulou-Åkermark, Gabriella Silvestrini, Kari Palonen, Paul-Erik Korvela, Jani Marjanen, Jan Harald Alnes, Mira Söderman and Konstantinos Bizas.

Finally, I would like to thank my parents, Loli and Andrés. From them I have learnt to find reward in steady work. I will never be able to repay them for all they do for me.

Málaga
September 2023

Contents

CHAPTER 1

Introduction: Examining Political Rhetoric in Spanish Constitutional Debates

This book appraises the innovations of the political language in Spain's constitutional debates during the nineteenth and the twentieth centuries which gave rise to new constitutions. Constitutional debates can be classified into three types: first, those dealing with constitutional issues, for example, the right to health care; second, those that entail a constitutional reform, for instance, to rewrite one or several constitutional articles; and third, those of constituent assemblies leading to the passing of new constitutions. This third type of debate is studied here.

'Constitutional Debates, Rhetoric, and Political Philosophy in Spain's Parliamentary History' aims to identify the conceptual contributions of MPs that led to political changes affecting the meanings of basic political concepts. Representatives endorsing a plurality of ideological views reinterpreted political philosophy ideas and models when adapting them to their institution-building designs. This book aims to identify the conceptual innovations produced in Spanish constitutional debates through the analysis of political philosophy arguments during the parliamentary history of the country. By doing so it is possible to distinguish historical tensions between constitutionalism and liberalism, on the one hand, and democracy and republicanism, on the other.

The Spanish Parliament (*Cortes*) has been the stage of the political modernization of the country. Constitutional debates have historically

F. J. Bellido, *Constitutional Debates, Rhetoric, and Political Philosophy in Spain's Parliamentary History*, Rhetoric, Politics and Society, https://doi.org/10.1007/978-3-031-56894-7_1

led to the gradual acknowledgement and broadening—though usually unevenly—of citizens' rights. Together with it, these debates have been opportunities for designing institutions and settling legal mechanisms to enforce rights and to distribute state resources.

Throughout Spain's parliamentary history, seven constitutions came into effect, those of 1812, 1837, 1845, 1869, 1876, 1931, and the current one of 1978. They followed a path to steadily advance political, civil, social, and economic rights. The debates that ended in the passing of these constitutions mirrored the social and political ups and downs of the country. A number of parliamentary constitutional speeches, for example those of the liberal representative Agustín de Argüelles between 1810 and 1812 to those of the centrist liberal rapporteur José Pedro Pérez-Llorca in 1978, should be regarded as outstanding pieces of argumentative innovation rooted in the history of political thought and not exclusively responsive to a national tradition.

In parliament, rhetorical interplay with present and past ideas and debates offers MPs manifold options for renewing the political vocabulary. Parliamentary speeches are the locus of the rhetorical use of parliamentary times and procedures that, as highlighted by Kari Palonen, are a fruitful field to draw on counter-intuitive arguments, to enhance improvisation, to assess constitutional rules from a technical point of view, and to ponder feasible alternatives of institution-making. When political alternatives to institution-building are handed over giving classic political concepts new meanings the parliamentary history of a nation becomes a resource to weigh up political newness.

Since the first constitutional debate of the country between 1810–1812, which gave rise to the Cadiz Constitution of 1812, representatives showed an extraordinary capacity to reshape the political vocabulary of the nation. Agustín de Argüelles, Diego Muñoz-Torrero, the Count of Toreno, Francisco Martínez de la Rosa, Antonio Alcalá Galiano, Juan Donoso Cortés, and Cándido Nocedal, among others, contributed to give classic political concepts new connotations. Their ideas were enriched by the influence of European political trends from the United Kingdom and France to a much greater extent than those from Germany, Italy, and Portugal.

In this line, the study draws attention to the international contexts that provide the background to constitutional debates in Spain. Liberal ideas from 1810 onwards underwent a process of transformation into an ideology and, to no lesser extent, into a set of reformist programmes at odds with an absolutism. In the second half of the nineteenth-century liberalism, republicanism, and traditionalism made sense of the political, social, and economic alternatives represented in parliament. The Spanish twentieth century gradually shaped the ideologies of liberalism and democratic socialism from its partisan meaning in 1931 to its pluralistic connotations in 1978 (Rosales 2016b).

1 Argumentative Clues

In this section I explain, firstly, the main features of constitutional debates and their argumentative relevance, and secondly, how they fit with the deliberative framework of parliamentary assemblies. The opportunities that constitutional debates which give rise to new constitutions offer for an interdisciplinary analysis range from the combination of ideological, legal, and political arguments to the mixing aspects of political philosophy and parliamentary history that new conceptual usages of classic political concepts entail. That argumentative thread expounds on how democratic institutions are envisioned by political representatives in their parliamentary contributions.

1.1 Exploring Constitutional Debates from a Political Philosophy Perspective

Political philosophy arguments during constituent assemblies have historically led to envisioning the practicalities of building new state institutions ranging from the territorial structure of the state to the scope of administrative institutions. In constituent assemblies, the argumentative performance of representatives is a precondition for making institutions feasible partly mirroring other constitutional experiences. To choose among competing argumentative alternatives of institution-making gives constitutional debates their preeminence as stages to test the practical outcomes of political philosophy ideas and concepts.

Following Kari Palonen's approach to parliamentary politics, it can be said that "in parliament, dissensus is institutionalized in its procedure, based on the idea of opposed points of views as a condition for a thorough understanding of the question" (Palonen 2019: 46). Constituent assemblies can be studied as sites of deliberative exercises in which representatives ponder over different alternatives in the creation of the institutions of a new political regime. That does not mean that parliamentary deliberations in constituent assemblies are rationally perfect, but that they rather work as a feasible institutional framework to channel political diversity.

1.2 *Innovative Political Concepts*

As highlighted by Michael Freeden, properly understanding political concepts demands bringing on other adjacent concepts that surround them (Freeden 2017: 120). Any researcher interested in identifying the changing meanings of concepts should answer what are the predominant meanings ascribed by political agents, the connotations that a concept has regarding ideological leanings, and their semantic fields. In parliamentary debates—especially during constitutional ones—representatives' persuasive aims give political rhetoric a pervasive relevance to make concepts mean what each representative wants them to mean. That is so in order to defend a certain stance, be that suasive attempt deliberately grounded in previous uses of that concept or not.

In parliamentary assemblies using the language to express new or old meanings in a different manner is much more relevant from the point of view of 'political literacy' than using concepts routinely (Palonen 2019: 59). The rhetorical resource of *topoi* (frequent argumentative assumptions), *inventio* (capacity to create new ideas and arguments), and *dispositio* (the organization of the discourse) form together the structure of any articulated political speech with persuasive aims (Palonen 2014: 23), as it is the case of parliamentary constitutional debates.

Without the resource of *dispositio* MPs' speeches in parliamentary assemblies would lack either their internal rationality or the possibility of their different points of view being understood by audiences. All these aspects of political creativity are precisely improved when new situations are regarded by professional politicians as opportunities for strengthening their own stances with new political arguments. Spanish constitutional debates provided huge chances for representatives to shape an innovative political language, indeed, to partly shape the features of the parliamentary vocabulary of the country, in opposition to previous practices and political ideas.

1.3 An Analysis of the Arguments Debated by a Constituent Assembly

Unlike other kinds of parliamentary assemblies and as a consequence of their argumentative character, constitutional debates usually demand from political representatives a higher degree of knowledge about political history, political thought and law; a sense of practical intelligence to reconcile the deliberative character of a parliamentary constitutional assembly with the accommodation of different demands from rival representatives and parties; rhetorical skills to defend their own stances; and the capacity to inform new political institutions. Thus, constitutional debates are opportunities for the modernization of state institutions and thereby address unsettled problems (Rosales 2016a: 278).

Furthermore, especially in constituent assemblies, legal and political expertise helps to improve the argumentative performance of representatives. Their overall historical accuracy when reinterpreting the political milestones that were considered relevant to the new democratic regime of Spain, together with the argumentative refinement of legal and political doctrines, should be remarked. These aspects strengthened the argumentative quality of parliamentary speeches. As reflected in the diary of sessions of parliament, these concerns prevailed over highly speculative views. It was so precisely because they were a necessary condition for the drafting of a constitution. Legal expertise and political imagination are inseparable when drafting and debating a new constitution that framed the process of democratic change.

The kind of parliamentary politics practised during the constitutional debate of 1977–1978 is far beyond the trends, visible in aged parliamentary regimes, that accentuate what Kari Palonen regarded as a narrow-minded view that reduces the complexity and chances of parliamentary politics to partisan disputes in electoral processes, municipalities and parliamentary institutions (Palonen 2019: 5).

2 Political Philosophy, Conceptual History, and Parliamentary History: An Interdisciplinary Method

Throughout this section, firstly, I address the relationship between political philosophy and parliaments. Secondly, I highlight the potential of parliamentary debates to look at argumentative and conceptual changes.

Thirdly, I focus on the potentialities of parliamentary politics as relevant to studying historical changes in the political language. Finally, I argue in favour of understanding parliamentary sources and materials to study constitutional debates in Spain as cases of political production of new ideas to be explored through their parliamentary discussions.

2.1 *Political Philosophy Applied to the Study of Constitutional Debates*

Prevailing approaches of political philosophy or theory have paid relatively minor attention to parliaments as the deliberative institutions which produce new political ideas. With a few exceptions that seem to keep growing in recent years, some scholarly contributions have been focused on the potentialities of parliamentary argumentations to understand and assess the development of parliamentary democracies as the deliberative loci par excellence (Palonen 2012: 13–4; Rosales 2014: 24). As a consequence, the procedures and unwritten rules of parliamentary institutions have been deemed almost irrelevant to the production of philosophical arguments.

Against that view, parliamentary debates offer instead broad chances to representatives to imaginatively use arguments and to play with the times and procedures of parliaments (Ilie 2022: 2). Accordingly, the approach assumed in this research brings conceptual history closer. Consequently, the variety of arguments, their quality, and the interpretations of individual representatives about political arguments and doctrines become patent. By the same token, conceptual history is understood as a discipline to explore the argumentative uses of classic political ideas, to compare the diversity of ideological and doctrinal interpretations by MPs.

The present approach of conceptual history focuses not just on the new meanings that are produced, but on how concepts turn out to be part of political controversies around the institutions of a constitutional state when rival meanings for the same political terms clash with each other. Following Giuseppe Duso, it can be said that modern and contemporary political and social concepts are the product of political philosophy arguments and ideas as publicly debated when informing state institutions and not as isolated intellectual contributions (Duso 2007: 61).

Since the mid-2000s Kari Palonen has defended the potentialities of parliaments for exploring their deliberative dimension. There, representatives have contributed historically to new understandings of political ideas and to the very practice of democracy. Together with other scholars, they have produced academic contributions about parliamentarism that open a path for future research: Palonen (2014, 2019), Palonen and Rosales (2015), Ihalainen et al. (2016), Rosales (2016a, b), and Wiesner et al. (2017). Parliamentary debates unveil "both adversarial and dissensual aspects" as parts of a proceduralized model of *pro et contra* deliberations (Finlayson 2017: 25–26). That practice can also be found, to a certain extent, in other sort of debates, for example, among scholars, journalists, or economists in meetings and other events (Wiesner et al. 2017: 16).

2.2 Conceptual History and Constituent Assemblies

From a methodological point of view, this research stems from a methodology of conceptual history to revise political philosophy arguments during the parliamentary history of Spain. It suggests an approach to political philosophy that attends to the argumentative rhetoric of constituent assemblies. Further, it understands conceptual history from the perspective of the historical semantics of constitutional debates between 1810–1812 and 1977–1978, with a special focus on those held during the twentieth century, 1931, and 1977–1978.

This entails contextualizing the argumentative features of constitutional debates and to analyse the uses of key political ideas such as 'nation', 'sovereignty', and 'constitution', among others, since the nineteenth century. From the perspective of international constitutionalism, appraising the political language of constitutional debates in nations with a lasting parliamentary tradition would clarify the historical development of key political concepts of constitutional democracies used with dissimilar meanings over time.

Semantic changes have informed the design of the country's political institutions over two centuries. Further, the diversity of parties and parliamentary groups in a constitutional debate can be interpreted as a requirement to strengthen the deliberative character of constituent assemblies as much as a necessity to pass a constitution which most citizens, irrespective of ideologies, can adhere to. Ideological diversity usually fosters argumentative chances to raise new arguments and ideas.

2.3 An Approach of Parliamentary History to Study Political Ideas in Action

Parliamentary history contributes to explaining the political and social changes that come about in a country over time. In this case, to explore two centuries of constitutional debates provides a broad outlook on the political vocabulary of Spain since the beginning of liberalism in the *Cortes* of Cadiz (1810–1812). During constitutional debates, parliamentary speeches make sense of innovations during the political history of a country that otherwise would be impossible to identify. Accurate and dispersed accounts of political institutions allow us to understand both political newness and ideological complexity. Polysemy is more a resource than a hindrance to examining the diversity of meanings for classic political concepts.

Political ideas are contrasted with each other regarding parliamentary speeches addressed to answer specific problems conducive to the passing of a constitution. Concepts receive new meanings when connected to partly new semantic fields and intertwined with other political, social, and economic ideas. The influence of foreign constitutions, political philosophy debates, and the history of political thought is a precondition for making parliamentary speeches and ideas intelligible. To deftly pinpoint the sources of new ideas is the task of parliamentary history research.

Parliamentary speeches are extensively reviewed in order to identify the conceptual changes in the political vocabulary of the country. The resulting political language is also the outcome of envisaging answers to pervasive problems of institutional design. Political ideas in parliament are not merely theoretical exercises, but practical actions aimed to build new institutions and lasting constitutional texts for a country.

2.4 Sources and Materials for an Interdisciplinary Analysis of Constitutional Debates

Delving into the analysis of constitutional debates entails arranging sources and materials ranging from the diaries of sessions to the secondary bibliography that can bring light into the argumentative complexity of constitutional debates. Interdisciplinary research about constitutional debates requires in this case to apply the methodology of conceptual history but also to undertake exhaustive research word by word through search engines of digitized bases. Parliamentary speeches, political arguments, and concepts are the three units of research.

By doing so, this interdisciplinary research surveys MPs' political philosophy arguments through a methodology of conceptual history aiming to identify the changing meanings given to political concepts during the parliamentary history of the country. Despite the usefulness of political dictionaries and specialized contributions, the complexity of the vocabulary of constituent assemblies does not exhaust the pervading polysemy and ideological ambiguities that political concepts acquire during constituent assemblies.

3 Structure of the Book

Chapters are organized in chronological order. Each one of them selects a set of differentiated controversies in the course of constitutional debates around conceptual disagreements and alternative projects of institution-making. By doing so, this book reconstructs the arguments that were successively used to shape the country's institutions. The distribution of the chapters' contents is explained below.

This first chapter, 'Examining Political Rhetoric in Spanish Constitutional Debates', has an introductory character and sets forth the structure and research aims of the book. It highlights the special deliberative framework of constitutional debates by advancing an interdisciplinary approach. Unlike other kinds of parliamentary debates, in constitutional debates speeches are not only addressed to persuade the audience, from electors to fellow representatives, or to promote specific reforms. In constitutional debates, the immediate goal is to provide a country with lasting institutions enshrined in a constitutional text. Constitutional debates have historically led, in varying degrees, to upgrading the political vocabulary of the country and to reforming institutions.

Chapter 2, 'A Survey of Constitutional Debates in Spain's Nineteenth Century', underscores the capital moments of conceptual innovation in constitutional debates of the nineteenth century. The chapter looks at the constitutional debates of 1812, 1837, 1845, 1869, and 1876 by selecting issues such as the foundation of Spain as a nation and the meaning of national sovereignty.

Firstly, the chapter focuses on the Cadiz constitutional debate between 1810 and 1812 to identify innovations in the political language of representatives. It presents the tensions between the rival ideologies of liberalism and conservatism. It assesses Agustín de Argüelles'—the most prominent liberal representative in the *Cortes* of Cadiz—performance defending liberal principles from both a technical and a scholarly perspective. Secondly, some remarks about the flawed ideas of the transaction during the constitutional debates of 1837 and 1845 are confronted with the meanings given to the concept of constitution. Thirdly, the chapter reviews the alternative projects of the state by republicans and monarchists regarding the idea of Spain as a nation in the constituent debate of 1869. Fourthly, the clashing concepts of constitution and nation held by liberal and conservative representatives to endorse the Constitution of 1876 finally passed are reviewed.

Chapter 3, 'The Historical Framework of Spain's Twentieth-Century Constitutional Debates', examines the settings in which the constitutional debates of 1931 and 1977–1978 took place. Unlike in 1931, when partisanship became prominent and hampered constitutional agreements, in 1977–1978 ideologies were regarded as part of the democratic logic of fair competition between diverse political options.

The chapter singles out the innovations of the political language produced by the parliamentary deliberations of Spain's twentieth-century constitutional debates. The new democratic regimes that resulted from the constituent assemblies of 1931 and 1977–1978 hastened political changes affecting as one of their results the meanings of basic political concepts. Each one of these constituent assemblies led to new assessments of the constitutional tradition of the country since the General and Extraordinary *Cortes* (*Cortes Generales y Extraordinarias*) of Cadiz in 1810, but also of contemporary trends of European constitutionalism.

Chapter 4, 'Understanding Democracy in the Constitutional Debates of 1931 and 1977–1978', compares the constitutional debates of 1931 and 1977–1978. It points out to which extent federalism and regional autonomy labelled different phenomena. In 1931 the so-called 'integral' state was meant to acknowledge in the Constitution those competences that solely belonged to the central administration, those that were to be exercised by regional governments and those that could be delegated from the former to the latter. Instead, in 1978 the Constitution left open the scope of competences that could be transferred to regional governments. That practice unleashed an everlasting process of decentralization of state competences well beyond many federal states.

The first section surveys to which extent the two models of that 'integral' state of 1931 and the autonomist state of 1977–1978 were heirs to federalism. It presents both designs as alternatives to a full decentralization of state competences which imitated a federal structure of the state without naming it as such. The second section attends to the rhetorical usages of the ideas of competences, faculties and self-rule. These concepts were used to justify the need to increase the capacity of regions to self-rule within the institutional framework that was finally acknowledged in both constitutions.

In the third section, the struggle for bargaining between different political agents is highlighted. As a consequence of the pressing necessity for political agreements, representatives such as Adolfo Suárez, of Union of Democratic Centre, and Santiago Carrillo, of the Communist Party of Spain, relinquished part of their electoral programmes to their cost as party leaders. The fourth section presents how the idea of reform was interpreted by constituent representatives in 1931. The fifth section highlights the endeavours to draft a democratic constitution in 1977 and 1978. Under the premise of pragmatism, political parties worked towards consolidating the democratic regime in the following years.

Chapter 5, 'Competing Meanings of the New Democratic State', seeks to understand, firstly, how the ideas of reform and revolution were interpreted both in 1931 and 1977–1978; secondly, the alternative views of state institutions presented by centre-right and centre-left political parties; and thirdly, the demands of state decentralization and more ambitious reforms by the Communist Party of Spain and nationalist parties in Catalonia and the Basque Country. Their understanding of Spain as a democratic nation was at odds with the readings of both moderate right-wing and left-wing parties. In a nutshell, the chapter looks over the resulting democratic regimes of both constitutional debates. In each case, it illustrates the changing meanings of concepts regarding ideological leanings.

Chapter 6, 'Constitutional State Powers', presents the constitutional functions of public powers as safeguards of national sovereignty and of the political unity of the country. The nation was portrayed by constituent MPs in 1978 as a shared political project for Spaniards of any ideology. State powers were designed accordingly to promote citizens' rights within the bounds of a social and democratic state and a strengthened rule of law.

The chapter surveys how state institutions were envisaged in the Constituent Assembly summoned between May and September 1978. The first section analyses the ideas of popular and national sovereignty, that were often interpreted as synonyms. The second section sheds light on how the idea of rule of law was widely accepted among centrist and right-wing MPs. It was appraised as the safeguard of democratic institutions, which only looked disputable to nationalist parties.

The third section clarifies the disagreements around the idea of sovereignty between the Spanish Socialist Workers' Party and the Communist Party of Spain. To the former, national sovereignty was one and indivisible but allowed the decentralization of state competences; to the latter parliament was the holder of sovereignty over the rest of state institutions. The last section focuses on the boundaries of the executive, the legislative, and the judicial powers. Representatives advised mechanisms of the legislative branch to counterbalance the executive power. Besides, the independence of the judiciary was widely deemed the stronghold of democratic institutions.

In Chapter 7, 'The Decentralization of Spain as a Political Nation', disagreements between majority parties and minority nationalist groups are set forth. The contrast between self-rule and self-determination as two distinct ideas was claimed by centre and right-wing parties. They were in favour of self-rule to satisfy regional demands, but against self-determination as a political idea implying a right to secession from Spain in Catalonia and the Basque Country. Regional parties aimed to enshrine in the Constitution the idea of *nationalities*[1] (*nacionalidades*) as a substitute for the idea of nation.

The chapter comprises the arguments of representatives in the Constituent Assembly about the new structure of the state, the concept of *nationalities* (as opposed to that of regions), and their insights into the Spanish nation. Firstly, it surveys the clashing viewpoints of regional autonomy by right-wing, centrist, and left-wing parties. There, it sets forth the disagreements between Union of Democratic Centre and Popular Alliance, on the one hand, and left-wing parties, on the other. Secondly, the chapter clarifies the rival meanings of the idea of *nationalities* (*nacionalidades*). To Union of Democratic Centre, Popular Alliance, the Aragonese Candidacy of Centre, and independent senators the concept of *nationalities* disguised nationalisms. Instead, the Spanish Socialist Workers' Party, the Communist Party of Spain, and nationalist

[1] In the specific Spanish constitutional and political concept, *nationalities* does not refer to the legal status of membership of the state, but to the so-called historical regions of Spain: Catalonia, the Basque Country and Galicia. That is why, in this book, it is always written in italics.

parties of Catalonia and the Basque Country regarded it as a sound constitutional concept, even though unsettled. Finally, it discerns the idea of Spain as a political nation from the alternative ethnic understanding of nations within Spain.

Chapter 8, 'Liberalism and Democracy in Contemporary Spain', presents some of the main challenges that Spanish contemporary democracy faces. Firstly, it underlines the tradition of liberal constitutionalism that characterizes Spain since the Constitution of 1812. Secondly, it compares the Portuguese, Greek, and Spanish transitions to democracy during the 1970s as tokens of the strength of political and social pluralism when joined to the defence of constitutional democracies. Thirdly, the chapter explains the interplay of Spain with the Council of Europe and the European Economic Community to become a member of the European Union in 1986. It argues that the reciprocal interests of these organizations and Spain favoured the country's steps towards democracy. Finally, the contemporary challenges to liberal democracy posed by populist anti-liberal rhetoric are underscored as forms of anti-pluralism that grant a privilege to nationalisms and partisanship to the expense of institutional stability, equality among citizens of different regions and the very existence of a constitutional state.

The conclusions summarize the contributions of constituent representatives to the language and institutions of liberalism and constitutionalism. That final section underlines the arguments that justify why constitutional debates were determined to understand the renewal of the political vocabulary. It resumes the main research question of the book: How did political philosophy arguments in the course of the constitutional deliberations encourage conceptual and ideological controversies and inform the institutions of the country?

The study of constitutional debates is addressed by selecting debates that affected the vocabulary of constitutionalism, liberalism, republicanism, and democracy in varying degrees. The outcome was the successive renewal of the political language of the country following identifiable historical contributions. Intellectuals and legal scholars acting as representatives revamped the political vocabulary and boosted institutional reforms. Very often those changes were not just innovative but resulted in conflicting interpretations of classic political concepts.

References

Duso, Giuseppe (2007). 'Politica e filosofia', in *La logica del potere. Storia concettuale come filosofia politica*. Milan: Polimetrica.

Finlayson, Alan (2017). 'What Is the Point if Parliamentary Debate? Deliberation, Oratory, Opposition and Spectacle in the British House of Commons', *Redescriptions: Political Thought, Conceptual History, and Feminist Theory*, 20(1), 11–31.

Freeden, Michael (2017). 'Conceptual History, Ideology and Language', in *Conceptual History in the European Space*, eds. William Steinmetz, Michael Freeden & Javier Fernández-Sebastián. New York: Berghahn.

Ihalainen, Pasi, Cornelia Ilie & Kari Palonen eds. (2016). *Parliaments and Parliamentarism: A Comparative History of Disputes on a European Concept*. New York: Berghahn.

Ilie, Cornelia (2022). 'How to Argue with Questions and Answers: Argumentation Strategies in Parliamentary Deliberation', *Languages*, 7(205), 1–19.

Palonen, Kari (2012). 'Parliamentary Procedure as an Inventory of Disputes. A Comparison Between Jeremy Bentham and Thomas Erskine May', *Res Publica. Revista de Filosofía Política*, 27, 13–25.

Palonen, Kari (2014). *The Politics of Parliamentary Procedure: The Formation of the Westminster Procedure as a Parliamentary Ideal Type*. Opladen, Berlin, & Toronto: Barbara Budrich Publishers.

Palonen, Kari (2019). *Parliamentary Thinking: Procedure, Rhetoric and Time*. Cham: Palgrave Macmillan.

Palonen, Kari & José María Rosales eds. (2015). *Parliamentarism and Democratic Theory: Historical and Contemporary Perspectives*. Opladen, Berlin, & Toronto: Barbara Budrich Publishers.

Rosales, José María (2014). 'On the Irrelevant Place of Parliamentarism in Democratic Theory: Antecedents', in *The Politics of Dissensus: Parliament in Debate*, eds. Kari Palonen, José María Rosales & Tapani Turkka. Santander & Madrid: Cantabria University Press & McGraw-Hill.

Rosales, José María (2016a). 'Parliamentarism in Spanish Politics in the Nineteenth and Twentieth Centuries: From Constitutional Liberalism to Democratic Parliamentarism', in *Parliaments and Parliamentarism: A Comparative History of Disputes on a European Concept*, eds. Pasi Ihalainen, Cornelia Ilie & Kari Palonen. New York: Berghahn.

Rosales, José María (2016b). 'From Partisan to Pluralist Ideology: The Changing Practices of Democracy Through Spain's 20th-Century Constitutional Moments', *Journal of Political Ideologies*, 21(3), 225–41.

Wiesner, Claudia, Taru Haapala & Kari Palonen (2017). *Debates, Rhetoric and Political Action: Practices of Textual Interpretation and Analysis*. London: Palgrave Macmillan.

CHAPTER 2

A Survey of Constitutional Debates in Spain's Nineteenth Century

This chapter enquires into the conceptual diversity, rhetorical strategies and arguments of nineteenth-century constitutional debates in Spain. It aims to show that these debates gave concepts such as nation, constitution, sovereignty, representation, constituent power and freedom new connotations over time connected to the modern language of liberalism. Despite the clear-cut similarities between constitutional debates, Spanish representatives refined their answers to problems such as the territorial unity of the country, economic backwardness, and lack of bourgeoise elites.

This first section sets forth some of the finest speeches of the *Cortes* of Cadiz from an argumentative perspective until the Constitution of 1812 was passed (24 September 1810–19 March 1812). It aims to contrast the use of contested concepts such as national sovereignty, constituent power, constituted power, division of powers, jurisdiction, and constitutional justice, conditioned by the clash of liberal and absolutist ideologies. The second section presents how moderate and progressive liberals negotiated during the constitutional debate of 1836–1837 around the idea of representative government. The third section delves into the clash between moderate, progressive and radical liberals during the constitutional debate of 1844–1845, which revolved around monarchy and the

F. J. Bellido, *Constitutional Debates, Rhetoric, and Political Philosophy in Spain's Parliamentary History*, Rhetoric, Politics and Society,
https://doi.org/10.1007/978-3-031-56894-7_2

nation. Their strong disagreements curbed transactions between these parliamentary groups.

The fourth section selects several speeches that make it patent the salient argumentative skills of representatives during the constitutional debate of 1869. Through an exercise of institutional envisioning, they shaped the political and moral vocabularies of the country to enhance civil and political freedoms. The last section surveys the meanings of sovereignty, constitution and nation that prevailed in the constitutional debate of 1876. It revises the answers of conservative and liberal deputies who underpinned their own understanding of those concepts. Constituent representatives usually aimed at resolving or lessening practical problems of constitution-making. By alternately raising or leaving aside ideological and strategic controversies, they assumed to varying degrees the language of early liberal constitutionalism when designing state institutions.

1 The Constitutional Debate of Cadiz: 1810–1812

This section contextualizes the arguments and concepts used by liberal representatives during the constituent assembly (*Cortes Constituyentes*) of Cadiz. It sheds light on the conflicting overtones of liberal reforms. To absolutists reformist policies were innovations that could tear down the building of ancient institutions. Against that surmise, liberal MPs vindicated a programme of constitutional and administrative reforms with the reinvigorated language of constitutional freedoms. In so doing they translated philosophical ideas into a set of practical outcomes.

1.1 Cortes *of Cadiz: Founding a Parliamentary Rhetorical Style*

Broadly considered a milestone of constitutional history and liberalism, the *Cortes* of Cadiz, officially named General and Extraordinary *Cortes* (*Cortes Generales y Extraordinarias*) were a scenario of intellectual resources and argumentative quality of speeches that were likely the most outstanding in the constitutional history of the country. 538 parliamentary sessions were held between 1810 and 1812 (Rosales 2018: 279). The issues discussed in *Cortes* very soon echoed abroad giving the term 'liberal' political connotations that it did not have before (Luengo and Dalmau 2018: 429).

Liberal representatives such as Agustín de Argüelles, the Count of Toreno, Diego Muñoz-Torrero, José Mejía Lequerica, Evaristo Pérez de Castro, José de Espiga and José María Calatrava, among others, exhibited their talents as supporters of a nascent tradition of political thought around the ideas of distribution and separation of political powers, equality of rights before the law, emancipation from arbitrary rule, individual freedoms and merit. Their political vindications were especially welcome in urban areas and there were endorsed by popular classes (Smith 2016: 57).

Three political groups coexisted after the Cadiz *Cortes* convened in 1808 (Müller 2016: 189). The first and largest political group was made up of the so-called liberals (*liberales*), roughly divided into two factions: those in favour of institutional reforms through a written constitution that would acknowledge individual freedoms and national sovereignty, and those others who aimed to reconcile the king's executive power with that of parliament. The second group was that of absolutists (*realistas*) in favour of the king's unbound power and medieval institutions such as social strata, enemies of any political reform that would alter the *status quo* before the French invasion of Spain (18 October 1807–17 April 1814). The third political group was that of Americans, representatives from overseas territories that distrusted the king's power and whose foremost goals were to grant equal representation in *Cortes* for American citizens and a higher degree of economic and administrative independence from the Iberian Peninsula's central power.

The constitutional commission in charge of writing the constitutional draft was made up of nine lawyers, six clergymen and five Americans. Liberal and absolutist tendencies within the commission were balanced (Escobar Fornos 2012: 175). The former had the initiative of constitutional wording; the latter kept up a reactive profile. Liberal representatives such as Agustín de Argüelles, the Count of Toreno and Juan Nicasio Gallego lavishly received the ideas of English and French iusnaturalism, the *philosophes* and Montesquieu, among other miscellany of authors and theories connected to French Enlightenment.

For instance, the Enlightenment thinker Gaspar Melchor de Jovellanos took inspiration from English constitutionalism as to hold a middle-ground answer between that of absolutists and impassioned liberals (Fernández Sarasola 2016: 52). However, Diego Muñoz-Torrero and José de Espiga were more reluctant than their peers to accept these foreign ideas if that meant to cast aside Spanish scholasticism and historicism (Varela Suanzes-Carpegna 2020: 55).

Liberal ideas did not correlate with a plain liberal language, but with the meddling of historical influences that mirrored a 'bridge period' (*Sattelzeit*), to use Reinhart Koselleck's insightful expression. Parliamentary speeches made it patent the conceptual diversity and rhetorical clashes between concepts and terms. Polysemy was hand in hand with conceptual hybrids denoting inaccurate or simply unarticulated meanings of political ideas. Rhetorical interplay between terms, historical references, and polemic meanings characterized the constitutional history of the country during the nineteenth century.

Liberal manners and liberality, understood as generous behaviour and friendly treatment with others, was translated from the social into the political language. The term 'liberal' was equated with the positive defence of individual freedoms against arbitrary rule. During the *Cortes* of Cadiz intellectual speeches were connected to the practical consequences of political ideas. There, to design lasting state institutions was overly regarded as indispensable to the success of constitutional reforms. Each MP had recourse to his own expertise about national and international affairs to defend constitutional models that echoed English and French institutions to varying degrees (Hijano Pérez 2016: 133).

Disguised as partial reforms by liberals such as Agustín de Argüelles, their proposals assumed dissimilar aims of political, social and economic reforms to dismantle the medieval institutions of the Ancient Regime. Liberal representatives argued that men should achieve social emancipation from wasted practices and institutions. Legal instruments such as written constitutions were the precondition for its success. Thus, liberal constitutionalism and subsequent constitutional rights entailed two ideals: equality of individuals before the law and freedom for any citizen to pursue their own goals without interfering with others' rights (Mirow 2010: 68–69).

The intellectual elites that welcomed liberal ideas in Spain were a young minority—mainly clergymen, lawyers, and civil servants—Fuentes (2010: 35) who regarded rights and constitutions as the fairest acknowledgement of individual freedoms and justice. Their demands appealed to a shared human nature. Individuals should not be subordinated to other authorities than consented ones. That individualistic mindset had to counterbalance individual freedoms with social bonds to prevent particular interests from overriding the public interest, that of the whole nation.

Organized around nations, municipalities, crafts, and families everyone should be free to search for their interests when in compliance with fair laws and basic rules of public morality. Positive laws were the instrument to prevent abuses and to safeguard political and civil rights. Nobody had the right to use their power against free countrymen. Laws were the best instrument available to constituent representatives to transform their far-reaching plan of liberal reforms into actual, even if limited, outcomes.

From a rhetorical perspective, representatives resorted to a new political language and argumentative devices because for the first time, the Spanish *Cortes* were summoned to represent all Spaniards from both hemispheres. That was not the case of the medieval *Cortes* where the modern concept of national representation was completely absent (Albaladejo 2013: 78). National representation and individual rights were to be joint.

Liberals demanded that the nation deemed a historical fact that consisted of individuals of different generations, was the bearer of sovereignty and the only source of legitimacy (Capellán de Miguel 2002: 613). Rivalry between historicism and individualism was mitigated if a broad concept of national sovereignty was accepted by both moderate and reformist liberals. National sovereignty was then embodied in the Constitution of 1812, supreme law endorsed by Spaniards (Timmermann and Müßig 2017: 112).

Conceptual disagreements were brought to light. For example, the concept of representation underwent a major transformation from medieval times to the first half of the nineteenth century. Representation shifted its meaning from a privative competence of delegated interests to a resource that justified differing opinions between represented and representatives without cancelling that representative bond. Hence the relevance of public opinion to encourage individual freedoms and political education (Fernández Sarasola 2010: 65).

The liberal understanding of representation meant a more efficient way of connecting shared interests, individual needs, and personal freedom with the political exercise of constitutional competences (Capellán de Miguel 2002: 614). To represent the nation implied that, with the words of Argüelles, "national representation cannot be but one, and this, solely recast in the *Cortes*, is the only one that can express the will of the peoples".[1]

1.2 Argüelles' Arguments for the Constitution

Representative Agustín de Argüelles was the champion of liberal reforms during the entire constitutional debate (24 September 1810–19 March 1812). He deployed his rhetorical resources and conceptual devices: uncomplicated grammar, combination and repetition of political terms and common-sense assumptions at the beginning together with short sentences at the end of his speeches. Argüelles endorsed the Constitution as an innovation that did not leave out the medieval political heritage of Spain, then disguising liberal reforms as scarcely innovative adjustments within an unchanging political tradition. When evading compromising himself with any foreign theory, Argüelles played rhetorically to test the reception of liberal ideas anticipating the replies of his adversaries and improvising answers to criticisms raised against him.

Argüelles' rhetorical style can be considered Gothic, though not Baroque (Camus 2015: 474). His style combined straightforward arguments with elegant logic. Unlike his opponents, Argüelles' oratorial technique bolstered up short effective arguments. From an argumentative perspective, his speeches are difficult to refute because he often proceeded either by endorsing a statement or principle to infer its logical consequences or to directly infer dangers, advantages, or contradictions in each practice, idea, or institution mentioned. If his premise is true or plausible, then the inference is sound: "against that sacred principle [sovereignty] no property, possession, prescription and no other titles can be put forward whatever those are".[2]

As this example shows, Argüelles put into practice a strategy to give preeminence to his arguments. The first sentence is usually clear, unambiguous, and intelligible to any educated person. Each political argument

[1] "*La representación nacional no puede ser más que una, y ésta, refundida solamente en las Cortes, es la que únicamente puede expresar la voluntad de los pueblos*" (DSCC, 12 January 1812: 2610).

[2] "[*C*]*ontra tan sagrado derecho* [*soberanía*] *no puede alegarse ni propiedad, ni posesión, ni prescripción, ni otros títulos, cualesquiera que ellos sean*" (DSCC, 6 June 1811: 1198).

is presented as a matter of fact, reasonable, and open to further development if needed. Following the first premise, the conclusion is emphatic and vehemently conveyed as to making clear that alternative courses of action were of little value. The comprehensive concept of nation works as a rhetorical way of *captatio benevolentiae*. Calls for political responsibility and for channelling disputes through adequate instruments, even when not mentioned explicitly, arise in his speeches in multiple occasions: "The nation is the object of all this great dispute, not single individuals".[3]

The French administrative model, heir to the revolutionary period, was foreshadowed by Argüelles as a model to be carefully imitated preventing provincial enmities to carving up the entire nation (Crawley 1939: 189). To make his arguments appealing Argüelles kept away from any positive endorsement of the French Revolution. In this sense, he pointed out that any break with legality by legitimate authorities should be resolved by invoking national sovereignty and removing them from public office: "That all citizens [know] that they should only resort to sovereignty when a true break against the law has been committed by supreme authorities".[4]

As indicated by Albaladejo, Argüelles is usually the representative that takes the initiative to defend a motion or to express his views (Albaladejo 2011: 48). The absolutist Francisco Javier Borrull and the more moderate Felip Aner were his two most prominent opponents. That adversarial practice made political speeches open to improvisation challenging the skills of representatives to straightforwardly and persuasively answer his rivals in a short span of time.

The reformist language of Argüelles does suggest a strategy to fight the unfavourable opinions of absolutists. The political nation and the monarchy, in that order, were aligned with the liberal endorsement of the so-called 'national will'. The final part of this fragment evinces the influence of Rousseau over Argüelles: "The nation has excluded in the most explicit way any form of government that is not monarchic [...]. How, then, could it offer in its project any article, any clause that included

[3] "*La Nación es el objeto de toda esta gran querella, no los individuos aislados*" (DSCC, 4 August 1811: 1577).

[4] "[*Q*]*ue todos los ciudadanos* [sepan] *que solo debían acudir a la soberanía cuando hubiese una verdadera infracción de ley por parte de las autoridades supremas*" (DSCC, 2 March 1811: 614).

the slightest idea contrary to the solemn and authentic declaration of the national will?".[5]

National sovereignty was the backbone of the political nation. That nation already existed in medieval times, as Argüelles and the bulk of representatives thought (DSCC, 12 September 1811: 1826). To Argüelles national sovereignty was "a political dogma" (DSCC, 16 October 1811: 2093). However, the procedure to summon the *Cortes* and enshrine individual rights in a written constitution was an innovation that Argüelles partly concealed. Being accused of Frenchified (*afrancesado*) could entail the end of his political career, as it finally occurred when king Fernando VII of Spain took power back in 1814. To partisans of absolutism there was an original unwritten bond between the king and the rest of Spaniards that no law or institution could infringe without jeopardizing the very existence of the Spanish nation (Gurpegui 2018: 17–18).

Uneven intellectual sources led Argüelles to assume the doctrines of both Jean-Jacques Rousseau and Emmanuel-Joseph Sieyès seeking to avoid the open contradictions between them. The very notions of constituent and constituted powers were, *prima facie*, ideas at odds with the existence of a *volonté générale* or a national will in terms of sovereignty. If the constituent power could be undone by resorting to a general will without limits, then it ceased to be politically efficacious. Argüelles combined those terms to harden his view. There was a continuity between constituent nation and constituted nation: "What is said by Mr. Terrero about the reasons on which the commission sets up the report, distinguishing constituent nation from constituted nation, are chimerical subterfuges, it comes from a mistake".[6]

Accordingly, the Spanish nation had the faculty to dismiss their ruling authorities by any political means at hand to undo "despotism and tyranny" (DSCC, 15 October 1811: 2088). His arguments entailed that it was possible to differ the sovereign authority of the nation among

[5] "[*L*]*A Nación ha excluido del modo más explícito toda forma de gobierno que no sea el monárquico* [...]. *¿Cómo, pues, podía ofrecer en su proyecto ningún artículo, ninguna cláusula que incluyese la menor idea contraria a la solemne y auténtica declaración de la voluntad nacional?*" (DSCC, 28 August 1811: 1709).

[6] "*Lo que dice el señor Terrero de que las razones en que la comisión funda al dictamen, haciendo distinción de Nación constituyente y Nación constituida, son quiméricos efugios, procede de una equivocación*" (DSCC, 28 September 1811: 1947).

its individuals. That vested faculty belonged to the historical nation and was to be exercised through parliamentary and constitutional means. By assuming it as a premise, the constitution ruled out any attempt to darken the division between political authorities enabled to exercise political power and sovereign authority. The former belonged to the elected representatives of the nation; the latter was a quality of the Spanish nation and could not be alienated (DSCC, 26 November 1811: 2479).

1.3 Cadiz Constitutionalism Beyond Parliamentary Rhetoric

From a historical perspective, liberal representatives of Cadiz constitutionalism were more worried about the duty-based rights of all Spaniards, baseline of the Constitution, than about itemizing each one of the corresponding civil and political rights (Pérez Ledesma 1991: 184). The representatives who debated the constitutional draft clarified the concepts of "constituent power, power to reform and legislative power" (Tajadura Tejada 2012: 258). To conceptualize the sources of legitimacy of the Cadiz Constitution led them to reshape the entire political vocabulary.

Legal and conceptual innovations revamped the language of reforms. Liberal representatives paved the way to fitting the modern language of institutional design with ideas such as efficiency, subjection to legal procedures, and constitutional justice. Constitutional rights known beforehand by citizens, to simplify and to modernize procedures for litigation, publicity, and a unitary system of justice were some of the features of the new state administration that should replace wasted practices of the Ancient Regime (DSCC, 19 April 1811: 894).

Despite the ties of Spanish liberalism with scholastic thought, the sort of political liberalism that liberal representatives upheld in the *Cortes* of Cadiz was also akin to modern theoretical contributions about individual freedoms and merit. Moderate liberals such as Francisco Javier Martínez Marina sought to reconcile foreign and national practices against despotism and arbitrary rule (Westler 2015: 396–397). Thus, freedom, equality, and property were the mainstay of the liberal motto. These three fundamental principles should enable new social and political relationships in which individuals and not classes or strata must be protected against arbitrariness (Artola 1973: 33).

To a similar extent, the liberal deputy José de Espiga illustrated that the existence of constitutional rights in the Constitution demanded to preclude feudal features. Feudal-like mentality hindered the effective working of the Constitution and the rest of the legal codes of the nation because ancient prerogatives curtailed the equal treatment of citizens before the law. If the threefold division of powers was a deep-rooted principle, then public authorities should comply with laws that applied to every citizen irrespective of any social or economic condition. Limits to powers were to be uncontested, constitutionally enforced through constitutional laws, and effective within a single jurisdiction (DSCC, 5 February 1811: 500).

Modern theories of political thought positively endorsed that ideal of equality, mainly after Montesquieu's *De l'esprit des lois* circulated in intellectual circles outside France. Subsequent refinements by liberals before and after the French Revolution, such as *Qu'est -ce que le Tiers-État?*, by Emmanuel-Joseph Sieyès, gave a boost to the meaning of liberal duties and legal checks of both the exercise of political power and discretionary measures by ruling authorities.

However, between 1790 and 1799 the *Gaceta de Madrid*, the institutional media to publish government laws, orders, and decrees, among other information, does not contain any of Rousseau's political writings (Aragón 1989: 262). That fact likely means that most foreign political books about politics circulated clandestinely or were read in French. Doctrinal quarrels brought political disagreements into focus. The absolutist Francisco Gómez Fernández raised doubts about the potential of the constituent and the constituted powers to be compatible with a single sovereign body. How to make sure for representatives which one of these powers was superior? (DSCC, 7 March 1811: 644).

The liberal representative Juan Nicasio Gallego upheld that national sovereignty could never be transferred or alienated (DSCC, 29 August 1811: 1717). To a similar extent, the American representative Mariano Mendiola summarized the features of national sovereignty in the *Cortes* of Cadiz: "Sovereignty, which essentially resides in the entire Nation, is the sum of all rights, both civil and political; whoever is part of this sovereignty also takes part proportionally in the entire sum of rights of which she [the nation] is formed".[7] The limits of powers were to be

[7] "*La soberanía, que reside esencialmente en toda la Nación, es la suma de todos los derechos, así civiles como políticos; el que es parte de esta soberanía, también participa proporcionalmente de toda la suma de derechos de que ella se compone*" (DSCC, 14 September 1811: 1850).

uncontested, enforced through constitutional laws and effective under an undivided jurisdiction (DSCC, 5 February 1811: 500).

For instance, the absolutist Francisco Javier Borrull underpinned sovereignty as its attribution to the nation and king Fernando VII together (DSCC, 28 August 1811: 1712). And, in a similar manner, the absolutist priest Juan Nepomuceno Lera argued that national sovereignty had to do with self-government and civil bonds in the absence of the king: "Once the Nation is constituted, it preserves in itself what is inseparable from every perfect civil community" (DSCC, 29 August 1811: 1721).[8]

Diego Muñoz-Torrero and José María Queipo de Llano, Count of Toreno, equated sovereignty and national sovereignty. The Spanish *Cortes* kept its legislative function, a delegated one exercised in the name of the whole Spanish nation, but they did not alienate any degree or part of sovereignty (DSCC, 15 November 1811: 2263; 17 January 1812: 2644). Sovereign power meant an undivided, unitary source of legitimacy to which any legal authority of the nation should be subordinated and responsible before courts of justice.

The concept of nation, central during the entire constitutional debate, was asymmetrically interpreted by constituent representatives. Either the nation was a "moral body" embodied by the king or it was the aggregate result of adding up the total number of individual citizens governed through the same laws and by the same legitimately consented authorities (Müller 2016: 188–89).

If the thesis of a moral body that consisted of the king and the people were accepted, then Francisco Suárez's scholastic idea of the "mystic body" (*cuerpum mysticum*) could be the hypothetical non-secular foundation of political authority (Müßig 2016: 42). Against that idea, a liberal understanding of the nation should dismiss body metaphors since they were not conducive to broader acceptance of individual constitutional rights.

National sovereignty, nation, constitutional rights, constituent power, constituted power and unitary jurisdiction of state powers were some of the ideas brought in the political vocabulary of the Spanish *Cortes*. The concept of nation was disputed to the extent of being accepted by all political tendencies despite its confusing meaning. Was freedom a quality of the nation, of individuals, or belonged to both, halfway liberalism and

[8] "*Constituida la Nación, conserva en sí lo que es inseparable de toda perfecta comunidad civil*" (DSCC, 29 August 1811: 1721).

historicism? (Luna-Fabritius 2012: 3–4). And if so, did historicism mean that traditional features of the medieval *Cortes* should prevail over any innovation?

The intellectual brilliance of liberal deputies does not hide the remarkable argumentative capacity of absolutists. This second group deemed new principles of public administration compatible with keeping up classic institutions, separate social strata, and king's sovereignty. Far from being merely rhetorical interplay of political ideas, the conceptual divergences of liberals and absolutists were the starting point of Spain's nineteenth-century constitutional debates.

2 Transactions in the Constitution of 1837

This section examines the political vocabulary of reformism and bargaining during the constitutional debate of 1836–1837 (17 October 1836–18 June 1837). It presents political controversies about the rights that should be enshrined in successive constitutions as the foreground of disagreements between moderates and progressives during the second third of the nineteenth century. Parliamentary speeches allow to distinguish arguments forecasting the practical consequences of adopting a constitution. Progressive representatives interpreted that the Constitution of 1837 could achieve that aim if agreeing with moderates on common constitutional grounds for both parliamentary groups.

2.1 *Rhetorical Devices of Moderates and Progressives*

By 1836 the political and moral vocabularies of moderates, progressives, and radicals were settled, to a great extent, in accordance with their interpretations of the Cadiz Constitution of 1812 (Romeo Mateo 1998: 46–47). Abstract concepts such as political representation and national sovereignty underwent a definite transformation that eroded optimistic views about the practicalities of direct political participation. Political representation was connected to the existence of middle classes which consisted of the urban bourgeoise, lawyers, teachers, journalists, professionals of medicine, and other members of liberal professions (Varela Suanzes-Carpegna 2020: 178).

Reformists aims were lessened after the failure of the revolutionary boost of the Cadiz Constitution of 1812. The Absolutist Six-Year Term (1814–1820), the Three Liberal Years (1820–1823), and the Ominous

Decade (1823–1833) that followed the passing of the Cadiz Constitution seemed to advice prioritizing constitutional and parliamentary stability over ambitious reforms. Pragmatic endeavours superseded the more philosophically sophisticated arguments of the Cadiz *Cortes* with concerns about institutional stability.

As a sign of political novelties, the very concept of representation after the 1820s was closer to the existence of a representative government in a broad sense. That qualified men would exercise their public function to benefit the nation was an appealing idea among political elites of the country (Sierra et al. 2006: 19). Most MPs were favourable to avoiding passionate stances in order to foster constitutional agreements and to pass an enduring constitution.

A general election was held in October 1836, aimed at settling a constituent assembly to write up a new constitution. It is difficult to itemize the results regarding parliamentary groups since affinities between elected deputies prevailed over partisan leanings. To sum up the results, leaving out independent representatives, 30 underpinned liberal radicalism; 90 were in favour of the Progressive Party, being the political centre of the chamber; and 70, in the right sector, had affinities with the Moderate Party (Marichal 1980: 135). Other calculations assign 213 seats to progressives and only 28 to the Moderate Party (Varela Suanzes-Carpegna 2020: 166).

Nevertheless, it would be inaccurate to classify the representatives in political parties during the constituent assembly of 1836–1837. At best there existed three political tendencies: a moderate one in favour of extending king's prerogatives and opposed to the individualistic rhetoric and constitutional reforms of Cadiz liberalism formed by representatives such as Francisco de Paula Castro y Orozco and Alejandro Mon; a progressive trend led by Agustín de Argüelles and Salustiano Olózaga, who despite regarding the Cadiz Constitution in a good light tempered their more radical demands; and a minority of impassioned liberals, named as radicals by adversaries, such as Fermín Caballero and José Gorosarri, who advocated to reinstate the Cadiz Constitution or, otherwise, to acknowledge individual rights as it was done in 1812, by restraining king's prerogatives and strengthening parliament (Varela Suanzes-Carpegna 2020: 166–67; Ramos Silgado 2022: 269–70). Indeed, many of the elected representatives were 'old liberals' who came back from exile such as Agustín de Argüelles, Antonio González and Evaristo San Miguel.

On 14 November 1836 a constitutional commission was appointed to reform the Constitution of 1812 (Fernández Segado 1983: 36). From a legal, but also from a political philosophical perspective, the existence of a constituent assembly was extensively cast off by the constituent representatives of 1837 (Fernández Segado 1983: 38). That circumstance reflected the lack of agreement about the special political relevance of a constituent assembly if compared to ordinary parliamentary sessions. The distinct functions of constituent assemblies were not acknowledged as such by part of parliament.

2.2 *Transactions Around the Idea of Representative Government*

During the constitutional debate of 1836–1837, there was a chance to include large mentions of other European constitutional texts and parliamentary practices (Vera Santos 2006: 172). The Constitution of 1837 bestowed on the monarch the capacity "to summon, to adjourn, to close and to dissolve the sessions of the Congress of Deputies" (Constitution of 1837, art. 26). Accordingly, representatives endorsed monarchy against any serious questioning raised by the new republican groups (Díaz Fernández 2006: 77). Any representative government was related to each individual of the nation, be her opinions the same or not that those of elected representatives. As the progressive deputy Agustín Armendáriz conveyed, freedoms were the pillar of representative government (DSCC, 20 October 1836: 17).

It makes sense to wonder whether the Constitution of 1837 was the necessary outcome of negotiating between moderates and progressives, or rather an achievement of progressives, the major group in parliament (Aquillué Domínguez 2015: 45–46). Even though a shared goal was to agree a constitution that would include individual rights and the existence of a representative government, a constitutional text would only endure if it was widely accepted by all political tendencies in *Cortes*. That fact made indispensable transactions with moderate liberals: a deal between moderates and progressives led to acknowledge of press freedom in Article 2 of the Constitution.

The parliamentary privilege of not being judged according to civil litigations sheltered deputies who in the exercise of their parliamentary function could be involved in legal processes. The exercise of political responsibility was overly regarded as crucial to fulfil the representative duties of the deputy. When lawsuits had nothing to do with their performance as members of the Congress of Deputies, the Spanish lower chamber, ministers should be protected in the exercise of their political functions (Núñez Rivero 1983: 155). In that vein, to be politically responsible entailed to be removed from office in case of misbehaviour, either through judicial ruling or direct dismissal, but also when lacking the confidence of parliament.

As a token of the idea of representative government, the military man and progressive liberal representative Luis de Sosa pointed out a concise outline of the foundations of any representative government. A nation could give rise to a representative government when electoral votes lead to electing deputies consented by individuals who did not rise in revolts against the constituted body of representatives. In that regard, heads of families were enough to count as individuals in political terms because they would represent themselves and their own families (DSCC, 29 January 1837: 1293).

Miguel Cabrera de Nevares, of progressive liberal affinities, upheld that national sovereignty was a political fact and no institution or person could curtail it without corrupting the very concept of sovereignty: *Cortes* were summoned to implement the reforms that the Spanish nation had demanded for years (DSCC, 22 November 1836: 362). The moderate priest Bartolomé Venegas voiced a similar viewpoint. To him sovereignty was undivided and rested upon the independence of the nation to enshrine the monarchic form of government in the Constitution, "fundamental law of the state" (DSCC, 17 January 1837: 1106, 1109). As the moderate liberal Francisco Javier Ferro Montaos had argued, public powers were to be subordinated to the Spanish nation since the king himself was a delegate power of the nation (DSCC, 9 April 1837: 2606).

Unlike previous accounts of representation in the Spanish context, the representative bond between representatives and represented shifted from holistic overtones that reified the idea of national representation to a more concrete philosophical foundation. Following that idea of representation of French doctrinaires, parliamentary politics was indebted to representative mandates in which the interests of the whole nation should prevail over partial ones. Ministers as well as the rest of deputies were politically responsible to the nation. They could be removed from office if losing parliamentary confidence.

Political responsibility began to be differentiated. There was legal protection for MPs whose involvement in trials during their term in office had nothing to do with their function as representatives of the nation. A truly representative government should protect representatives in the exercise of their functions. This is conceptually relevant because political and legal responsibilities admitted two different channels through courts of justice to make it possible the exercise of one's own political responsibility. That newness was partly indebted to Benjamin Constant's defence of separated responsibilities for ministers in the exercise of their function in order to preserve political stability.

On 7 April 1837 the main issue of debate was to clarify whether the king was part of *Cortes* or a separated institution and, if so, what were the consequences for the legislative power (García Atance 1983: 180). For example, the moderate liberal Francisco Martínez de la Rosa reluctantly accepted the Constitution of 1837. He admitted its potential to reconcile opposite points of view between those who advocated national sovereignty to the detriment of the crown and those who underpinned both the nation and the crown as the only bearers of national sovereignty (Tomás Villarroya 1983: 19–20). In a similar vein, the moderate Nicomedes Pastor Díaz spoke in favour of the Constitution to say that it was the result of "a transaction between all parties" (Varela Suanzes-Carpegna 1983: 95–96).

The speaker of the Congress of Deputies (*Presidente del Congreso de los Diputados*) in 1836, José María Calatrava, a classic liberal who took part in the constitutional debate of the Cadiz Constitution, spoke on behalf of moderate liberals to say that the new constitution to be passed as "fundamental law" was compatible with tempered passions and would bolster a fair administration of justice (DSCC, 24 October 1836: 32). As the progressive liberal representative Luis de Sosa made patent in his speech, constituent power was the most prominent power of the nation, the source of legitimacy among differentiated powers including the municipal and the moderate ones belonging to provinces and the monarch respectively (DSCC, 7 April 1837: 2545).

In 1836 and 1837 MPs were concerned about the institutional mechanisms to counterweigh state powers without diminishing the capacity of the executive and the legislative powers to exercise their functions. As Agustín Armendáriz, progressive liberal, admitted, the meddling of state powers undermined any representative government (DSCC, 10 November 1836: 196). The representative bond between the nation and *Cortes* was falsified in those cases in which the executive power invaded the rest of the powers. Even worse, regardless of the relationship between nation and *Cortes* there was no attempt to outline the features of the modern Spanish *Cortes* as compared to medieval *Cortes* or to foreign parliaments (Medina Muñoz 1976: 181).

The relationship between political representation and the exercise of a parliamentary function by elected representatives began to be controversial during the constitutional debate of 1836–1837. The very idea of political representation was discussed to reflect individual representation. The political nation, Spain, consisted of individuals with colliding interests. For the first time in Spain's constitutional history, the concept of representation was grounded as a political idea with clear outlines.

3 The Constitutional Debate of 1844–1845

This section delves into the constitutional debate of 1844–1845 (10 October 1844–23 May 1845). First, it contextualizes that debate by outlining the different parliamentary tendencies in the Congress of Deputies, the Spanish lower chamber: moderate liberals, conservatives and progressives. Second, it surveys how constitution, monarchy and nation were intertwined ideas that received their meanings in tune with the political stances of representatives of each parliamentary tendency.

3.1 The Predominance of Moderate Liberals

By 1844 the exclusive right to vote for owners was positively regarded by moderate MPs, as the conservative Fernando Calderón Collantes admitted. To him, as to the bulk of moderate liberals, that was the only path to establish a lasting representative government without proletarian uprisings (Varela Suanzes-Carpegna 2005: 118). Moderate liberals hampered constitutional agreements between political tendencies. That parliamentary group revised the political foundations of parliamentary politics in Spain to enshrine shared sovereignty between *Cortes* and the crown instead of national sovereignty (Iñesta 2010: 42).

Consequently, the Constitution of 1845 instituted shared sovereignty of *Cortes* and king, as the Secretary of the Constitutional Commission, Juan Donoso Cortés, a moderate liberal by that time, wanted to include it within the preamble of the Constitution (Varela Suanzes-Carpegna 2014: 131). National sovereignty was not acknowledged in the Constitution because it was interpreted as a setback to the prerogatives of the crown and the stability of the parliamentary regime. Progressive tendencies were almost completely excluded from the constitutional agreement, unlike what happened during the constituent assembly of 1836–1837, in which the moderate minority could include part of its demands into the constitutional wording.

The Constitution of 1845 replaced the constitutional text of 1837 and by doing so it set a doubtful precedent according to which a constitution could be left to the discretionary power of a political group to the detriment of its rivals. In practice, that institutional practice was against the very idea of a lasting constitutional agreement between different political tendencies (Varela Suanzes-Carpegna 1983: 104). The fact that ministers could be elected as members of the legislative power affected negatively the division of powers as conceived of in 1812 (Baro Pazos 1987: 61).

During the constitutional debate of 1844–1845, three political groups should be differentiated within the same political party, the Monarchic-Constitutional Party. The first of them advocated shared sovereignty between King and *Cortes* and gradual reforms. Some of their most prominent members were Francisco Martínez de la Rosa, Antonio Alcalá Galiano, Alejandro Mon and Juan Donoso Cortés. The second group, a conservative one akin to Carlist vindications was led by Manuel González de la Pezuela, Marquis of Viluma. The third tendency was made up of the closest group to progressive MPs, led by Joaquín Francisco Pacheco, Francisco Javier Istúriz, Antonio de los Ríos Rosas, and José Posada Herrera, whose intellectual concerns were more ambitious when compared to the rest of groups (Varela Suanzes-Carpegna 2020: 2010–12).

Parliamentary groups disagreed about the wording of constitutional articles. Progressive deputies sought to imitate the Constitution of 1837, whereas moderate deputies preferred to set limits to constitutional freedoms and regarded the Constitution on an equal footing with other laws. The predominance of moderate liberals gave rise to conceptual disputes about the very idea of Spain as a nation. Nation and constitution became keywords of the political vocabulary.

3.2 *Constitution, Monarchy and Nation*

As Nicomedes Pastor Díaz, member of the Liberal Union, blatantly expressed, that all parties or political groups would agree on the same constitution meant to establish common grounds for all Spaniards to accept it. Stability was consequently considered a determinant precondition for constitutional success (DSC, 30 October 1844: 149). Without stable institutions, the Spanish nation was left alone to face permanent threats of civil coexistence. If that was the case, legality and representative government were compromised over time. Constitutions were instruments to channel the demands of political changes by active citizens in tune with gradual reformism. That aim precluded trailblazing accounts of constitutions.

Nicomedes Pastor Díaz stated that "the constitutional chart of a country cannot be as high as the Throne".[9] Then, it was patent that to moderate liberals the crown should not be subordinated to the Constitution. In fact, any constitutional agreement should begin by casting aside any doubts about the supremacy of the king or queen in the constitutional order. Constitutional articles were a dogma to be enhanced through ordinary laws. The positive view on constitutions by moderate liberals was strictly instrumental: a means to safeguard the crown beyond partisan leanings.

José Posada Herrera, a prominent legal scholar and moderate liberal by that time, said in an outspoken style that the constituent power was superior to the ordinary constituted powers, essential to elaborate a constitution in accordance with the sovereignty of the Spanish nation (DSC, 31 October 1844: 165). Sovereignty was to him compatible with constitutional agreements. But the constituent power had competences to be qualified as a special power to elaborate a constitution that could not be easily reformed through ordinary laws.

National sovereignty relied on a constitutional text that would set down the rights of Spaniards and constituted powers. Posada Herrera bestowed on the constituent power a special faculty that differentiated the constitution from the rest of the legal order and subordinated ordinary laws to it. This aspect was far from being obvious during nineteenth-century liberalism. Indeed, that view did not crystallize until the passing of the Constitution of 1931.

Miguel Puche y Bautista, moderate liberal, clarified that "the Spanish nation is constituted, it has a constitution, it does not need to constitute

[9] "*La Carta constitucional de un país no puede estar tan alta como el Trono*" (DSC, 30 October 1844: 151).

itself, what this is about is just to make some reforms".[10] Transactions were meant to set out the validity of the constitution. Yet these agreements were not just difficult to attain, but they unleashed clashing views about the pace of reforms and the existence of a constituent power. Disagreements led moderate representatives, a majority in the Spanish *Cortes* formed in 1844–1845, to pass a constitutional text that was portrayed as insufficient and mistaken by progressive representatives. To negotiate the constitution pervaded the parliamentary practice of constitutional loyalty among parties with extraordinary negative consequences for the political stability of the country.

Unlike Miguel Puche y Bautista, the radical liberal José María Orense claimed that constitutions were instruments to make it possible happiness for citizens through good governments against the reluctant endorsement of constitutions by moderate liberals (DSC, 7 March 1845: 1687). To Orense the distrust of constitutions by moderate liberals was unjustified and contrary to the endeavours of the rest of the chamber. Constitutions made it possible for the nation to exist under a single jurisdiction for all territories. But constitutions were also means to ease citizens' lives through positive measures by governments that should always remain loyal to the nation.

When depicting the Constitution of 1845 to be passed, Ramón María Narváez, moderate liberal and head of government (*Presidente del Congreso de Ministros*) by that time, pointed out that the chief aim of the *Cortes* was to strengthen the Constitution, "fundamental law of the monarchy" (DSC, 23 May 1845: 2722). Transactions were regarded as positive when endorsing the monarchic form of government. Nevertheless, any efforts to question executive prerogatives of the monarch or to enhance constitutional rights were deemed inconsistent with the institutional history of the country.

Ramón María Narváez spoke to defend the new Constitution to say before *Cortes* that "your first work [...] was the reform of the Constitution [...], received by the Nation with that respect and trust that should inspire the agreement of the supreme powers of the state, engaged in

[10] "[*L*]*A Nación española está constituida, tiene Constitución, no necesita constituirse; únicamente de lo que se trata es de que se hagan algunas reformas*" (DSC, 26 November 1844: 646).

strengthening and improving the fundamental law of the Monarchy".[11] His speech summarized the moderate liberal motto of crown and constitution as cooperative bodies. Monarchy was the form of government of the Spanish nation and no constitution which deserved that name could abolish it. Thus, to moderate liberals the monarchy was a precondition for the existence of a constitution. To say Spanish monarchy was to uphold the existence of the Spanish nation; to say constitution was to endorse the fundamental law of the monarchy.

4 The Constitution of 1869: A Strongly Ideological Debate

In this section, the conceptual affinities of the ideas of nation, monarchy, and democracy are compared with each other as reflected in the constitutional debate of 1869 (11 February 1869–1 June 1869). The clash between democrats and republicans, on the one hand, and moderate and progressive liberals, on the other, gave rise to a closer relationship between individual rights and political nation which lessened the unfriendliness of moderate liberalism towards the full acknowledgement of constitutional rights. Consequently, the supremacy of the constitution over ordinary laws began to be seriously considered as the best instrument to shelter individual rights.

4.1 Republicanism and Monarchism as Ideologies

The Revolutionary Sexennium (1868–1974) gave democrats and republicans an opportunity to revamp exhausted political institutions, firstly, by dethroning Isabel II, secondly, by improving the political education of popular classes through an electoral vote, and thirdly, by contriving a programme of economic and social reforms to gradually modernizing the institutions of the country.

The Constituent Assembly of 1869 began its sessions on 11 February 1869, after a general election through universal suffrage for adult males was held between 15 and 18 January that year in the Iberian Peninsula.

[11] "*Vuestra primera obra* [...] *fue la reforma de la Constitución* [...], *acogida por la Nación con aquel respeto y confianza que debía inspirarle el acuerdo de los supremos Poderes del Estado, ocupados en robustecer y mejorar la ley fundamental de la Monarquía*" (DSC, 23 May 1845: 2722).

The Progressive Party and the Democratic Party received a large number of votes, enough to agree to the passing of a new constitution that would be closer to the one of 1837 than to the moderate one of 1845. Article 32 enshrined national sovereignty; Article 33 acknowledged the monarchic form of government; and Article 35 handed the executive power to the king, though its exercise fell on his appointed ministers.

Four political groups are to be distinguished during the constitutional debate of 1869: moderates, progressives, unionists, and democrats. Within these parliamentary factions, rival trends competed to impose their political views in the constitution (Bolaños Mejías 1998: 185–86). On 2 March 1869 the Constitutional Commission that wrote the constitutional draft discussed in parliament was made up. 15 MPs belonged to it: Salustiano Olózaga, Eugenio Montero Ríos, Cristóbal Valera, Joaquín Aguirre and Pedro Mata (Progressive Party); José Posada Herrera, Antonio de los Ríos Rosas, Manuel Silvela, Augusto Ulloa Castañón and Antonio Aguilar Correa (Liberal Union); Cristino Martos, Segismundo Moret, Vicente Romero Girón, Manuel Becerra, and Carlos Godínez de Paz (Democratic Party) (Varela Suanzes-Carpegna 2020: 272–73).

During parliamentary debates, the quarrel around monarchic rule was addressed on many occasions to the point of darkening more pressing debates about the economy and society. Those moderate liberals who did not join the Liberal Union were in practice excluded from parliamentary negotiations. The fact that both moderate liberals and republicans were left in the margins of the party system led the former to seek agreements with the Liberal Union and the latter to carry out an obstructionist practice through long and calculated parliamentary speeches by Francisco Pi i Margall, Estanislao Figueras and Emilio Castelar (Vilches 2015: 241–43).

Since Republicans were not included in the Democratic Party, being considered a threat to political stability, the election of a new king was a matter of concern for the bulk of political representatives. Freedom of worship, individual rights, and form of government were the issues that gave republican representatives advantages over their opponents (Vilches 2015: 245). To republican deputies, any irresponsible monarch before the *Cortes* was an unbounded sovereign power who contradicted national sovereignty.

In the context of changing parliamentary majorities during 1868 and 1869 monarchy meant “democratic monarchy” (Pascual Sastre 2020: 2). In that political circumstance, monarchy should be subordinated to democratic legality. Men of any class should have the right to vote in order to choose among political alternatives. Neither progressives nor moderates could endorse the Bourbon dynasty without electoral costs. To vest monarchy with more prerogatives would have been desirable to the parliamentary minority that consisted of moderate liberals, but scarcely practical from a political perspective (Pascual Sastre 2020: 10).

For instance, to the republican leader Emilio Castelar, monarchy was directly opposed to democracy and republicanism because kings and queens embodied the privileges that no other group of individuals or families could enjoy (Saiz Valdivieso 1999: 176). Republicanism worked as an ideology gathering hostile groups against monarchy and turned out to be the strongest political organization in urban areas of the country. To endorse a republican form of government was to assume democratic reforms for the country.

4.2 *Nation, Monarchy, and Democracy*

Following the political benchmark of republicans and democrats, monarchy was considered a moderating and regulatory power that made it easier for the legislative, the executive, and the judicial powers to work in balance with each other (Nieto Sánchez 2017: 76). At least it was so for liberal democrats, the Liberal Union and the Moderate Party. Indeed, the existence of organic laws to implement constitutional articles could lead to the election of a new monarch in parliament, as it finally occurred when Amadeo I of Savoy was elected king on 2 January 1871 (Vallejo Fernández de la Reguera 1993: 686).

As Joaquín Varela Suanzes-Carpegna has suggested, in 1869 the Spanish nation created a monarchy and not the other way around (Varela Suanzes-Carpegna 2006: 212–13). Monarchy had to be subordinated to the Spanish nation and its office regulated through law to ensure a truly moderating power (Varela Suanzes-Carpegna 2006: 220). That moderating power meant that the king was not allowed to make decisions that would compromise the independence of the executive, the legislative, and the judicial powers. His functions should be those written in the constitution, far afield from prerogatives to meddle in parliamentary politics. The monarchy was endowed with a symbolic power that for the first time in the history of Spain was seriously questioned, deemed inefficient, and opposed to constitutional freedoms by broad social groups of democratic and republican leanings.

The parliamentary behaviour of the republican minority was remarkably indomitable and very often exceeded their authority as elected representatives in parliament (Vilches 2015: 239). As the federal republican José María Orense voiced, "individual rights will always be superior to the *Cortes* and the nation itself; even when we admit this, the power of the *Cortes* is always an important power".[12] In that same regard, the democrat Nicolás María Rivero argued that to talk about a Spanish revolution was to put national sovereignty and universal suffrage above the rest of political axioms of modern times (DSCC, 22 February 1869: 84).

"National sovereignty, individual rights and administrative decentralization" were some of the keywords that the republican MP and lawyer Ramón Castejón endorsed as innovations of the new political time that Spain faced (DSCC, 10 March 1869: 403). Political changes were positively regarded because democratic and republican aims were compatible with a new territorial organization for Spain. Getting rid of the monarchic rule seemed an alternative to the lack of political and economic reforms implemented by moderate liberal representatives.

Following that new boost of political reformism, the Spanish nation was portrayed as a society of mutual insurance to which its members should contribute with their best performance as free citizens (DSCC, 23 March 1869: 640). The experienced liberal Antonio Méndez de Vigo, of the Liberal Union, sketched the idea of sovereignty as factual sovereignty to which all representatives, willingly or not, had to commit themselves in order to be loyal to the country (DSCC, 29 April 1869: 1462).

The constitutional debate of 1869 made it patent the necessity of political reforms. A discredited monarchy opened the path to claims for a decentralized political nation. From that moment onwards the Spanish nation, understood as a unitary political nation embracing Spaniards of any social and economic condition began to compete against two rivals: the monarchic endorsement of a centralized political nation, as understood by moderate liberals during the nineteenth century, and the rise of nationalist demands in Catalonia and the Basque Country.

[12] "[*L*]*os derechos individuales serán siempre superiores a las Cortes y a la Nación misma; aun cuando concedamos eso, el poder de las Cortes siempre es un poder importante*" (DSCC, 17 February 1869: 55).

4.3 An Assessment of State Institutions

Summing up underwent changes of state institutions, it is fair to affirm that the Constitution of 1869 relied on Enlightenment iusnaturalism as its philosophical source (Nieto Sánchez 2017: 73). Luis del Río y Ramos, who in 1873 became minister of grace and justice, was an example of these trends. He argued that individual rights had an innate base that legality should acknowledge as such (DSCC, 11 May 1869: 1813). If individuals were gifted with similar capacities such as reason and speech, then individual rights belonged to everyone even when laws would not acknowledge them.

Fundamental laws, public freedoms, and democracy were keywords associated with the political vocabulary of progressives, republicans, and democrats that filled a conceptual gap in the parliamentary vocabulary, reinvigorated since 1868 (Souto Paz 2002: 125). Legal mechanisms to protect and to enforce political and civil rights were some of the novelties included in the Constitution of 1869, even beyond the Belgian Constitution of 1831 and the French Constitution of 1848, from which the Spanish Constitution took inspiration (Souto Paz 2002: 131).

Augusto Ulloa Castañón, of the Liberal Union, was convinced about broadening the scope of individual freedoms. In his view citizens should be responsible for their public and private behaviour leaving aside the state, which had to manage other "undivided" issues such as providing means for the existence of an efficient legal justice and ensuring constitutional rights (DSCC, 13 May 1869: 1912). Individual freedoms and a system of justice to fight crimes were to him the milestones of new state institutions.

"Common legality" and "transaction" were terms that members of the Liberal Union such as Antonio de los Ríos Rosas used in their speeches when bringing up liberal standpoints that could enhance national prosperity and prevent violent uprisings against the constitutional order (DSCC, 20 May 1869: 2138). In that regard there was no sovereign power that could violate individual rights: that was equivalent to tyranny (DSCC, 26 May 1869: 2347).

During the constitutional debate of 1869 the left-wing of the Congress of Deputies, from progressive to democrats and republicans, argued that individual rights and political freedoms should prevail over discretionary cutbacks perpetrated by political elites. If individual rights enshrined in the Constitution were limited through ordinary or emergency laws, these rights were just empty declarations without practical outcomes.

For the first time since the *Cortes* of Cadiz individual rights were not interpreted as a result of but as a requirement for the existence of a parliamentary regime. Among the far-reaching consequences of this dogma, the existence of individual rights was correlated with the improvement of the living conditions of excluded groups: citizens without lands or other properties. Spanish society witnessed the rise of social, economic, and political organizations that made civil and political bonds growingly complex. The mainstay of Spanish classic liberalism, namely, monarchy, nation, parliament and constitution, were questioned.

5 Debating the Constitution of 1876

This section delves into the conceptual disputes around the concepts of sovereignty and nation during the constitutional debate of 1876 (15 February 1876–30 June 1876). First, it outlines the political context of that debate by regarding the two main political parties: the Liberal-Conservative Party, or simply Conservative Party, led by Antonio Cánovas del Castillo, and the Constitutional Party led by Práxedes Mateo-Sagasta. The former assumed liberal policies regarding the endorsement of a parliamentary regime based individual freedoms while keeping conservative policies against pressing social and economic changes. The latter was more receptive to political, social, and economic changes in order to gradually modernize the country.

Second, this section contrasts two concepts of sovereignty with each other: one with popular democratic features; the other with historicist overtones as defended by conservatives. Third, it draws attention to the concept of nation, which in case of dismissing conservative features was to be filled with new meanings. Two findings are summarized. First, the bearer of political sovereignty was confused with the exercise of sovereignty as if the monarchy would be a representative institution in a historicist sense, undermining parliamentary channels to deliberate. Second, the clashing views of national sovereignty made the concept of nation undefined for left-wing groups, but coherent to liberal conservatives.

5.1 *A Constitutional Debate Determined by Personalities*

A general election was held between 20 and 24 January 1876 through universal male suffrage. The Liberal-Conservative Party headed by Cánovas obtained 333 seats in parliament; the Constitutional Party led by Mateo-Sagasta only 28; the so-called intransigent moderates secured 12 seats; and democratic republicans such as Emilio Castelar and Juan María Anglada had seats in the Congress of Deputies, as also the monarchic democrat Ángel Carvajal Fernández de Córdoba, Marquis of Sardoal, did (Varela Suanzes-Carpegna 2020: 336).

The political groups which took part in the constitutional debate of 1876 were the majoritarian Liberal-Conservative Party, led by Antonio Cánovas del Castillo; the Moderate Party headed by Claudio Antonio Moyano, among other prominent personalities; the Constitutional Party, led by Práxedes Mateo-Sagasta and Manuel Ruiz Zorrilla; the centralists, led by Manuel Alonso Martínez; the republican groups led by Emilio Castelar; Carlists, led by Cándido Nocedal; and workers' parties (Álvarez Conde 1978: 82–84). Cánovas had an outstanding role during constitutional deliberations. Only the constitutional leader, Mateo-Sagasta, and the centralist head of the party, Alonso Martínez Alonso, partly outshined the leading position of Cánovas.

Since 1874 Cánovas and Mateo-Sagasta agreed on a restored monarchy to grant civil coexistence among Spaniards (Lario 2021: 82). Despite their disagreements, both aimed to establish a system of individual rights in the Constitution of 1876. Despite Cánovas' Burkean affinities, he underscored the perspective of doctrinaires avoiding what he regarded as excesses of both democratic republicans and Carlists favourable to the Ancient Regime (Martínez Sospedra 1981: 72–73). The doctrinaire influence as understood by Cánovas made it possible to reconcile the precapitalist social mentality of rural areas with the liberal mentality of the largest cities of the country in a precarious balance (Pérez-Prendes 1981: 28).

Cánovas summarized his political targets in an outspoken style: "constitutional monarchy" and "conservative principles" meant to preserve historical features of the Spanish nation that stood up over time against democratic attempts, deemed "demagoguery" and "utopia". Democracy was then equated to violence and anarchy. To rebuild the royal institution was not merely a rhetorical exercise. To him, monarchy was an institution preceding the constitutional text (DSC, 8 March 1876: 312). The existence of a monarchic regime was precondition for the existence of Spain as a political nation that no written constitution could dismiss.

As Alonso Martínez pointed out, to say that the nation owned itself was not the same that to question the monarchic form of government that would correspond to the country, something demanded by democratic and republican groups (DSC, 7 April 1876: 696). Cánovas and Mateo-Sagasta agreed on the Constitution of 1876 as the best means to get rid of the pervasive contestation of the country's institutions by democrats and republicans. None of them seriously challenged the idea of an 'internal' or 'material' constitution consisting of ancient customs and institutions that outlasted over time. Then, any written constitution should acknowledge those features to be legitimate.

5.2 Opposed Concepts of Sovereignty and Constitution

The Constitution of 1876 acknowledged both *Cortes* and king as cooperative powers in line with a historicist perspective that the Constitution of 1812 rejected (López Sánchez 2014: 192). Liberals who took part in the constitutional debate of the Cadiz Constitution refused to accept that national sovereignty could be replaced by shared sovereignty between *Cortes* and king. Despite that fact, doctrinaire constitutionalism in Spain remained strong even by 1876. Indeed, in the Constitution of 1876 the faculty of law-making was finally handed to *Cortes* with the king without explicitly mentioning sovereignty (Constitution of 1876, Article 18).

Nevertheless, historicism also had empirical roots according to which a decision in favour of monarchy was interpreted as a better answer than republican government in order to maintain political, social, and economic progress in the country. To sum it up, it can be said that Cánovas' idea of sovereignty was halfway historicism and the doctrine of moderating power elaborated by Benjamin Constant. To say sovereignty was to underline the unitary sense of the Spanish nation and its constitution. There was no sovereignty without bringing into focus the history of Spanish institutions, be that attempt a merely rhetorical device or an honest attempt to look over the historical institutions that could benefit stability and civil coexistence among Spaniards.

In that vein, any constitutional text could either mirror that social reality of a plurality of groups and ideas that should coexist with each other or be looked on as a fake agreement against the only true bearer of sovereignty, the Spanish nation. The problem, however, remained. Yet national sovereignty could lead to understanding that the nation was the only bearer of sovereignty, that circumstance did not mean the acknowledgement of political and civil rights in the constitution. How national sovereignty could entail a different content of constitutional rights without breaking with an individualistic conception of those rights?

The ideal of the full exercise of political and civil freedoms was not problematic to Cánovas insofar as he viewed both of them as necessarily kept within the bounds of institutional rules (Sánchez Ferriz 1998: 40). Public freedoms were conducive to liberty among citizens if the mainstay of civil peace among Spaniards was not threatened. Then, the very existence of the Spanish nation required agreements between parties whose ideological differences would be lessened as much as possible. To build a lasting nation meant to strengthen the political and civil bonds of citizens channelled through responsible parties and useful institutions. To put the nation before particular interests was to avoid violent authoritarian drifts and popular uprisings.

The progressive MP José Moreno Nieto admitted that after the revolutionary period of 1848 the "classic age of constitutionalism" vanished. In his view, after that revolutionary momentum, popular movements against institutions and demagoguery prevailed across Europe with terrible consequences for citizens' lives (DSC, 25 February 1876: 194). In a similar way, the conservative deputy Fernando Calderón Collantes contended that the nation has its own rights, "legitimately represented in the *Cortes* with the king" (DSC, 2 March 1876: 238). A historicist approach assumed that the nation and not merely individuals had rights.

The radical democrat Ángel Carvajal Fernández de Córdoba, Marquis of Sardoal, resorted to Spanish history to mention Juan de Mariana, Diego Saavedra Fajardo and the theologian Juan Márquez as previous authors that did not endorse absolute monarchy but a sort of national sovereignty (DSC, 11 March 1876: 363). This forced interpretation of classic Spanish thought aimed at justifying the constitutional reforms carried out by democrats against the enshrinement of a dual sovereignty shared between *Cortes* and king. In order to be rhetorically effective, democrats used Spanish thinkers as authorities, even when historical accuracy was completely distorted.

Augusto Ulloa Castañón, member of the centralist party and closer to the liberal-conservative group than he was in the past, held that the distinct feature of national sovereignty was to exclude any individual or family as its bearer (DSC, 19 April 1876: 813). In that regard, the liberal Ricardo Alzugaray assumed an institutional perspective about the very idea of a nation to say that sovereignty lies on written constitutions and decisions made by public powers. If the sovereignty of the nation and the monarch was to be accepted, that entailed to prevent the meddling of their faculties with each other (DSC, 24 April 1876: 893).

If national sovereignty was a historical feature of Spanish constitutions, then each one of the constitutional texts expressed contradictory views on sovereignty and political power that only the passing of time could repair. If a written constitution enshrined sovereignty as a shared or undivided attribute, then it was a matter of changing political balances between political groups in parliament. Even if that was true, secular meaning of national sovereignty and shared institutions around constitutional rights was the source and backbone of public powers. Whether that would mean admitting a historical, internal or material constitution was a different issue.

5.3 Constitutional Rhetoric Around the Unity of the Political Nation

Moderate and progressive rhetoric overemphasized the connection between federalism and anarchy, remarkably noted since the collapse of the Spanish First Republic (1873–1874). Secessionist threats seemed to rise during those years and almost encouraged by public authorities with republican and federalist trends. Thus, the rivalry between monarchic and republican groups grew over time.

Conceived by Cánovas as a political system of double confidence of *Cortes* and king, political parties should remain loyal to the Constitution and to the king or queen as well as to the *Cortes* promoting "conciliatory" demands with governing parties (Ramos Rovi 2000: 98). Not calling for upheavals against the legitimate power was a political duty to safeguard civil peace. Opposition parties had to respect the constitutional rules agreed upon and fighting government policies through public discussion, without having recourse to inflammatory speeches. No political group saw it as a legitimate option to jeopardize the unity of Spain as a nation.

Sánchez Ferriz suggests that the doctrine of shared sovereignty between *Cortes* and king implied an organic view of the Spanish nation. Alonso Martínez argued that Cánovas' concept of the nation collided with the national sovereignty of individuals, who had the right to express their views and to make decisions through electoral participation and by exercising their rights (Sánchez Ferriz 1979: 188). Individual rights could be dismissed as secondary if that union between *Cortes* and king was threatened.

In that regard, the liberal leader Práxedes Mateo-Sagasta advocated that national sovereignty was nothing else but the source of legitimacy to agree on political and social institutions for all Spaniards without distinction of class (DSC, 15 March 1876: 433). The unitary character of the Spanish nation was implied because of the existence of national sovereignty, one and undivided. To deny national sovereignty would unleash political cleavages between Spaniards. Without that premise, the existence of the Spanish nation lacked any sense and political institutions could be arbitrarily condemned as illegitimate leading to civil discord among citizens.

As the republican Emilio Castelar pointed out, "national sovereignty is a principle raised face to face against ancient monarchy and, consequently, an essentially liberal, democratic and modern principle".[13] That democratic stance casts aside any attempt to discredit political institutions, including parliament and monarchy, as exhausted and unfair. Liberal principles were at odds with a national sovereignty that did not correspond to individual freedoms.

The political institutions of the Spanish nation belonged to all Spaniards and were the result of political decisions made in parliament and then, endorsed by citizens. To overturning them was an unequivocal sign of an illegitimate uprising against the Spanish nation. Universal suffrage was a step forward to strengthen and enhance that legitimacy, but it should never be used as a plea to raze to the ground the institutions that people's endeavours had built for centuries. The rhetoric of shared sovereignty between *Cortes* and king was anti-liberal insofar as it could erode the baseline of constitutional rights for individuals in emergency periods.

[13] "*El principio de la soberanía nacional es un principio levantado frente a frente de la antigua Monarquía, y por consiguiente, un principio esencialmente liberal, democrático y moderno*" (DSC, 16 March 1876: 460).

Bibliography

Albaladejo, Tomás (2011). 'Los discursos del conflicto y los conflictos del discurso. Análisis interdiscursivo y retórica cultural', in *Vozes, Discursos e Identidades em Conflito*, eds. Ana Gabriela Macedo, Carlos Mendes de Sousa & Vítor Moura. Braga: Húmus.

Albaladejo, Tomás (2013). 'The Cortes of Cadiz: Discourses for the Constitution and for the Everyday Life', in *1812 Echoes: The Cadiz Constitution in Hispanic History, Culture and Politics*, eds. Stephen G. H. Roberts & Adam Sharman. Newcastle upon Tyne: Cambridge Scholars Publishing.

Álvarez Conde, Enrique (1978). 'La Constitución española de 30 de junio de 1876. Cuestiones previas', *Revista de Estudios Políticos*, 3, 79–100.

Aquillué Domínguez, Daniel (2015). 'La Constitución de 1837, ¿una Constitución transaccional?', *Revista Historia Autónoma*, 6, 45–49.

Aragón, María Aurora (1989). 'Traducciones de obras francesas en la "Gaceta de Madrid" entre 1790 y 1799', in *Imágenes de Francia en las letras hispánicas* [Symposium held at the University of Barcelona, 15 to 18 November 1988], 261–70. Barcelona: Promociones y Publicaciones Universitarias.

Artola, Miguel (1973). 'Guerra y revolución', in *La burguesía revolucionaria (1808–1874)*. Madrid: Alianza.

Baro Pazos, Juan (1987). 'Hacia la consolidación del régimen parlamentario en España. El Congreso de los Diputados en la Constitución de 1837', *Revista de Estudios Políticos*, 57, 55–106.

Bolaños Mejías, Carmen (1998). 'Soberanía nacional y soberanía compartida en la estructura política de la Constitución española de 1869', *Boletín de la Facultad de Derecho*, 13, 183–99.

Camus García, Estela (2015). *En torno al liberalismo de Agustín Argüelles. Una aproximación a la construcción política e intelectual de la idea de España.* Doctoral Thesis. Dir. Jesús M. Rodés. Barcelona: Universidad Autónoma de Barcelona.

Capellán de Miguel, Gonzalo (2002). 'Representación', in *Diccionario político y social del siglo XIX español*, eds. Javier Fernández Sebastián & Juan Francisco Fuentes. Madrid: Alianza.

Crawley, Charles W. (1939). 'French and English Influences in the Cortes of Cadiz, 1810–1814', *The Cambridge Historical Journal*, 6(2), 176–208.

Díaz Fernández, Paloma (2006). 'La Constitución de 1837. ¿Qué tipo de Monarquía queremos?', *Historia Contemporánea*, 18, 73–89.

Escobar Fornos, Iván (2012). 'La Constitución de Cádiz. Modelo de constitucionalismo', *Anuario Iberoamericano de Justicia Constitucional*, 16, 165–89.

Fernández Sarasola, Ignacio (2010). 'La opinión pública. De la Ilustración a las Cortes de Cádiz', *Ayer. Revista de Historia Contemporánea*, 80(4), 53–81.

Fernández Sarasola, Ignacio (2016). "So, You Want Us to Be Englishmen…': Jovellanos and British Influence on Spain's First Modern Parliament (1808–1810)', *Comparative Legal History*, 4(1), 51–81.

Fernández Segado, Francisco (1983). 'Pragmatismo jurídico y concertación política. Dos ideas-clave en la obra de los constituyentes de 1837', *Revista de Derecho Político*, 20, 33–65.

Fuentes, Juan Francisco (2010). 'Las Cortes de Cádiz: Nación, soberanía y territorio', *Cuadernos de Historia Contemporánea*, 32, 17–35.

García Atance, María Victoria (1983). 'Crónica parlamentaria de la Constitución de 1837', *Revista de Derecho Político*, 20, 171–83.

González Rodríguez, Hortensia (2002). 'La forma de gobierno en el debate constituyente de 1869', *Revista de Derecho Político*, 55–56, 365–410.

Gurpegui, José Antonio (2018) 'Historical Determinism in the Constitutions of the United States and the Spanish of 1812', *Complutense Journal of English Studies*, 26, 9–25.

Hijano Pérez, Ángeles (2016). 'Las claves de la monarquía en las Cortes de Cádiz', *Rúbrica Contemporánea*, 5(9), 123–44.

Iñesta, Emilia (2010). 'The Spanish Parliament and Legislative Delegation (1844–1849)', *Parliaments, Estates & Representation*, 30(1), 41–56.

Lario, Ángeles (2021). 'The Consolidation of the Constitutional Monarchic System (1874–1902)', in *Monarchy and Liberalism in Spain: The Building of the Nation-State, 1780–1931*, eds. David San Narciso, Margarita Barral-Martínez & Carolina Armenteros. London & New York: Routledge.

López Sánchez, Carmina (2014). 'La soberanía compartida de 1876 frente a la soberanía nacional de 1812', *Revista de Historiografía*, 20, 189–98.

Luengo, Jorge & Paul Dalmau (2018). 'Writing Spanish History in the Global Age: Connections and Entanglements in the Nineteenth Century', *Journal of Global History*, 13, 425–45.

Luna-Fabritius, Adriana (2012). 'Defining the Borders for an Interpretation of the Concept of Liberalism in Cádiz's Constitutional Moment 1810–1812', Working Paper, Centro de Investigación y Docencia Económicas (CIDE), 78, 1–22.

Marichal, Carlos (1980). *La revolución liberal y los primeros partidos políticos en España: 1834–1844*. Madrid: Cátedra.

Martínez Sospedra, Manuel (1981). 'Las fuentes de la Constitución de 1876. Continuidad y cambio en el constitucionalismo español del siglo XIX', *Revista de Derecho Político*, 8, 71–96.

Medina Muñoz, Miguel Ángel (1976). 'Las Cortes en la Constitución de 1845', *Revista de Estudios Políticos*, 208–209, 131–48.

Mirow, Matthew C. (2010). 'Visions of Cadiz: The Constitution of 1812 in Historical and Constitutional Thought', *Studies in Law, Politics and Society*, 53, 59–88.

Müßig, Ulrike ed. (2016). *Reconsidering Constitutional Formation: National Sovereignty. A Comparative Analysis of the Juridification by Constitution*. New York: Springer.

Müller, Marius (2016). 'The Notion of Sovereignty in the Constitutional Process of Cádiz', *Ivs Fvgit. Revista de Cultura Jurídica*, 19, 177–208.

Nieto Sánchez, Carlos (2017). 'Soberanía nacional y monarquía. La oposición republicana a la opción monárquica en la Constitución de 1869', *Fides et Ratio*, 2, 65–78.

Núñez Rivero, José María Cayetano (1983). 'Inviolabilidad e inmunidad en la Constitución de 1837', *Revista de Derecho Político*, 20, 151–59.

Pascual Sastre, Isabel María (2020). 'Teoría y práctica de la monarquía nacional y democrática. La Constitución de 1869 y su forma de gobierno', *Bulletin d'Histoire Contemporaine de l'Espagne*, 55, 1–18.

Pérez Ledesma, Manuel (1991). 'Las Cortes de Cádiz y la sociedad española', *Ayer*, 1, 167–206.

Pérez-Prendes, José Manuel (1981). 'Continuidad y discontinuidad en la Constitución de 1876', *Revista de Estudios Políticos*, 8, 21–32.

Ramos Rovi, María José (2000). 'La Constitución de 1876 a través de los discursos parlamentarios', *Revista de Historia Contemporánea*, 9–10(1), 85–100.

Ramos Silgado, Héctor (2022). 'El clero en las Cortes constituyentes de 1836–1837', *Anuario de Historia de la Iglesia Andaluza*, 15, 259–96.

Romeo Mateo, María Cruz (1998). 'Lenguaje y política del nuevo liberalismo moderado y progresista, 1834–1845', *Ayer*, 29, 37–62.

Rosales, José María (2018). 'Parliamentarism in Spanish Politics in the Nineteenth and Twentieth Centuries: From Constitutional Liberalism to Democratic Parliamentarism', in *Parliament and Parliamentarism: A Comparative History of a European Concept*, eds. Pasi Ihalainen, Cornelia Ilie & Kari Palonen. New York: Berghahn.

Saiz Valdivieso, Alfonso Carlos (1999). 'Don Emilio Castelar en las Cortes Constituyentes de 1869 (Apuntes para conmemorar un centenario olvidado)', *Estudios de Deusto*, 47(2), 171–84.

Sánchez Ferriz, Remedio (1979). 'Aproximación al concepto de soberanía en el pensamiento de Cánovas y su consideración en las Cortes de 1876', *Estudis. Revista de Historia Moderna*, 8, 177–91.

Sánchez Ferriz, Remedio (1998). 'Cánovas y la Constitución de 1876', *Revista de Estudios Políticos*, 101, 9–44.

Sierra, María, Rafael Zurita & María Antonia Peña (2006). 'La representación política en el discurso del liberalismo español (1845–1874)', *Ayer*, 61, 15–45.

Smith, Angel (2016). 'The Rise and Fall of 'Respectable' Spanish Liberalism, 1808–1923: An Explanatory Framework', *Journal of Iberian and Latin American Studies*, 22(1), 55–73.

Souto Paz, José Antonio (2002). 'Las libertades públicas en la Constitución de 1869', *Revista de Derecho Político*, 55–56, 107–58.

Tajadura Tejada, Javier (2012). 'La problemática de los límites del poder de reforma constitucional en la Constitución de Cádiz. Límites materiales y limitación temporal', *Historia Constitucional*, 13, 257–70.

Timmermann, Andreas & Ulrike Müßig (2017). 'Sovereignty Doctrines in the Constitutional Debates Around the Cadiz Cortes: Transition of Monarchical Sovereignty to National Sovereignty', *Giornale di Storia Costituzionale*, 34, 105–35.

Tomás Villarroya, Joaquín (1983). 'La publicación de la Constitución de 1837', *Revista de Derecho Político*, 20, 15–31.

Vallejo Fernández de la Reguera, Jesús (1993). 'Ortografía y heterografía constitucionales (1869)', *Anuario de historia del derecho español*, 63–64, 615–700.

Varela Suanzes-Carpegna, Joaquín (1983). 'La Constitución española de 1837. Una Constitución transaccional', *Revista de Derecho Político*, 20, 95–106.

Varela Suanzes-Carpegna, Joaquín (2005). 'Propiedad, ciudadanía y sufragio en el constitucionalismo español (1810–1845)', *Historia Constitucional*, 6, 105–23.

Varela Suanzes-Carpegna, Joaquín (2006). 'La monarquía en las Cortes y en la Constitución de 1869', *Historia Constitucional*, 7, 209–28.

Varela Suanzes-Carpegna, Joaquín (2013). 'La Constitución de 1876 y la organización territorial del Estado', *Iura Vasconiae*, 10, 11–37.

Varela Suanzes-Carpegna, Joaquín (2014). *Política y Constitución en España (1808–1978)*, 2nd ed. Madrid: Centro de Estudios Políticos y Constitucionales.

Varela Suanzes-Carpegna, Joaquín (2020). *Historia constitucional de España*, ed. Ignacio Fernández Sarasola. Madrid: Marcial Pons.

Vera Santos, José Manuel (2006). 'La influencia del constitucionalismo francés en la fase de reafirmación constitucional española (1837–1845)', *Revista de Derecho Político*, 67, 167–210.

Vilches, Jorge (2015). 'Entre el parlamentarismo y la insurrección. La minoría republicana en las Cortes Constituyentes de la revolución (1869-1871)', *Historia y Política*, 34, 239–67.

Westler, Brendon (2015). 'Between Tradition and Revolution: The Curious Case of Francisco Martínez Marina, the Cadiz Constitution, and Spanish Liberalism', *Journal of the History of Ideas*, 76(3), 393–416.

CHAPTER 3

The Historical Framework of Spain's Twentieth-Century Constitutional Debates

This chapter appraises the innovations of the political language produced by the parliamentary deliberations of Spain's twentieth-century constitutional debates. The new democratic regimes that resulted from the constituent assemblies of 1931 and 1977–1978 hastened political changes affecting the meanings of basic political concepts. Both constitutional debates resulted in two parliamentary regimes in line not only with the constitutional tradition of the country since the General and Extraordinary *Cortes* (*Cortes Generales y Extraordinarias*) of Cadiz in 1810, but also with the contemporary trends of European constitutionalism. In 1931 parliamentary democracy was inseparable from a partisan understanding of democracy, whereas in 1978 democratic pluralism was fairly interpreted as compatible with the adversarial practice of parliamentary democracy.

F. J. Bellido, *Constitutional Debates, Rhetoric, and Political Philosophy in Spain's Parliamentary History*, Rhetoric, Politics and Society, https://doi.org/10.1007/978-3-031-56894-7_3

1 The Constituent Assembly of 1931

This section presents the main features of the Constituent Assembly of 1931. Firstly, it pays attention to the context of that Constituent Assembly. Secondly, it clarifies its similarities to interwar constitutionalism. Finally, as a token of the conceptual changes in that assembly, it surveys some of the concepts to whose semantic renewal they contributed: religious freedom, freedom of education, and freedom of conscience.

1.1 Contrasting Ideological Alternatives

The Spanish Second Republic and the Constituent Assembly of 1931 were originally characterized by their political and intellectual elites as the result of a popular revolution. The declared aims of republican politicians were to break with oligarchy, chieftainship (*caciquismo*), and other misuses of the past that deteriorated parliamentary institutions, discrediting national politics (Ben-Ami 1978: 231). Bourgeois political elites of the past, the army, and the Catholic Church were deemed by an increasing number of groups incapable of revamping the Spanish political system.

Local elections in April 1931 were interpreted as a plebiscite against the monarchy. Their results led to proclaiming the Spanish Second Republic. The new republican democracy meant the refusal of general Miguel Primo de Rivera's dictatorship (1923–1930) and to the Bourbon Restoration (1874–1931) (García Canales 1977: 181). It was a sudden break with the past that intended to answer the longing for democracy, freedom, and republic in Spanish society that kept growing almost since the beginning of Primo de Rivera's authoritarian rule.

The Constituent Assembly of 1931, held between August and December 1931, resulted in a constitution passed on 9 December. It was aimed to promote ambitious economic and social policies that challenged traditional institutions and increased the role of the state against the liberal state of nineteenth-century Spain. The ideological trends of democratic socialism, social radicalism and centre radicalism of French roots, classic liberalism, and traditionalism provided their own answers to rebuild the state.

Interwar constitutionalism's main features were assumed by Spanish MPs during the constitutional sessions in parliament during 1931. The control of the executive power to strengthen the legislative branch and the constitutional control of laws were thought to prevent authoritarian drifts. The Constitution and its enforcement followed a general model to rationalize political powers based to a great extent on the theories of the Russian-French scholar Boris Mirkine Guetzévitch (Corcuera Atienza 1991: 17). The Spanish Constitution was undoubtedly interpreted as the supreme law of the country to which other laws should be subordinated.

1.2 Theoretical Backgrounds to the Constituent Assembly of 1931

Spanish MPs used arguments that were grounded in public and administrative law. Many of them, such as Fernando de los Ríos (Spanish Socialist Workers' Party, democratic socialism), Niceto Alcalá-Zamora (Progressive Republican Party, classic liberalism), Antonio Royo Villanova (Popular Agrarian Minority, liberal conservatism), Rafael Guerra del Río (Radical Republican Party, centrist republicanism), Melquíades Álvarez (Liberal Democratic Republican Party, liberal reformism), Ángel Galarza (Radical Socialist Republican Party, social liberalism inspired by French Jacobin trends), Mariano Ruiz Funes (Republican Action Party, left-wing reformism), Manuel Rico Avello (Group at the Service of the Republic, intellectual reformism) or Joaquín Beunza (Basque-Navarre Minority, traditionalism), were scholars with different legal backgrounds. They addressed conceptual issues connected with each one of the questions raised during the constitutional sessions. These representatives combined argumentations rooted in the history of legal and political thought, be their focus on the national history of Spain or transnational exchanges.

Their contributions relied on their own interpretations of interwar constitutionalism and public law. Their capacity to revamp the Spanish political vocabulary in a democratic sense keeps some similarities with the constitutional debate of 1977–1978. First, both constitutional debates produced the only two democratic constitutions of Spain in the twentieth century, which came after dictatorships. Second, both debates were embedded in the European legal and political experiences of constitutionalism and the political thought of interwar and post-World War II respectively.

Different understandings of the institutional checks of the republican regime led to irreconcilable viewpoints between left-wing and right-wing political parties. It was a source of polarization, and precisely because of that, an explanatory tool of ideologies and concepts. The case of the religious question is representative of this controversy. Revising the role of political parties and representatives during the parliamentary sessions about religious freedom, freedom of education, and freedom of conscience clarifies the defence of or the refusal to accept the autonomy of Catholic institutions in the context of state secularization which determined some of the conceptual controversies in that Constituent Assembly.

2 Comparing the Constitutional Debates of 1931 and 1977–1978

This section, firstly, outlines how MPs followed dissimilar strategies in both constitutional debates to establish democracy. Secondly, it analyses the implications of the constitutional debate of 1977–1978 in national politics bearing in mind its main differences when compared to the one of 1931. Thirdly, it argues in favour of acknowledging the influence of the constitutional debate that resulted in the current Constitution of Spain over the modernization of the political vocabulary. That renewal of the political language is itself a resource to be explored by means of political philosophy and conceptual history. Finally, it highlights that representatives built part of their arguments on both a selection of contributions to the history of political thought and on their own interpretations of the parliamentary history of the country.

2.1 Two Moments of Democratization

The aforementioned constitutional debates entailed two processes of political democratization after dictatorships. The constitutional debate of 1931 was based on a partisan style of democracy where negotiations between parties were often regarded as a way to relinquish electoral commitments with the electorate, thus seeming to jeopardize the moral principles of ideologies. The constitutional debate of 1977–1978, instead, replaced momentarily that partisan understanding of democracy with a pluralist practice in which parties and ideologies were acknowledged as the channels of political representation.

The Constituent Assembly of 1931 exemplified the start of an interrupted but valuable process towards democratization. In the Spanish transition to democracy initiated 46 years afterwards representatives such as for example the centrist José Pedro Pérez-Llorca, together with the socialist Gregorio Peces-Barba, resumed some of the political, intellectual and legal contributions of 1931 to further develop them.

Parliament's representative character was enshrined in Article 66 of the Constitution of 1978: "The *Cortes Generales* [parliament] represent the Spanish people and consist of the Congress of Deputies and the Senate".[1] Members of the Congress of Deputies are usually named as deputies; members of the Senate, as senators. Unlike the constitutional debate of 1977–1978, in the Constituent Assembly of 1931 there was only a parliamentary chamber, the Congress of Deputies. Articles 1 and 5 of the Constitution of the Spanish Second Republic enshrined, respectively, popular sovereignty and the Congress of Deputies as the institution in which citizens' representatives exercised the legal authority of law-making.

A majority of deputies after the election of 15 June 1977, from right-wing to left-wing ideologies, agreed that the Constitution of 1931 was a milestone of the country's constitutional history. From a practical point of view, as much as from an intellectual perspective, that constitutional text did not represent a truncated democratic experience, but a worthy part of the history of Spain, necessary to recast the language and the institutions of democracy.

2.2 *Reinterpreting the Legacy of the Constituent Assembly of 1931*

The changes brought about as a result of a democratic process in 1977 and 1978, albeit with its own distinctive features, ran parallel to the relatively sudden reconceptualization of the political vocabulary. Three years after the death of Francisco Franco the political vocabulary of the dictatorship had been totally discredited. By 1978 its lexicon had almost completely vanished from parliamentary politics keeping a very reduced presence in the public debate.

Many representatives after the general election of 15 June 1977 were qualified lawyers and scholars trained in the European political culture of the 1950s and the 1960s, such as Gabriel Cisneros, José Pedro Pérez-Llorca, Óscar Alzaga, Joaquín Garrigues, and Francisco Fernández Ordóñez, of Union of Democratic Centre; Gregorio Peces-Barba, Eduardo Martín Toval, Virgilio Zapatero and Enrique Múgica, of the Spanish Socialist Workers' Party; and Miquel Roca Junyent, of the Democratic Pact for Catalonia.

[1] "Las Cortes Generales representan al pueblo español y están formadas por el Congreso de los Diputados y el Senado" (Spanish Constitution of 1978, art. 66).

By 1978 deputies of different parties agreed that two prominent flaws of the Constitution of 1931 were the regulation of the so-called religious issue (Articles 25, 26, and 27) and the confusing wording to define the constitutional role of the president of the republic regarding the executive and the legislative powers (from Article 67 to Article 85). Freedom of worship was limited, and the Jesuit religious order was banned in 1932. Some of the constitutional competences of both the president of the republic and government could be interpreted by the courts of justice as if they were contradictory with each other, then compromising the effective functioning of institutions.

Unlike in 1931, in 1977 and 1978 parliamentary politics meant a very particular sense of consensus: a momentary phase of the Spanish democratic transition to democracy when MPs accepted negotiations and were professionally committed not just to parties and ideologies, but to the building of democratic institutions. In that vein, the partisan understanding of democracy as the clash between irreconcilable ideological aims in 1931 was replaced by a pluralist consensus considered by most political actors as the only path available to build democratic institutions and to safeguard civil peace. That assumption made it possible the practice of adversarial democracy in Spain after 1978 (Rosales 2016b: 225–26).

Moderate representatives of right-wing and left-wing ideologies agreed that the argumentative profile of the constitutional deliberations of 1931 should be imitated in parliament during 1977–1978. Precautions against partisanships that could undermine the consensual character of the Constitution of 1978 were the main lessons to be learned from 1931. By the same token, the deliberative character of debates should be strengthened, making possible disagreements, be they either ideological or pragmatic, as a nuclear aspect of consensus.

Deputies understood the democratic sense of professional politics as an irreducible pluralistic activity. Their speeches, often relying on theoretical contributions of the history of political thought, were at some moments vindications of the parliamentary history of Spain during the nineteenth and the first three decades of the twentieth century. It was so in the light of a process that through democratic means should finish the brotherly hatred provoked by the Spanish Civil War (1936–1939) and, in the aftermath of the Spanish Second Republic (1931–1939), Franco's dictatorship (1939–1975). Since the end of the Spanish Second Republic

Spain's role in the international realm was marginalized (Rosales 2014: 137). However, the democratic transition to democracy and, more specifically, the constitutional debate of 1977–1978 showed that Spain could follow the example of other European democracies.

3 The Context of Political Changes Before the Constitutional Debate of 1977–1978

This section seeks to clarify the political changes that made the constitutional debate possible. Firstly, it explains the legal changes that hastened the downfall of the institutions of Francoism. Secondly, it presents the chronology of events from the death of the dictator until the general election held on 15 June 1977. Thirdly, the analysis describes the distribution of seats in parliament regarding ideological trends. Fourthly, it presents to which extent the threat of terrorism had the effect of strengthening the politics of consensus between parties. Finally, it summarizes the consensus practised since the Moncloa Pacts (*Pactos de la Moncloa*) of October 1977.

3.1 First Political Changes

The so-called Francoist *Cortes* (*Cortes franquistas*), namely, the Spanish Parliament during the dictatorship, was in fact a corporate, organic system of fascist inspiration and not truly representative. Neither political parties nor pluralist elections existed. Separation of powers was excluded, and the sovereign power was held by the head of state, the dictator Franco himself. Nevertheless, since the 1960s some groups within the regime advocated political reforms to make Spain gradually closer to European democracies.

Two days after the death of the dictator Juan Carlos I was proclaimed king of Spain and head of state. Even though he confirmed Carlos Arias Navarro, a regime insider, as head of government (*presidente del gobierno*), on 1 July 1976 the king himself demanded Arias Navarro resign. Juan Carlos I appointed Adolfo Suárez, another regime insider, as head of government. Against the negative prospects of democrats, Suárez showed a high capacity to dialogue with democratic groups with the promise of transforming Spain into a democracy comparable to others in Europe.

Suárez, in collaboration with Torcuato Fernández-Miranda, another regime insider in favour of democracy, conceived of a strategy to break the foundations of the Francoist legality from within. The so-called Law for Political Reform devised by Fernández-Miranda was passed on 18 November 1976 and came into force on 4 January 1977 after a referendum. It allowed the democratic transition by dissolving the legal framework of Francoism and by calling for a general election, held on 15 June 1977.

3.2 *Electoral Results, the Threat of Terrorism, and the Making of Consensus*

Regarding the results of the election in June 1977, the centrist Union of Democratic Centre obtained 34.7% of the vote and 165 seats in parliament; the social democratic Spanish Socialist Workers' Party received 33.7% of the vote and 124 seats; the Communist Party of Spain obtained 9.2% of the vote and 20 seats; the conservative Popular Alliance[2] received 8.3% of the vote and 16 seats; the moderate centre-right Democratic Pact for Catalonia obtained 2.8% of ballots and 11 seats; the Basque Nationalist Party obtained 1.6% of the vote and 8 seats. In the Senate the results favoured the most voted party, Union of Democratic Centre, which obtained 34.7% of the vote (Gunther 1986: 42).

From an ideological perspective, the results of the general election of June 1977 benefited the moderate parties of Union of Democratic Centre and the Spanish Socialist Workers' Party. Although the Communist Party of Spain and Popular Alliance were a communist and a conservative party respectively, both assumed the defence of democratic institutions as a commitment with Spanish citizens. In that regard, a high sense of political responsibility and respect towards ideological diversity became two ideals. Each one of them entailed mutual concessions to reach agreements and the acknowledgement of parliamentary politics as inseparable from the deliberation about ideological alternatives.

The country had to face terrorism, prominently by the revolutionary-Leninist Basque terrorist organization ETA (*Euskadi Ta Askatasuna*, Basque Country and Freedom). Other terrorist groups such as GRAPO, Group of Anti-Fascist Resistance First of October (*Grupo de Resistencia*

[2] In academic books and articles the most frequent name for the party is People's Alliance. However, a more accurate translation of *Alianza Popular* is Popular Alliance.

Antifacista Primero de Octubre), the also Catalan organization Free Land (*Terra Lliure*) and the far-right Warriors of Christ the King (*Guerrilleros de Cristo Rey*) also threatened civil peace during the late 1970s. Terrorist violence was usual during the time span of the constitutional debate (Conversi 2002: 226–27).In fact, ETA's violence was one of the major threats to Spain's democratization (Bermeo 1997: 309).

Terrorism had the unintended effect of easing the accommodation to a democratic language of communists in exile and conservative democratic groups. They relinquished the use of inflammatory speeches that could be viewed as endorsing violent means since that could lead to the break of civil peace. Partly as a consequence of that shared goal, the democratic aims of excluding violence kept rival political groups in permanent negotiations despite their evident ideological and instrumental differences regarding how the democratic process should be accomplished. For instance, peripheral nationalist parties and government had recurrent conversations about the pace of democratic reforms during the entire transition to democracy (Aguilar 2002: 160).

The distribution of the political agenda, combining permanent negotiations between parties and with strategic decision-making by political agents would become key for the success of the Spanish transition to democracy (Colomer 1995: 78–9). The secrecy of some proceedings in the committee during the preparation of constitutional drafts was open to individual provisions by constitutional rapporteurs. However, parliamentary groups were not allowed to present their own entire drafts. That circumstance promoted mutual concessions to reach consensus (Elster 1995: 387).

The first landmark of that ideal of consensus is to be found in the Moncloa Pacts, an agreement of political, economic, and social policies to accelerate the process of political changes and to ensure a certain degree of economic stability to fight inflation. Union of Democratic Centre, the Spanish Socialist Workers' Party, the Communist Party of Spain, the nationalist parties of Catalonia and the Basque Country, and Popular Alliance—this party endorsing just the economic aspects of the deal—signed the agreement together with trade unions.

The Moncloa Pacts were signed on 25 October 1977 and ratified in the Senate on 11 November. That deal lasted from the beginning of the transition led by the centrist politician Adolfo Suárez in 1976 until the end of the constituent legislative period (Elkins et al. 2009: 70). After 1977 Suárez successfully headed the transformation of a "transitional parliament into a pluralist arena" (Rosales 2016a: 288). In that process of political negotiations, parliamentary deliberations reflected the existing political pluralism of Spain throughout the constitutional sessions.

4 The Constitutional Debate of 1977–1978 and Spanish Democratic Constitutionalism

This section focuses on the influences over MPs of various traditions of political and legal thought. Firstly, it surveys in a selective manner democratic constitutionalism after World War II, which sheds light on the institutional system adopted. Secondly, it highlights the German Basic Law of 1949, interpreted by Spanish representatives as a preferential mirror to design the state institutions of the country. Thirdly, it presents how they interpreted the institutions of the new democracy relying on, to a certain extent, the contributions of twentieth-century classic authors such as Max Weber, Joseph A. Schumpeter or Friedrich Hayek, among others. Finally, it emphasizes the adversarial politics of consensus carried out by Spanish MPs, with very few exceptions among left-wing and right-wing radicals, as an argumentative understanding of parliamentary politics.

4.1 Democratic Interpretations About Post-war Constitutionalism

During the constitutional debate recent experiences of democratic constitutionalism were considered. That was partly a consequence of the scholarly training of representatives, and partly the result of the receptive environment in Spain towards the political influence of European countries such as the United Kingdom, Germany and France. The national past of Spain, more remarkably, through the constitutional debate that resulted in the Constitution of 1931, was relevant. But also recent international experiences of constitution-making after World War II were taken into account, chiefly the Basic Law (*Grundgesetz*) of the Federal Republic of Germany of 1949, the Italian Constitution of 1948, and the French Constitution of 1958. Spanish deputies and senators drew inspiration from them when writing both the Preliminary Draft of the Constitution (*Anteproyecto de la Constitución*) that was submitted to the Congress of Deputies in May 1978 and the Constitutional Draft (*Proyecto de Constitución*) that was submitted to the Senate three months later, in August.

The constitutional debate of 1931 in Spain and the Basic Law of the Federal Republic of Germany of 1949 entailed deliberate decisions to break with the previous political past of Miguel Primo de Rivera's dictatorship (1923–1930) and Nazi totalitarianism (1933–1945) respectively. For the Spanish representatives of 1977–1978 the Constitution of 1931 and the German Basic Law of 1949 were regarded as milestones, historical lessons on how to build democratic institutions anew. For example, the constitutional debate of 1931 and the ensuing Constitution were regarded as democratic endeavours to be improved, aiming to prevent a new failed experience of democracy in Spain.

Some solutions promoted by Spanish MPs imitated the German Basic Law of 1949, for instance, regarding the decentralization of the state. German constitutionalism was understood as the mirror of the constitutional wording that should inspire the Constitution of 1978. That is to say, it was conceived of as a model of parliamentary democracy that could be consolidated in the long run through a strengthened system of freedoms, constitutional limits to public powers, and effective courts of justice.

4.2 *Parliament as Mirror of Ideologies*

Parliament, as the channel of the political plurality of Spaniards, became undoubtedly the representative institution par excellence. MPs refused to accept a model of participative democracy, deemed a setback to the representation of social pluralism. They endorsed, instead, a representative model of democracy in the Constitution. Through the acknowledgement of representative democracy political representatives aimed to ease governability and to preclude authoritarian drifts by either regional or central governments (Article 23 of the Constitution).

In the constitutional debate the variety of ideologies and scholarly influences contributed to intensive performances and hurriedly adapted speeches when deliberating about the wording of the articles that would be included in the Constitution. Most deputies were aware that the future of democracy in Spain, their own political prestige and—for some of them—their intellectual credentials demanded a high capacity for reaching agreements with other political groups. Those efforts between parties do not contradict that ideological and strategic disagreements were visible throughout the constitutional debate. Neither biased arguments nor electoral aims diminished the average high intellectual quality of parliamentary speeches.

Parliamentary speeches expressed different or simply irreconcilable aims during political argumentations. These speeches were often improvised, but many other times they were thoroughly pondered, foreseeing aspects of political contestation. Constitutional rapporteurs dealt with the most conflicting aspects of the political agenda once and again in the course of the constitutional sessions. The structure of the state and a mixed economic model with the capacity of state intervention in the economy were two salient issues.

At least forty-two speeches should be described as interpretations of democratic institutions and of democracy itself by means of intended rhetorical usages of the history of political thought. For instance, classic doctrines and authors of interwar Europe were mentioned. Parliamentary speeches highlighted contributions to democratic constitutionalism after the passing of the Spanish Constitution of 1931 and after World War II in Europe.

Furthermore, representatives interpreted the doctrinal improvements in democratic theory made by leading international scholars of the twentieth century such as Hans Kelsen, Carl Schmitt, Otto Kirchheimer, Friedrich Müller, Ernst-Wolfgang Böckenförde, or Santi Romano, among others. By doing so, representatives pondered over the best institutional solutions regarding the recent political experience available. Very often they drew inspiration from scholarly contributions to defend their own stances by responding to the objections of other MPs.

The deliberative context of the constitutional debate demanded the accommodation of alternative viewpoints about almost any aspect of the parliamentary agenda: from the territorial organization of the country to the electoral system. In that situation, adversarial politics entailed a model of politics that normalized the parliamentary practice of democracy through a highly argumentative practice. Deliberating about different party and social interests with some shared aims was cleverly understood as a resource by the constitutional rapporteurs. Even deputies outside the Constitutional Commission that prepared the Preliminary Draft of the Constitution agreed on the priority of passing a democratic constitution to properly acknowledge the social and political pluralism of Spain.

5 The Making of the Constitution of 1978

Throughout this section, the process to prepare the Constitution of 1978 is sketched. I highlight four different moments. First, the analysis brings in the Commission of Constitutional Affairs and Public Freedoms (*Comisión de Asuntos Constitucionales y Libertades Públicas*) in the Congress of Deputies. Second, it explains how the Preliminary Draft of the Constitution was debated in the Congress of Deputies and the Senate. Third, it briefly describes the phases of deliberations in two additional commissions: the Constitution Commission (*Comisión de Constitución*) in the Senate, and the Joint Commission of Deputies and Senators (*Comisión Mixta de Diputados y Senadores*). Finally, it sets forth the passing of the Constitution by popular referendum on 6 December 1978, ratified by king Juan Carlos I on 27 December of that year.

The Law for Political Reform (*Ley para la Reforma Política*), promoted by the reformist insiders Torcuato Fernández-Miranda, Landelino Lavilla and Adolfo Suárez, came into force on 4 January 1977. It dismantled the legal framework of the Francoist regime by allowing a general election on 15 June 1977 paving the way for the gradual legalization of political parties. Together with it, that law established that the Spanish parliament would consist of two chambers: the Congress of Deputies (lower chamber) and the Senate (higher chamber).

On 1 August 1977 the Commission of Constitutional Affairs and Public Freedoms was formed. Its president was Emilio Attard, of the Union of Democratic Centre. Thirty-six representatives took part in it. Also on 1 August the same commission appointed the seven constitutional rapporteurs that prepared the Preliminary Draft of the Constitution that should be submitted to parliament: Gabriel Cisneros, Miguel Herrero y Rodríguez de Miñón, and José Pedro Pérez-Llorca, who belonged to Union of Democratic Centre; Gregorio Peces-Barba, of the Spanish Socialist Workers' Party; Manuel Fraga, of Popular Alliance; Jordi Solé Tura, of the Communist Party of Spain; and Miquel Roca Junyent, of the Democratic Pact for Catalonia, who also defended the positions of the Basque Nationalist Party (Varela Suanzes-Carpegna [2007] 2014: 584).

The Constitution of 1978 was the result of different phases of parliamentary deliberations. The seven constitutional rapporteurs appointed by political parties debated in private sessions between 26 July and 1 August 1977 (Hernández Gil 1983: 22–23). Indeed, the Constitutional Commission that prepared the Preliminary Draft of the Constitution was formed just one month before, on 27 June 1977 (Freixes Sanjuán 1984: 103). That Commission held 29 sessions in private meetings between August and December 1977. On 5 January 1978, the Preliminary Draft of the Constitution was officially published and open to amendments. More than three thousand were presented to the Preliminary Draft of the Constitution that was submitted to parliament.

The work of the Commission of Constitutional Affairs and Public Freedoms in twenty-four sessions held in the Congress of Deputies between May and June 1978 had as a result a text with new amendments. The Preliminary Draft of the Constitution was also submitted to the Senate. During seventeen sessions between 18 August and 14 September 1978 the Constitution Commission in the Senate deliberated on the new draft. Immediately after, ten sessions were held in the plenary meetings of the Senate between 25 September and 5 October. There, senators produced a different draft compared to the one that resulted from the Congress of Deputies. Aiming to conciliate them, a joint commission of both chambers held a series of private meetings.

A final version was agreed and then passed on 31 October 1978 in the Congress of Deputies (350 seats) and the Senate (207 seats). There were just 11 votes against the passing of the Constitution. On 6 December 1978, the Constitution was submitted to referendum. The Constitution was endorsed by 87.78% of votes. On 27 December 1978 King Juan Carlos I ratified the Constitution in a solemn joint session of the Congress of Deputies and the Senate. Finally, the Constitution was published on 29 December 1978 and came into force that same day.

6 An Argumentative Framework for the Constitutional Debate

This section presents, firstly, that the Provisional Standing Orders of the Congress of Deputies (*Reglamento Provisional del Congreso de los Diputados*) and the Provisional Standing Orders of the Senate (*Reglamento Provisional del Senado*) made it possible the participation of all parties in parliament. Secondly, it sheds light on how the argumentative capacity of representatives such as Gabriel Cisneros, Enrique Múgica, Miquel Roca Junyent, or Carlos Ollero was indispensable to understanding the new democratic institutions. Thirdly, it shows how Spanish democracy was envisaged as a highly decentralized state with broad competences to be distributed between the central government and the regions. Finally, this section suggests that the constitutional debate of 1977–1978 represented a historical opportunity to rethink not just the institutions and the vocabulary of the new democratic regime, but also its theoretical premises.

As to the effective procedures of parliamentary debates, the Provisional Standing Orders of the Congress of Deputies and the Provisional Standing Orders of the Senate came into force on 26 October 1977. As a token of the regulations, Article 20 of the Provisional Standing Orders of the Congress of Deputies read that political groups could only be formed with a minimum of fifteen deputies or if they would have a 20% of the total number of seats in the lower chamber. That means to consider all the electoral districts (*circunscripciones*) in which they present their lists of candidates. Article 98 allowed two speeches in favour and the other two against the motion delivered. It was also possible for a government minister to use an extra speech. Article 99 established one speech in favour and another against to debate partial amendments.

José Pedro Pérez-Llorca and Gabriel Cisneros, of Union of Democratic Centre; Manuel Fraga and Licinio de la Fuente, of Popular Alliance; Gregorio Peces-Barba and Enrique Múgica, of the Spanish Socialist Workers' Party; Santiago Carrillo and Jordi Solé Tura, of the Communist Party of Spain; Miquel Roca Junyent, of the Democratic Pact for Catalonia; together with Carlos Ollero and Luis Sánchez Agesta, independent senators by royal designation, showed their capacity to deliberate with a deep sense of practical intelligence about the effects of accepting the wording of those constitutional articles about the structure of the democratic state. When delivering speeches in the Constituent Assembly and when negotiating with each other, these representatives kept loyalty towards the principles of parliamentary fair play.

Representatives had to learn to play with the times and rules of parliamentary democracy as much as with its practices without a previous professional experience of parliamentary politics. That process led to representatives such as José Pedro Pérez-Llorca, Manuel Fraga, and Carlos Ollero to provide old political terms with new meanings. For example, it was so when describing Spain as the only political nation of all Spaniards. Despite that, it also provoked the rise of keywords that were absent in the political vocabulary of the dictatorship, such as pluralism, regional autonomy, or popular sovereignty. As a result, in the constitutional debate of 1977–1978 representatives gave expression to sharp concerns about the present and future of Spanish politics. In that regard, some parliamentary speeches of the constituent period should be considered intellectual contributions as well. To a large extent, they also entailed refined argumentative exercises envisioning democratic institutions.

Parliament's ideological diversity did not diminish the contrast of alternatives about the structure of the state and the meaning given to the political concepts that were finally enshrined in the Preliminary Title of the Constitution: freedom, justice, equality, political pluralism, national sovereignty and parliamentary monarchy. Representatives were aware that these concepts would have a constitutional interpretation by the Constitutional Court (*Tribunal Constitucional*) in cases of institutional conflicts between government and regions, or of conflicts regarding basic rights.

The building of democratic regimes was considered dependent on institutions that could ensure political pluralism and channel social dissensus. Different mechanisms were envisaged to consolidate the rule of law acknowledging the accommodation of the political ideologies and the internal tensions of the executive, the legislative, and the judiciary powers as part of democracy. The consensus that characterized the constituent period between 1977 and 1978 became a sort of 'dissentient pluralism' soon afterwards, partly as a result of the alternation of different political parties in government (Rosales 2016b: 238).

Broad possibilities to negotiate and to cleverly play with the limited times of parliamentary politics were available (I adapt from Palonen 2008: 29). Nevertheless, in the constitutional debate of 1977–1978 the circumstances for the entire renewal of democratic institutions and the public debate provided representatives with very accentuated historical conditions of opportunity, risk, and contingency of what Max Weber characterized as a political chance (Weber [1922] 2019: 65). With other words, that constitutional debate was understood as a kairós (*καιρός*), a critical chance for political transformation, by those who played a leading role in it.

Bibliography

Legal Sources

Constitución Española de 1978. Available at: http://www.congreso.es/docu/constituciones/1978/1978_cd.pdf

Provisional Standing Orders of the Congress of Deputies [*Reglamento provisional del Congreso de los Diputados*], 13 October 1977. Available at: https://www.boe.es/buscar/doc.php?id=BOE-A-1977-25701

Provisional Standing Orders of the Senate [*Reglamento provisional del Senado*], 14 October 1977. Available at: https://www.boe.es/buscar/doc.php?id=BOE-A-1977-25702

Spanish Constitution of 1978. Available at: http://www.congreso.es/portal/page/portal/Congreso/Congreso/Hist_Normas/Norm/const_espa_texto_ingles_0.pdf

References

Aguilar, Paloma (2002). 'The Memory of War and the Lessons of Peace in the Democratic Transition', in *Memory and Amnesia: The Role of the Spanish Civil War in the Transition to Democracy*, trans. Mark Oakley. New York: Berghahn.

Ben-Ami, Shlomo (1978). *The Origins of the Second Republic in Spain*. Oxford: Oxford University Press.

Bermeo, Nancy (1997). 'Myths of Moderation: Confrontation and Conflict During Democratic Transitions', *Comparative Politics*, 29(3), 305–22.

Colomer, Josep M. (1995). *Game Theory and the Transition to Democracy: The Spanish Model*. Aldershot & Brookfield: Edward Elgar Publishing.

Conversi, Daniele (2002). 'The Smooth Transition: Spain's 1978 Constitution and the Nationalities Question', *National Identities*, 4(3), 223–44.

Corcuera Atienza, Francisco Javier (1991). 'El constitucionalismo de entreguerras y la Constitución española de 1931', *Historia Contemporánea*, 6, 15–46.

Elkins, Zachary, Tom Ginsburg & James Melton eds. (2009). 'What Makes Constitution Endure?', in *The Endurance of National Constitutions*. Cambridge: Cambridge University Press.

Elster, Jon (1995). 'Forces and Mechanisms in the Constitution-Making Process', *Duke Law Journal*, 45(2), 364–96.

Freixes Sanjuán, María Teresa (1984). 'Crónica de una Constitución consensuada', *Revista de Estudios Políticos*, 40, 101–22.

García Canales, Mariano (1977). *La teoría de la representación en la España del siglo XX*. Murcia: Universidad de Murcia.

Gunther, Richard (1986). 'El proceso constituyente español', *Revista de Estudios Políticos*, 49, 33–61.

Hernández Gil, Antonio (1983). 'Facetas de dos procesos cwonstituyentes', *Revista de Estudios Políticos*, 31–32, 11–24.

Palonen, Kari (2008). *The Politics of Limited Times: The Rhetoric of Temporal Judgment in Parliamentary Democracies*. Baden-Baden: Nomos.

Rosales, José María (2014). 'On the Irrelevant Place of Parliamentarism in Democratic Theory: Antecedents', in *The Politics of Dissensus: Parliament in Debate*, eds. Kari Palonen, José María Rosales & Tapani Turkka. Santander & Madrid: Cantabria University Press & McGraw-Hill.

Rosales, José María (2016a). 'Parliamentarism in Spanish Politics in the Nineteenth and Twentieth Centuries: From Constitutional Liberalism to Democratic Parliamentarism', in *Parliaments and Parliamentarism: A Comparative History of Disputes on a European Concept*, eds. Pasi Ihalainen, Cornelia Ilie & Kari Palonen. New York: Berghahn.

Rosales, José María (2016b). 'From Partisan to Pluralist Ideology: The Changing Practices of Democracy Through Spain's 20th-Century Constitutional Moments', *Journal of Political Ideologies*, 21(3), 225–41.

Varela Suanzes-Carpegna, Joaquín ([2007] 2014). *Política y Constitución en España (1808–1978)*, 2nd ed. Madrid: Centro de Estudios Políticos y Constitucionales.

Weber, Max ([1922] 2019). *Economy and Society*, trans. Keith Tribe. Cambridge, MA & London: Harvard University Press.

CHAPTER 4

Understanding Democracy in the Constitutional Debates of 1931 and 1977–1978

This chapter examines the two constitutional debates in Spain's twentieth century. The first section surveys to which extent the two models of an integral state in 1931 and an autonomist state in 1977–1978 were heirs to federalism. It presents both designs as alternatives to a full decentralization of state competences. Both of them imitated a federal structure of the state without naming it as such. The second section attends to the rhetorical usages of the ideas of competences, faculties and self-rule. These concepts were used to justify the need to increase the capacity of regions to self-rule when keeping their loyalty to the institutions that were finally acknowledged in both constitutions.

In the third section, the process of negotiating between different political agents is highlighted. Section four presents how the idea of reform was interpreted by representatives in 1931. Finally, the fifth section highlights the endeavours to draft a democratic constitution between 1977 and 1978. Under the premise of pragmatism political parties worked to build a new democratic regime in the following years.

F. J. Bellido, *Constitutional Debates, Rhetoric, and Political Philosophy in Spain's Parliamentary History*, Rhetoric, Politics and Society,
https://doi.org/10.1007/978-3-031-56894-7_4

1 Regional Autonomy: Two Models of Federalism

This section compares the constitutional debates of 1931 and 1977–1978 to focus on how a new democratic state would be understood. First, it aims to answer how the Constituent Assembly of 1931 shaped an innovative alternative to federalism: the integral state. Second, it underlines that in the Constituent Assembly of 1977–1978 the integral state was reinterpreted as a precedent to the state of autonomies (*estado de las autonomías*), as it was expressed in the Constitution of 1978. Finally, it surveys the features of a federal system proposed by constituent representatives. By paying attention to the degree of decentralization of state competences, I argue that the autonomist design of Spain surpassed that of federal regimes.

1.1 *The Integral State of 1931*

Regarding the structure of the state, the constitutional debate of 1931 had, as a result, the so-called 'integral state'. According to Luis Jiménez de Asúa, socialist representative and leader of the Constitutional Commission (*Comisión de Constitución*) that arranged the constitutional draft to be debated in parliament, the integral state was adequate to the political context of Spain. Additionally, the experience of federal and centralist regimes in Spain and the rest of Europe advised to go against merely echoing old political trends. According to his words, it should be agreed that "both unitarianism and federalism are in clear theoretical and practical crisis".[1]

The members of the Constitutional Commission understood the acknowledgment of regional autonomy as the best alternative to both federalism and centralism. The integral state meant in practice an interpretation that followed some of the reformist plans of the Weimar Constitution of 1919 (Demarchi 2016: 15). As a precondition, it was necessary a legal framework to distribute competences between administrations, keeping a number of them to be decided by the government.

It is indispensable to emphasize that during a short period of the constitutional deliberations, Article 1 read that Spain was an "integral state with federate tendency" (*Estado integral de tendencia federativa*,

[1] "[T]anto el unitarismo como el federalismo, [sic] están en franca crisis teórica y práctica" (DSCCRE, 27 August 1931: 645).

quoted by Lavilla Rubira 1998: 93). It was the representative and intellectual José Ortega y Gasset who suggested to change that article (Lavilla Rubira 1998: 92–93). However, neither the Preliminary Draft of the Constitution included that expression mentioning a federal affinity, nor did it the Constitution of 1931.

In line with the stances of Luis Jiménez de Asúa, of the Spanish Socialist Workers' Party, and Claudio Sánchez-Albornoz, of the Republican Action Party, the design of the state finally ruled out federalism. It imitated a degree of decentralization of state competences similar to the one enshrined in the Weimar Constitution of 1919. Representatives of the centrist Radical Republican Party, such as Basilio Álvarez, minority left-wing parties, and nationalist parties of Catalonia, the Basque Country and Galicia vindicated federalism as a legitimate choice for Spain. Nonetheless, the leader of Republican Left of Catalonia, Lluís Companys, who accepted the idea of an integral state, argued that the terms "regionalism, federalism, autonomy and decentralization" were subject to "technical and legal interpretation" (DSCCRE, 4 September 1931: 771).

As a token of that discussion, José María Gil Robles, leader of the conservative Popular Agrarian Minority, argued that there was an intermediate option between a federal and a centralized state that could respect the territorial unity of the Spanish nation (DSCCRE, 15 September 1931: 923). It was not incompatible with a certain degree of political autonomy for the regions. Accordingly, the integral state should increase the loyalty to Spain and its institutions in those regions with nationalist trends, namely, Catalonia, the Basque Country and, to a lesser degree, Galicia.

The integral state, as designed in the Constitution of 1931, was partly planned as an alternative to the complete federalization of the country. It should safeguard its political unity by lessening the tensions between peripheral nationalist parties and those who advocated a unitary state without any degree of decentralization. Federalist measures, such as providing a higher level of self-government to the regions, were widely regarded as feasible and not detrimental to the territorial unity of the country.

First, constituent MPs agreed that the regional autonomy of the regions could be acknowledged in autonomy statutes when complying with constitutional procedures (Spanish Constitution of 1931, art. 12). Second, the integral state meant that the Spanish government should refrain from making decisions that could affect the degree of self-rule of the regions with the exception of those cases in which the Constitutional

Court (*Tribunal de Garantías Constitucionales*) would decide otherwise (Spanish Constitution of 1931, art. 19).

1.2 Autonomist Demands in 1977–1978

During the constitutional debate of 1977–1978 the Spanish Socialist Workers' Party, the Communist Party of Spain, the Democratic Pact for Catalonia, the Basque Nationalist Party, Republican Left of Catalonia and Euskadi's Left (*Euskadiko Ezkerra*) voiced a break with the highly centralized state of Franco's dictatorship. In a nutshell, these parties fostered a model of state whose structure should be similar to the one adopted in the Constitution of 1931.

A centralized state, as defended by the conservative Popular Alliance responding to autonomist parliamentary groups, was impossible to agree with other parties. Basque and Catalan nationalist representatives broadened their demands regarding political self-rule for Catalonia and the Basque Country beyond a federal state, with the exception of the constitutional rapporteur of the Democratic Pact for Catalonia, Miquel Roca Junyent. His defence of the decentralization of state competences—at least theoretically—was compatible with strengthened state institutions: "Without a strong and efficient state, there is no possibility to consolidate democracy and, without democracy, the exercise of the autonomy, the right to autonomy of the different nationalities and regions that form Spain is not possible".[2]

The Spanish Socialist Workers' Party and the Communist Party of Spain focused on a strategy of regional demands that were to be accomplished gradually through their acknowledgement in the Constitution. Against that strategy, the only representative of the nationalist party

[2] "[S]in un Estado fuerte y eficaz no hay posibilidad de consolidar la democracia y, sin democracia, el ejercicio de la autonomía, del derecho a la autonomía de las diferentes nacionalidades y regiones que integran España no es posible" (DSLC, 16 June 1978, Congress: 3382). Nationalities was an agreed name by constituent representatives to avoid identifying Spanish regions with nationalist trends as nations. It partly resumed the idea of nationalities defended by Francisco Pi i Margall, a prominent federal politician and writer of the nineteenth century.

Euskadi's Left, Francisco Letamendía, feared that the number of competences for the regions would have been "smaller than those that the Constitution of 1931 established, which were already weak".[3]

Instead, the Basque Nationalist Party led negotiations with Union of Democratic Centre to acknowledge the so-called 'historical rights' in the Constitution (Spanish Constitution of 1978, First Additional Provision). These so-called historical rights were described as if they had an original character rooted in cultural features different from the rest of Spain (Solozábal 1992: 109). Initially, the negotiations with the Basque Nationalist Party were intended to ensure its support to the Constitution of 1978, though Union of Democratic Centre failed in that purpose.

The Basque Nationalist Party, both through one of its leaders, Xabier Arzalluz, and Marcos Vizcaya, argued in favour of the idea of historical rights. They meant a vague outline of the territorial rights of Basque citizens, hard to justify in terms of individual or social rights. The very concept of historical rights was reminiscent of the medieval charters (*fueros*) of the Basque Country and Navarre, incompatible with a modern understanding of rights belonging to individuals and not to territories.

Likely unfair distribution of public economic resources for citizens of different regions of Spain could follow an asymmetric status of regions, some of them with constitutional privileges. From a fiscal point of view citizens in the Basque Country could enjoy a better distribution of resources through the Basque economic agreement (*concierto económico vasco*) between the regional government of the Basque Country and the government of Spain. Licinio de la Fuente, of Popular Alliance, insisted that Spain could not accept different fiscal statuses for regions without damaging the equality of citizens before the Constitution (DSLC, 12 May 1978, Congress: 2273).

As a consequence of the complex territorial structure of Spain, the regime of Autonomous Communities (*Comunidades Autónomas*) is closer to the federal regime of Germany, as the provisions of Art. 151 and Art. 152 in the Spanish Constitution illustrate. These Autonomous Communities have high courts of justice for each one of them. The German *Länder* does not have broader competences than the Spanish Autonomous Communities in that regard (Simón Tobalina 1981: 187).

[3] "[M]ás pequeñas que las que establecía la Constitución de 1931, que ya de por sí eran débiles" (DSLC, 8 June 1978, Congress: 3319).

In that sense, to talk about a quasi-federal system in Spain, though not openly named as federal, is not completely imprecise.

1.3 The Federal Features of Spain's Political System

Representatives such as Gregorio Peces-Barba, of the Spanish Socialist Workers' Party (DSLC, 11 May 1978, Congress: 2170) and José Pedro Pérez-Llorca, of Union of Democratic Centre (DSLC, 14 June 1978, Congress: 1537–38) were against the federalization of the country as much as against its centralization. Discrepancies between nationalist parties and national parties remained about how to regulate the process to decentralize state competences.

Unlike a federal design, as the Basic Law of the Federal Republic of Germany illustrates, the Spanish one does not acknowledge a 'constituent competence' to regions or *nationalities*[4] as it is the case of the *Länder* (Ariño Ortiz 1985: 280–81). In fact, the autonomist design of Spain leaves open contradictions on how the Constitutional Court should proceed in cases of administrative conflict (Canosa Usera 1992: 40).

The lack of precision in the constitutional articles has produced conflicts between administrations since the beginning of the 1980s. Consequently, a new political vocabulary to defend the accommodation of autonomist demands arose. It was inspired by nationalist and federal demands in the case of peripheral nationalist parties, even though autonomist vindications were understood by Union of Democratic Centre, the Spanish Socialist Workers' Party, and the Communist Party of Spain as a necessary step towards the fulfilment of citizens' rights in regions with nationalist parties.

2 The Evolution of Political Language: Faculties, Competences and Self-Rule

This section outlines the evolution of the political vocabulary around the terms 'faculties', 'competences', and 'liberties'. First, it sketches how representatives in the Constituent Assembly of 1931 envisaged the idea of

[4] In the specific Spanish constitutional and political concept, nationalities does not refer to the legal status of membership of the state, but to the so-called historical regions of Spain: Catalonia, the Basque Country and Galicia. That is why, in this book, it is always written in italics.

faculties as part of the political language that could justify a decentralization of state competences in the context of an integral state with features of federalism. Second, it pays attention to the idea of competences and liberties in the Constituent Assembly of 1977–1978.

I argue that the idea of preserving equal freedoms for all Spaniards prevailed in the case of the Union of Democratic Centre over an understanding of regional competences in terms of an acknowledgement of 'nations within Spain', defended by the socialist rapporteur Peces-Barba. The territorial unity of the country was interpreted by the centrist Pérez-Llorca as inseparable from the equality of all Spaniards before the law, linking the idea of political autonomy with the respect for the constitutional freedoms enshrined in the Preliminary Draft of the Constitution.

2.1 State Faculties According to the Constituent Assembly of 1931

In the Constituent Assembly of the Spanish Second Republic the competences of the *Reichstag* in the Weimar Constitution of 1919 were pondered by Luis Jiménez de Asúa when he assessed its "legislative faculties" as "very debatable" (DSCCRE, 27 August 1931: 646). The term 'faculty' and its plural, 'faculties', were part of the political vocabulary employed to defend the decentralization of state competences.

Melquíades Álvarez, of the centre-reformist and minority Liberal Democratic Republican Party, used the term 'faculties' to refer what are nowadays understood as competences. He emphasized that the government and the Spanish Socialist Workers' Party "have endowed the regions with the faculty to make their own statutes to determine what constitutes their own life; but that a region decides on the faculties of the nation state is as much as to suppose that the region is sovereign".[5]

When talking about faculties, Spanish representatives focused on the necessity to distinguish them, to organize them in the Constitution, but it also entailed to design a more complex state administration. The Spanish government in 1931, formed by a large coalition of parties, aimed to build the state around the coexistence of regional authorities acknowledged

[5] "Vosotros habéis concedido a las regiones la facultad de elaborar sus Estatutos para determinar lo que constituye su vida propia; pero desde la región señalar las facultades del Estado nacional, [sic] es tanto como suponer que la región es soberana" (DSCCRE, 9 September 1931: 820).

in the Constitution together with a central administration, strengthened from a legal and economic point of view to undertake economically ambitious policies.

The existence of regional governments with the capacity to execute part of the ordinary laws promoted by the state was sometimes understood as a potential threat of secession in Catalonia and the Basque Country. The regional governments had the constitutional capacity to legislate on a number of issues that were not previously detailed in Article 14 and Article 15 of the Constitution. That exclusive competence to execute and to legislate belonging to the regional governments was enshrined in Article 16 (Constitution of 1931).

2.2 *State Competences and Self-Rule in the Constituent Assembly of 1977–1978*

The parliamentary debate developed between 1977 and 1978 in the second Constituent Assembly of Spain's twentieth century resumed the disagreements around the organization of the state debated in 1931. Representatives of the Union of Democratic Centre and the Spanish Socialist Workers' Party appealed to the need to reform state institutions after dictatorship and to create new ones.

Pérez-Llorca, of Union of Democratic Centre kept his commitment to the design of a decentralized state in the Preliminary Draft of the Constitution that rejected the idea of understanding autonomies in nationalist terms (DSLC, 9 May 1978, Congress: 2106). The autonomist state should work to distribute competences between administrations in terms of institutional loyalty. That fact entailed full respect towards the liberties that were to be acknowledged in the Constitution by both regional governments and the government of Spain.

As an alternative, Gregorio Peces-Barba, of the Spanish Socialist Workers' Party, held a different opinion to defend autonomism in national terms for some regions of Spain. He said that "the existence of nations-communities should not lead us to [think] that every nation should be an independent state".[6] The argument proposed by Peces-Barba can be interpreted as a concession to nationalist parties. However, the existence of nations within the Spanish nation could threaten the territorial unity of

[6] "[L]A existencia de esas naciones-comunidades no debe llevarnos a [pensar] que cada nación debe ser un Estado independiente" (DSLC, 11 May 1978, Congress: 2170).

the country, as Pérez-Llorca had claimed on 9 May 1978 in the Congress of Deputies.

In the newspaper *El País*, the essayist Fernando Chueca wrote an article titled 'Centralism or pluricentralism' to argue that despite the refusal of progressive groups to accept a centralist state, that should not lead to suppression a necessary debate about the advantages and drawbacks of a decentralized state (*El País*, 23 August 1977). Far from being evident, the political and economic consequences of decentralizing Spain were uncertain.

The language of state faculties was replaced. The term 'competence' was used instead. If political competences to legislate and to execute laws conflicted with constitutional freedoms, that would mean that the Constitution should prevail over any attempt to challenge the political institutions of the country. Strengthening the autonomy of regions in Spain was intended to comply with two aims. First, it was a choice to grant self-rule to Spanish regions that could improve the inefficiencies of a centralized state. Second, it was an answer to nationalist parties to keep them loyal to the laws of the Spanish nation.

3 From Constitutional Decisions Based on Parliamentary Majorities in 1931 to Negotiations in the Spanish Constitutional Debate of 1977–1978

This section explores the negotiations in the drafting process of the Preliminary Draft of the Constitution. First, it briefly surveys the idea of constituent power and focuses on how representatives interpreted the constitutional process in Spain. Second, it clarifies the meaning of political negotiations by MPs, compatible with argumentatively detailed constitutional deliberations in the Congress of Deputies, the Senate, and the Joint Commission of Congress and Senate. Finally, it underlines the framework of the Preliminary Draft of the Constitution to understand the subsequent process of parliamentary debates as leading to pervasive changes in the political vocabulary thereafter.

3.1 *The Constituent Power in 1977*

According to Carlos Ollero, independent senator by royal designation, the Spanish *Cortes* of 1977 were a constituent assembly though "no constituent act was produced strictly speaking" (Morodo 1984: 170–71). The institutional framework of the dictatorship was invalid to be interpreted as the legal structure of a constituent act of a democratic kind. The Constitution to be written had a different normative character: resuming the constitutional tradition of Spain and, more precisely, getting inspiration from the democratic institutions which ensued the Constitution of 1931 (Muñoz Machado 2004: 62).

The constituent power that gave rise to the Constituent Assembly of 1977–1978 was legitimized by its ends: transforming state institutions into democratic ones and producing a Constitution endorsed by Spanish citizens (Porras Nadales 1981: 195–96). In the words of the socialist representative Javier Solana, "the constituent process was necessary to fill the [...] political gap [after Franco's dictatorship], in which the popular will played a leading role" (*El Socialista*, 7 May 1977: 8). In parallel with that transformation the new democratic regime "was early on identified with its constitutional order" (Rosales 2016: 232).

Contributions of constituent representatives in 1931 such as the philosopher José Ortega y Gasset, of the Group at the Service of the Republic, and Julián Besteiro, of the Spanish Socialist Workers' Party, were mentioned in the course of the constitutional sessions in 1978 (Tusell 2007: 41). The second Constituent Assembly of twentieth-century Spain mirrored, to a great extent, the need not to repeat the political events that triggered the Civil War initiated in 1936.

The shared belief of not using the past as a weapon of political confrontation was clearly understood by all representatives. It did not darken the democratic struggle of republican representatives to build a constitutional state. The political commitment of elected representatives in 1977 was to shape democratic institutions. For instance, the monarchic institution, considered a hindrance against political, social, and economic modernization in 1931, reappeared as a key to the success of the transition to democracy between 1975 and 1978 (Fusi 2017: 118).

Party leaders took advantage of their positions in organizations to impose their strategies against discrepancies from within (Montero 1981: 59). Nevertheless, in Union of Democratic Centre some senators lacked in discipline to accept the commitment of their party with the Spanish

Socialist Workers' Party regarding, for instance, religious issues. That fact provoked the adoption of a more rigid method to prevent agreements from being broken by fellow party members (Gunther 1986: 47–48). The need to unite votes in both chambers was cleverly grasped by José Pedro Pérez-Llorca, of the Union of Democratic Centre, and Alfonso Guerra, of the Spanish Socialist Workers' Party. Both were responsible for coordinating their parties' strategies in the deliberative process.

3.2 Negotiations Between Parties and Between Representatives

Certainly, the general election of 15 June 1977 reflected to a great extent a proportion between the number of seats in parliament and the number of votes obtained by the larger parties. That was in part the consequence of the demands of the opposition. Adolfo Suárez and his collaborators took them into account to favour an electoral system that would not erode a minimum standard or proportion between votes and seats (Urdánoz 2019: 26).

Suárez had in mind two priorities for his government. First, he thought that the drafting process of the Constitution could be entrusted either to an expert committee to be led by Miguel Herrero y Rodríguez de Miñón or to a committee excluding deputies and senators. Second, Suárez thought to call a new general election immediately after the passing of the Constitution (Abella 2006: 292). Only the second one was accomplished.

Peces-Barba, of the Spanish Socialist Workers' Party, wondered about the possibilities of the Preliminary Draft of the Constitution to be prepared by one or by several commissions formed by politicians. He distrusted Adolfo Suárez's initial intention to create a technical commission excluding elected representatives (Peces-Barba 1988: 16–17). To the socialist rapporteur that hypothetical commission by then should be formed by professional politicians.

In the private meetings held during November 1977 Miquel Roca Junyent, of the Democratic Pact for Catalonia, made a deal with the three constitutional rapporteurs of Union of Democratic Centre, Miguel Herrero y Rodríguez de Miñón, José Pedro Pérez-Llorca, and Gabriel Cisneros. The subjects to be regulated exclusively in the Constitution "except as provided by law" (*con reserva de la ley*) meant that a number of those subjects could not be regulated through other laws than the Constitution itself.

Peces-Barba, of the Spanish Socialist Workers' Party, and Jordi Solé Tura, of the Communist Party of Spain, opposed that agreement considering that it contradicted "the legislative autonomy of the *nationalities* [*nacionalidades*]" (*Cuadernos para el Diálogo*, 26 November 1977: 14). In an editorial published by *El País*, 'Nationalities, the first cornerstone of the debate about the Constitution', the idea of *nationalities* was deemed one of the most troublesome issues for constitutional agreements (*El País*, 27 December 1977). "We have made a long, ambiguous, transactional (*de compromiso*) but enduring Constitution", Herrero y Rodríguez de Miñón said after the private meetings among the constitutional rapporteurs finished, in an article titled 'The men of the Constitution' (*ABC*, 12 January 1978: 9).

Those words illustrate that the constituent process relied on a strategy of reciprocal concessions between parties. To negotiate each article of the Constitution led rapporteurs to abandon part of their political programmes. In order to agree on it, they had to relinquish some of their political demands. Agreements were built to preclude sectarianism from the constitutional text.

3.3 The Constitutional Debate After the Preliminary Draft of the Constitution

As a consequence of a thorough revision of the Preliminary Draft in both chambers, the constitutional debate lasted roughly twelve months. Five phases should be distinguished. Firstly, the constitutional rapporteurs met in private meetings between June 1977 and January 1978 to write the Preliminary Draft of the Constitution. Secondly, after being submitted to parliamentary amendments, 24 sessions between May and June 1978 were held to prepare a new text for the so-called Commission of Constitutional Issues and Public Freedoms. Thirdly, new amendments were included in the text during the plenary debates in the Senate between August and October 1978. Fourthly, the Joint Commission of the Congress of Deputies and the Senate were summoned to write the final text of the Constitution that was submitted to vote in both chambers. Finally, a referendum was held on 6 December 1978: the Constitution was endorsed by the majority of Spaniards and entered into force on 29 December 1978 after King Juan Carlos I sanctioned it.

Pérez-Llorca explained that the efforts of the two main negotiators, Fernando Abril Martorell, of Union of Democratic Centre, and Alfonso

Guerra, of the Spanish Socialist Workers' Party, were crucial to achieving consensus. Nonetheless, the constitutional rapporteurs wrote the draft that was debated in parliament (Pérez-Llorca 2003: 208). According to Pérez-Llorca, there was an implicit process to make decisions responding to unexpected or unforeseeable circumstances and, together with it, an explicit process of regular meetings and parliamentary discussions in which representatives constantly contrasted their views with each other.

The arrival in Spain of the Catalan political leader in exile Josep Tarradellas and his legal acknowledgement as a political authority was part of the implicit process. The frequent meetings that resulted in gradual agreements between MPs inside and outside parliament were the explicit process (Pérez-Llorca 2018: 643). Pérez-Llorca regarded the good relationships and discretion between the politicians of different parties that were members of the Constitutional Commission as part of the success of the drafting process (Pérez-Llorca 1998: 34; Pérez Herrera 2020: 32).

The parallel series of negotiations between different parties and political circumstances such as the autonomist demands in Andalusia or the internal differences in parties shaped the constitutional process. That process also affected the political vocabulary of representatives, who in the case of moderate parties such as Union of Democratic Centre and the Spanish Socialist Workers' Party were often reluctant to use political expressions with straightforward meanings. Since an exercise of political clarity was not always recommendable when using expressions such as autonomy, *nationalities*, pluralism, or consensus, an effect of reconceptualization of terms with new meanings was produced.

4 The Constitution of 1931: Fundamental Law of a Democratic Republic

This section highlights some of the main conceptual and ideological goals that shaped the understanding of democratic institutions in the Constituent Assembly of 1931. First, it draws attention to the ideal of reform shared by MPs by briefly addressing the political changes envisioned by the ideas of reform and sovereignty. Second, it summarizes the ideological disagreements about the number and extent of reforms that were possible to accomplish.

4.1 The Reformist Potential of the Constitution

In 1931 political parties were the result of the associations between individuals with similar interests and ideologies. Unlike in nineteenth-century Spain, during the Second Republic parties aimed to reflect and coordinate social interests and demands. That political understanding had no precedent in the constitutional history of Spain. Until the Spanish Second Republic parties were never considered state institutions (Fernández Sarasola 2009: 246).

The idea of reform through the political parties that brought democracy in Spain obtained the support of the middle classes and workers in the cities. By the 1930s, democracy had a broad acceptance in the political vocabulary. It fully reflected the ideological contrast between left-wing and right-wing parties (Fernández-Sebastián and Rosales 2018: 135). Democracy and revolution had positive meanings that entailed new meanings for other political concepts such as sovereignty, freedom of conscience, and semi-presidentialism.

Sovereignty began to be used to mean both popular sovereignty and the realms of autonomy for political and civil institutions. Freedom of conscience was connected to different strategies of state secularization for parties with conflicting ideologies. Semi-presidentialism is defined as a democratic system designed to reconcile the idea of limiting both the executive power of government and the legislative function of parliament.

4.2 A Fundamental Law to Build Democratic Institutions

At the beginning of the political transition since 1976 democracy was understood in terms of expectations. Uncertainty corresponded with the fear of a backward step that could end that gradual process of democratization (Del Águila and Montoro 1984: 66–67). Democracy meant political pluralism and coexistence as opposed to any kind of authoritarian rule (Del Águila and Montoro 1984: 253). Both left-wing and right-wing parties appealed to reconciliation, a shared aim (De Santiago Guervós 1992: 39–41). Newspapers, with just a few exceptions, broadly endorsed the peace among Spaniards of any ideology and contributed to the success of the transition to democracy (Zugasti 2012: 214).

In contrast, to build a republican democracy in 1931 was not solely regarded as a means to promote ideological diversity, but also to improve the scope of state intervention in the economy and society. The first coalition government of the Spanish Second Republic planned to improve the liberal state of nineteenth-century Spain by strengthening political and social institutions. Ideological commitments were in many cases interpreted as priorities over the necessity of transactions between different parties. Sectarianism was one of the main accusations between left-wing and right-wing parties against each other during the Spanish Second Republic. It decreased during the transition to democracy in the 1970s, though not completely (De Santiago Guervós 1992: 52).

5 The Constitution of 1978: Fundamental Law and Gradual Democratic Transformation of State Institutions

In this section, I seek to shed light on the understanding of the very practice of parliamentary democracy by representatives. First, I distinguish how the Spanish Constitution was thought of as a political project achieving the agreement of all political parties and parliamentary groups. Second, this section presents the legal framework of democratic institutions relying on political pragmatism. Ideological disagreements were contrasted with each other but also calculated according to the real chances that each political party had to satisfy part of its demands.

5.1 *A Constitution to Safeguard Democracy*

The Constitution of 1978 was prepared from its beginning to its final version without excluding any political group. There were disputes about each one of the issues, especially about the autonomist design of Spain that imperilled the endorsement of constitutional articles by national parties. Unlike the four months of constitutional debate in 1931, more than one year of debates and negotiations were necessary to produce this new Constitution (Hernández Gil 1983: 24).

One of the reasons for holding those prolonged meetings and debates was the examination of drafts by several commissions in both chambers of parliament. Besides, the preliminary versions that were produced in the Congress of Deputies and the Senate led constitutional rapporteurs to rewrite a sole draft that respected the contents agreed in both chambers. The Constitution of 1978 was almost unanimously interpreted as the fundamental law to transform the country in a democratic sense.

There are ideologically relevant changes when comparing the constitutional debates of 1931 and 1977–1978. In the former, centrist parties had a residual importance. In the latter, the Union of Democratic Centre was the party with more votes. That capacity of the party to join both liberal-conservative stances and social demands in a mass party was an almost unprecedented case in the history of Spain.[7]

The Spanish Socialist Workers' Party, the Basque Nationalist Party, and the Republican Left of Catalonia were the only three parties represented in both constituent assemblies, 1931 and 1977–1978. The poor political culture of democracy among members of parties had as a consequence that the transition to that regime had some of the features of a prolonged trick by conjurers: skilled individuals that benefited to a certain extent from "the fragility of ideologues" to achieve their goals and ambitions (Morán 2015: 21).

5.2 *The Constitution of 1978: Reforming Institutions from Within Francoist Legality*

The legal framework of the Spanish transition to democracy started with the Francoist laws. That legal base was radically transformed into the legality of a democratic regime (Del Águila 1982: 109). Despite that context, a fifth of representatives, roughly 119 from about 598 (summing both chambers), had held some political positions in the Francoist regime (Ramírez 1989: 46). However, the endorsement of democracy was unanimous.

The boost of foreign policies through the ministers, ambassadors, diplomats, and businessmen since Suárez became head of government (appointed initially in July 1976) contributed to the support of his policies (Pereira 2008: 93). The democratic transition itself was considered a real hope in other European countries such as France, the United Kingdom

[7] Only at the beginning of the Bourbon Restoration (1874–1931) the Liberal-Conservative Party and the Constitutional Party, led respectively by Antonio Cánovas del Castillo and Práxedes Mateo-Sagasta, conciliated their views. Nevertheless, none of these parties fits the conditions of a mass organization.

and, especially, Germany. Regarding international relations, the government led by Helmut Schmidt in Germany endorsed Suárez's strategy and had a remarkable role in improving the international image of Spain (Muñoz Sánchez 2017: 204).

The Spanish Constitution of 1931, the Italian Constitution of 1947, the Portuguese Constitution of 1976, to a lesser extent the Constitution of Greece of 1975, and especially the Basic Law of the Federal Republic of Germany of 1949 were the constitutional texts mostly examined by constituent representatives in the drafting process of the Constitution (Rubio Llorente 1997: 31).

Legal scholars such as Jorge de Esteban and Luis López Guerra also regarded the Constitution of 1958 in France as a relevant text to Spanish constitutional rapporteurs (*Cuadernos para el Diálogo*, 26 November 1977: 19). For instance, Article 9.2 of the Spanish Constitution was translated from Article 3.2 of the Italian Constitution (Tomás Villarroya 1979: 69). Together with them, the Universal Declaration of Human Rights and the protocols of the European Convention on Human Rights were considered as basic legal references as well (Peces-Barba et al. 1978: 7).

The ideological distribution was quite similar to the system of parties of other European countries such as Italy and France. Liberalism, democratic socialism, conservatism, and communism were the main ideological families. Political parties clarify their electoral aims insofar as the constituent process moves forward; parties against the monarchy had a setback in the general election of June 1977; parliamentary groups with more than twenty representatives tended to include minority parties within them, whereas small parliamentary groups experienced frequent internal divisions; and all communities but the Basque Country in their later regional elections reproduced a similar distribution of votes to the results at the national level (Ramírez 1989: 27).

The heated speeches that highlighted ideological differences at the cost of party negotiations during the last period of the Spanish Second Republic before the Civil War (1933–1936) were left aside in the transition to democracy. The leaders of Union of Democratic Centre and the Spanish Socialist Workers' Party, the Communist Party of Spain and Popular Alliance understood that pragmatism was irreplaceable in politics (Ramírez 1989: 143–44). Party agreements outside parliament were recurrent and in some cases contributed to shortening parliamentary debates (Díez-Picazo and Elvira Perales 2008: 27).

Some of the weaknesses of the Constitution of 1978 were the regulation of the vote of no confidence (*voto de censura*), which can simply be used to erode government; the enquiry commissions, that are dependent on parliamentary majorities; government with almost an exclusive capacity to settle the parliamentary agenda; a system that benefits closed and blocked electoral lists of candidates; and the strength of parliamentary speakers to the detriment of broader use of speeches by representatives (Cotarelo 1992: 206).

Those regulations aimed at improving political stability through an enhanced role of political parties. Deliberations about European constitutionalism after World War II advised increasing the capacity of parties to safeguard constitutional freedoms and pluralism. By strengthening the executive power regarding law-making a majority of constituent representatives, in particular constitutional rapporteurs, thought it as the best choice to prevent the threat of antidemocratic trends and to imitate other European countries such as Germany, France, and Italy in that regard.

Partly as the consequence of the heterogeneous aims of the groups and individuals that took part in the constitutional debate, partly as the result of the political transformation of the country from a dictatorship to a democratic regime, the Constitutional Draft that was debated had its origin outside parliament (Lucas Verdú 1978: 16). Paradoxically, that peculiarity made it possible to produce a text that imitated other European constitutions, thus preventing political experiments in the context of the worsening of an economic crisis in the second half of the 1970s that provoked high rates of unemployment and inflation.

Bibliography

Legal Sources

Constitución Española de 1978. Available at: http://www.congreso.es/docu/constituciones/1978/1978_cd.pdf

Proceedings of the Constituent Assembly, 1977–1979 [*Diario de Sesiones de la Legislatura Constituyente, 1977–1979*, DSLC]. Available at: https://www.congreso.es/web/guest/indice-de-publicaciones?p_p_id=publicaciones&p_p_lifecycle=0&p_p_state=normal&p_p_mode=view&_publicaciones_selectedLeg=0

Proceedings of the Constituent Assembly of the Spanish Second Republic [*Diario de Sesiones de las Cortes Constituyentes de la República Española*, DSCCRE]. Available at: https://app.congreso.es/est_sesiones/

Spanish Constitution of 1978. Available at: http://www.congreso.es/portal/page/portal/Congreso/Congreso/Hist_Normas/Norm/const_espa_texto_ingles_0.pdf

Newspapers

ABC (1903–).
Cuadernos para el Diálogo (1963–1978).
El País (1976–).
El Socialista (1886–).

References

Abella, Carlos (2006). 'El primer gobierno de UCD', in *Adolfo Suárez. El hombre clave de la Transición*. Madrid: Espasa.

Aja, Eliseo (1989). 'La distribución de competencias entre el Estado y Comunidades Autónomas en España. Balance y perspectivas', *Revista del Centro de Estudios Constitucionales*, 4, 233–54.

Ariño Ortiz, Gaspar (1985). 'El Estado de las autonomías', in *La España de las autonomías*, ed. Fernando Fernández Rodríguez. Madrid: Ministerio de Administración Territorial.

Balaguer Callejón, Francisco (1988). 'Soberanía popular y democracia en la Constitución española de 1978', in *Jornadas de estudio sobre el Título Preliminar de la Constitución*, vol. II. Madrid: Ministerio de Justicia.

Canosa Usera, Raúl (1992). *Legitimación autonómica en el proceso constitucional*. Madrid: Trivium.

Chueca, Fernando (1977). 'Centralismo o pluricentralismo', *El País*, 23 August, https://elpais.com/diario/1977/08/23/opinion/241135209_850215.html

Cotarelo, Ramón (1992). *Transición política y consolidación democrática, España (1975–1986)*. Madrid: Centro de Investigaciones Sociológicas.

Cuadernos para el Diálogo Reportage (1977). 'Esta es la Constitución', *Cuadernos para el Diálogo*, 26 November, 14.

Del Águila, Rafael (1982). 'La Transición a la democracia en España. Reforma, ruptura y consenso', *Revista de Estudios Políticos*, 25, 101–27.

Del Águila, Rafael & Ricardo Montoro (1984). *El discurso político de la transición española*. Madrid: Centro de Investigaciones Sociológicas.

Demarchi, Giacomo (2016). *Provincia y territorio en la Constituyente española de 1931. Las raíces europeas del Estado integral*. Madrid: Universidad Carlos III de Madrid.

De Santiago Guervós, Javier (1992). *El léxico político de la transición española*. Salamanca: Universidad de Salamanca.

Díez-Picazo, Luis María & Ascensión Elvira Perales (2008). *La Constitución de 1978*. Madrid: Iustel.

El País Editorial (1977). 'Las nacionalidades, primera piedra de toque para el debate de la Constitución', *El País*, 27 December, https://elpais.com/diario/1977/12/27/espana/252025202_850215.html

El Socialista Editorial (1977). 'Por la senda constitucional', *El Socialista*, 7 May, 8, http://archivo.fpabloiglesias.es/files/Hemeroteca/ElSocialista/1977/5-1977/3.pdf

Fernández Sarasola, Ignacio (2009). *Los partidos políticos en el pensamiento español. De la Ilustración a nuestros días*. Madrid: Marcial Pons.

Fernández-Sebastián, Javier & José María Rosales (2018). 'A Conceptual History of Democracy in Spain Since 1800', in *Democracy in Modern Europe: A Conceptual History*, eds. Jussi Kurunmäki, Jeppe Nevers & Henk te Velde. New York & Oxford: Berghahn.

Fusi, Juan Pablo (2017). 'De la dictadura a la democracia', in *Espacios de libertad. La cultura española bajo el franquismo y la reinvención de la democracia en España (1960–1990)*. Barcelona: Galaxia Gutenberg.

Gunther, Richard (1986). 'El proceso constituyente español', *Revista de Estudios Políticos*, 49, 33–61.

Hernández Gil, Antonio (1983). 'Facetas de dos procesos constituyentes', *Revista de Estudios Políticos*, 31–32, 11–24.

Herrero y Rodríguez de Miñón, Miguel (1978). 'Los hombres de la Constitución', *ABC*, 12 January, 9.

Lavilla Rubira, Juan José (1998). 'El problema regional en tiempos de la II República', in *Terceras Jornadas Niceto Alcalá-Zamora y su época*, ed. José Manuel Cuenca Toribio. Córdoba: Patronato Niceto Alcalá-Zamora.

Lucas Verdú, Pablo (1978). 'La singularidad del proceso constituyente español', *Revista de Estudios Políticos*, 1, 9–27.

Montero, José Ramón (1981). 'Partidos y participación política. Algunas notas sobre la afiliación política en la etapa inicial de la transición española', *Revista de Estudios Políticos*, 23, 33–72.

Morán, Gregorio ([1991] 2015). *El precio de la transición*, 2nd ed. Madrid: Akal.

Morodo, Raúl (1984). *La transición política*. Madrid: Tecnos.

Muñoz Machado, Santiago (2004). 'La configuración histórica de las principales características de la Constitución como norma jurídica', in *Constitución*. Madrid: Iustel.

Muñoz Sánchez, Antonio (2017). 'Un padrino en Europa. La República Federal de Alemania y España durante la presidencia de Adolfo Suárez', in *Adolfo Suárez y la transición política*, ed. Manuel Redero San Román. Salamanca: Universidad de Salamanca.

Peces-Barba, Gregorio (1988). *La elaboración de la Constitución de 1978*. Madrid: Centro de Estudios Constitucionales.

Peces-Barba, Gregorio et al. (1978). *La izquierda y la Constitución*. Barcelona: Taula de Canvi.

Pereira, Juan Carlos (2008). 'The International Dimension of the Spanish Transition', in *The International Politics of Democratization: Comparative Perspectives*, ed. Nuno Severiano Teixeira. New York & Abingdon: Routledge.

Pérez Herrera, Gema (2020). *José Pedro Pérez-Llorca. Una biografía política*. Madrid: Centro de Estudios Políticos y Constitucionales.

Pérez-Llorca, José Pedro (1998). 'Veinte años después. Reflexiones de los padres constituyentes', in *La Constitución Española de 1978. 20 años de democracia*. Madrid: Centro de Estudios Políticos y Constitucionales.

Pérez-Llorca, José Pedro (2003). '¿Balance o liquidación?', in *Reflexiones de los ponentes de la Constitución española (1978–2003)*, ed. Gabriel Cisneros Laborda. Pamplona: Aranzadi.

Pérez-Llorca, José Pedro (2018). 'Reflexiones de un ponente constitucional', *Revista de las Cortes Generales*, 103, 637–51.

Porras Nadales, Antonio (1981). 'Notas sobre la teoría del poder constituyente y la experiencia española', *Revista de Estudios Políticos*, 24, 175–200.

Ramírez, Manuel (1989). *Partidos políticos y Constitución. Un estudio de las actitudes parlamentarias durante el proceso de creación constitucional*. Madrid: Centro de Estudios Constitucionales.

Rosales, José María (2016). 'From partisan to Pluralist Ideology: The Changing Practices of Democracy Through Spain's 20th-Century Constitutional Moments', *Journal of Political Ideologies*, 21(3), 225–41.

Rubio Llorente, Francisco (1997). *La forma del poder. Estudios sobre la Constitución*. Madrid: Centro de Estudios Constitucionales.

Simón Tobalina, Juan Luis (1981). *El Estado autonómico y sus matices federales*. Madrid: Instituto de Estudios de la Administración Local y Autonómica.

Solozábal, Juan José (1992). 'Sobre el Estado autonómico español', *Revista de Estudios Políticos*, 78, 105–29.

Tomás Villarroya, Joaquín (1979). 'Proceso constituyente y nueva Constitución. Un análisis crítico', *Revista de Estudios Políticos*, 10, 59–86.

Tusell, Javier (2007). *La transición a la democracia (España, 1975–1982)*. Madrid: Espasa.

Urdánoz, Jorge (2019). 'El origen del modelo representativo de la Constitución de 1978', *Revista de Estudios Políticos*, 186, 13–44.

Zugasti, Ricardo (2012). 'A Forge of Consensus: The Press During the Transition to Democracy in Spain', *Media History*, 18(2), 207–17.

CHAPTER 5

Competing Meanings of the New Democratic State

This chapter explores how the new democratic regime was understood in the debates of the Constituent Assembly of 1977–1978. The first section illustrates the changing meanings of the concepts of reform and revolution during the transition to democracy and, especially, through the deliberative sessions of the Constituent Assembly. The second section throws light on the ideologies of Union of Democratic Centre and the Spanish Socialist Workers' Party, the two biggest parties, around their projects to reform institutions in a democratic sense.

The third section clarifies the commitment to democracy of the Communist Party of Spain and the conservative Popular Alliance. It emphasizes their dissimilar understandings of Spain as a democratic nation. The last part surveys how nationalist parties of Catalonia (Democratic Pact for Catalonia and Republican Left of Catalonia), and of the Basque Country (Basque Nationalist Party and Euskadi's Left) conceived of the new democratic regime. Their stances ranged from a complete federalization of the country to a wholly decentralized state that would acknowledge self-determination to the so-called historical regions of Spain: Catalonia, the Basque Country, and Galicia.

F. J. Bellido, *Constitutional Debates, Rhetoric, and Political Philosophy in Spain's Parliamentary History*, Rhetoric, Politics and Society,
https://doi.org/10.1007/978-3-031-56894-7_5

1 The Ideas of Reform and Revolution in the Political Vocabulary of Representatives

This section reviews the meanings of reform and revolution during the Constituent Assembly of 1977–1978. First, it clarifies the idea of reform associated to institutional changes that resulted in the new democratic regime. Second, it illustrates the connotations of the term 'reform' in the constitutional debate. There, that term meant gradual changes as much as institutional transformation lessening its rhetorical proximity to the idea of revolution. However, the idea of reform became ambivalent and closer to the break (*ruptura*) with authoritarian institutions.

Far from being discarded in the Constituent Assembly, the idea of reform was standardized to express gradual changes towards a democratic regime. It worked as a sign of how reforms were plainly assumed as the right procedure to reach democracy. Finally, this section explains the scarce rhetorical appeal of the term 'revolution', equated with disorder and violence. As a consequence, the term 'revolution' was secondary in parliamentary speeches during the constitutional debate keeping just positive connotations for two left-wing political parties: the Communist Party of Spain and Euskadi's Left (*Euskadiko Ezkerra*).

1.1 Reforming Institutions Through Gradual Changes

Reform was a keyword that denoted the adversarial and deliberative practice of parliamentary democracy with barely negative connotations by 1978. It was so because each one of the political parties could give to reform the contents that fitted their aims better. Reform meant democratic transformation of institutions through both immediate and gradual changes in ordinary laws ensuring civil and political freedoms, against uncertain radical transformation, to centre and right-wing parties. That ambiguity worked positively to join forces from opposed ideologies to build democratic institutions, though it left open how the organization of the state would be settled. For example, it led representatives to freely interpret the degree of state decentralization and the legal procedure to decide on conflicts between regional administrations and the central administration of the state.

From a chronological perspective, reform indicated, firstly, institutional improvements immediately after Francisco Franco's death in November 1975; secondly, it referred to the changes that were possible within legality; and finally, it entailed the advancing of democracy through negotiations between parties and their leaders (Del Águila and Montoro 1984: 241). Since 1976 onwards terms such as 'democracy', 'civil liberties', 'autonomy', 'elections', 'referenda', and 'reconciliation' were widespread in the political vocabulary (Zugasti 2012: 210).

Between 1976 and 1977 the term 'reform' was considered insufficient by those parties that sought major changes in institutions. The rhetorical use of the term 'reform' by regime insiders that had political responsibilities during the Francoist dictatorship provoked the rejection of that idea by the democratic opposition. To democrats outside the regime the term 'break' (*ruptura*) had more agreeing connotations (Fuentes 2008: 1037).

Reform was a way to appealing to channel political disagreements through democratic means. With more precision, it entailed to use parliamentary deliberations and political negotiations with the aim of transforming the existing institutions, not of tearing them apart. What very often were presented as gradual reforms, for example, the legalization of political parties, had the effect of a radical transformation of politics since 1976.

Almost any change that was interpreted as gradual or as a significant alteration that would not jeopardize institutions could be endorsed. The positive view about reformist policies was the main reason of the viability of the political changes that transformed Spanish politics into a pluralist arena. Through reforms, balanced agreements were planned to amend institutions in a gradual manner. That language was appealing enough to arouse the support of ideologically diverse political groups.

As a token of conceptual changes, the meanings of the terms 'reform' and 'negotiation' became closer to each other. To reform institutions and to negotiate policies were irreplaceable steps of policy-making precisely because the so-called 'politics of consensus' entailed a dissensual understanding of democracy, though rarely acknowledged as such. Parliamentary democracy relied upon the renewal of institutions and the capacity to negotiate the conditions that made it possible. In order to make parliamentary politics functional, representatives assumed that disagreements and rival stances should lead to constant negotiations between parties.

1.2 The Concept of Reform During the Constitutional Debate of 1978

Reform was a political concept with overall positive overtones among representatives of right-wing and left-wing ideologies, except for the Basque Nationalist Party and Euskadi's Left. To revamp political institutions was part of the very process of building the democratic regime. The constitutional debate was an irreversible step in that direction. To pass the Constitution meant to enshrine democracy and its institutions to further consolidate them after 1978.

Union of Democratic Centre, the Spanish Socialist Workers' Party, the Communist Party of Spain, Popular Alliance, the Democratic Pact for Catalonia, and the Basque Nationalist Party kept negotiations with each other between 1977 and 1978. They aimed to achieve a constitutional project supported by most parties. After the general election of 15 June 1977 the new democratic government had to implement reforms which necessarily hanged on the passing of the Constitution of 1978.

In the constitutional debate at the Congress of Deputies, Gabriel Cisneros, of Union of Democratic Centre, argued that there were "two senses of parliamentary reform, the rigid and the flexible".[1] The term 'reform', when applied to parliamentary improvements was never pejorative. Additionally, any parliamentary democracy has reformist aims. Reform and democracy are inseparable from each other. Without gradual enhancement of institutions parliamentary democracy would lack its rationale.

Ramón Bajo Fanlo, senator for the Basque Nationalist Party, identified the constitutional process with a more ambitious practice than reforming institutions: "Want it or not, right now we are not making a political reform, we are making a political break, and I am pleased about it".[2] Reform seemed to contradict a sudden break. The legal changes resulted in the vanishing of authoritarian institutions, even though initially within the dictatorship's legality.

[1] "[*D*]*os sentidos de reforma parlamentaria, la rígida y la flexible*" (DSLC, 20 June 1978, Congress: 3463).

[2] "[*Q*]*ueramos o no, en este momento no estamos haciendo reforma política; estamos haciendo ruptura política, y de ello me congratulo*" (DSLC, 18 August 1978, Senate: 1589).

Both reform and break could mean different things or just the same. The reform of institutions in a democratic sense was not interpreted as revolutionary. Rather, it was understood as the necessary outcome of replacing authoritarian institutions by democratic ones, then characterized as the most reasonable way of recasting political institutions. The passing of the Constitution was the legal innovation that with citizens' endorsement left authoritarianism behind.

1.3 The Limited Uses of Revolution in a Positive Sense

During the constitutional debate the idea of reforming institutions gained acceptance, whereas the idea of revolution was not appealing because of its anti-democratic overtones. For instance, representatives of the Communist Party of Spain used the term 'revolution', though its leader, Santiago Carrillo, did not completely refuse the benefits of gradual changes. To him democracy was not the result of a social revolution but the return of democracy "through a series of steps corresponding to a policy of reconciliation".[3]

Unlike the renewal of institutions, revolutionary means were understood as leading to a radical drift far from democracy (Hernández Gil 1983: 13–14). The idea of revolution had connotations that resembled the heated speeches during the Spanish Civil War (1936–1939). Further, revolution indicated social clashes that made political agreements between rival ideological groups much harder to accomplish. Revolution had a non-parliamentary meaning.

The only meanings of revolution that had positive overtones when used in parliamentary speeches were those that claimed for more ambitious changes. For example, among federalist and nationalist representatives, the complete federalization of Spain by acknowledging self-rule for some regions such as the Basque Country and Catalonia entailed more than a reform in the political history of the country. Francisco Letamendía, of Euskadi's Left, expressed in the second parliamentary session of the debate in the Congress of Deputies this revolutionary trend: "I want to be the voice not just of those who in Euskadi [the Basque Country] chose

[3] "[*P*]*or una serie de pasos que corresponden a una política de reconciliación*" (DSLC, 5 May 1978, Congress: 2037).

me to represent them, but also of all revolutionary forces of the state that are not represented in parliament".[4]

Although reform and consensus shared a similar semantics, consensus gained prestige over the idea of reform (Fuentes 2008: 1039). Enrique Tierno Galván, leader of the Popular Socialist Party, clarified that the term 'revolution' had a negative meaning for representatives, since it was connected to violent upheavals of the past, mainly during the Spanish Civil War. To Tierno Galván the idea of revolution seemed to directly attack any liberal and democratic understanding of political freedoms (DSLC, 20 June 1978, Congress: 3484). Revolution and democracy conflicted with each other. A social and political revolution could be the reason of political transformation towards democracy in other countries. But in Spain the transition to democracy was a process of continuous legal reforms, very often in the margins of the legal system, without wholly breaking the previous legality.

Furthermore, the idea of revolution denoted to radically renew institutions in a hasty way. As that was not the case of Spain, any appeal to revolution lacked a realist warning against revolutionary demands that could exceed legal possibilities. If the constitutional debate was a process to write a new Constitution, then its references were to be found in other constitutional texts and not in any revolutionary event. To advocate a different understanding of Spanish democracy was considered equivalent to endangering the success of the constitutional debate because it meant to put one's own interests before those of Spaniards.

In a similar vein, Carlos Ollero, senator by royal designation, pointed out how the process to modify organic laws—those laws that are passed through the vote of the majority of parliament and are in compliance with the Constitution—should be more demanding than what was suggested in Article 75 of the Preliminary Draft of the Constitution: "With that it is clear, of course, that no revolutionary novelty would be introduced in our legal order".[5] Revolution was then understood as a deep type of change that would go beyond the Spanish constitutional tradition. For

[4] "[*Q*]*uiero ser la voz, no sólo de los que en Euskadi* [País Vasco] *me eligieron para representarles, sino también de todas las fuerzas revolucionarias del Estado que no tienen representación en el Parlamento*" (DSLC, 8 May 1978, Congress: 2083).

[5] "*Con ello queda claro, por supuesto, que no se introduciría en nuestro ordenamiento ninguna novedad revolucionaria*" (DSLC, 5 September 1978, Senate: 2267).

most representatives revolution seemed to indicate irresponsible changes that would lead to instability and disruptive uprisings.

To Carlos Ollero the constitutional and parliamentary traditions of Spain showed that any success of political reforms was the consequence of gradual political and social adjustments. Radical innovations in the constitutional text were unadvisable because they meant to assume higher risks than by imitating other European constitutions. A democratic regime should not be object of political experiments. The priority was to build a democratic regime with the resources of contemporary constitutionalism. It was deemed irrational to design institutions disregarding the legality that granted a greater degree of stability when compared to weak parliamentary regimes of the past. Unlike in 1931, in 1977 and 1978 revolution was not the cause of bringing in democracy.

Luis Sánchez Agesta, independent senator by royal designation, wrote about this question an article in *La Vanguardia*, a newspaper published in Barcelona. He argued that the Constitution was possible thanks to a figurative "revolution through law" that by initiative of the people who held the political power after 1975 and by means of reforms established a dialogue with other organizations, thus making the constitutional process feasible (*La Vanguardia*, 20 December 1978: 19).

Constitutional articles were intended to pave the way for the ensuing reforms. In practice, legal improvements had the result of recasting the previous institutions into democratic ones. That could be interpreted as a revolutionary event. But the transition to democracy did not take place because of a revolution, but through clever and timely reforms, sometimes very gradual and some other times faster than expected.

Revolution was excluded from the parliamentary vocabulary of Union of Democratic Centre, the Spanish Socialist Workers' Party, and Popular Alliance because its rhetorical usage did not benefit representatives and their parties' interests. Any appeal to revolution was unlikely to arouse the endorsement of the middle classes, but even among citizens with lower incomes the idea of revolution had a bad reputation because of its association with the Spanish Civil War. Perhaps nationalist supporters were the only exception to that rule. Only in the Basque Country a defence of political revolution was interpreted with some favourable nuances by left-wing nationalists.

2 The State According to the Centrist and Centre-Left National Reformist Parties in 1978: Union of Democratic Centre (*Unión de Centro Democrático*) and Spanish Socialist Workers' Party (*Partido Socialista Obrero Español*)

This section examines the stances of Union of Democratic Centre and the Spanish Socialist Workers' Party in the Constituent Assembly. First, it argues that Union of Democratic Centre conceived of institutions assuming that Spain was a pluralist society in which nationalist trends conditioned the structure of the state. From that perspective, representatives of the centrist party argued that constitutional freedoms were dependent on the design of institutions. The unity of the Spanish nation was to a great extent the historical result of its parliamentary and constitutional traditions. Second, this section aims to shed light on the arguments of the Spanish Socialist Workers' Party to emphasize that representatives of this party combined an ambiguous defence of nations within Spain with the constitutional loyalty to the unity of the Spanish nation. Thus, public powers should protect autonomous regions improving their self-rule gradually as a condition to safeguard the unity of Spain.

2.1 Union of Democratic Centre During the Constitutional Debate: Revamping Institutions to Defend a Liberal Democracy

Union of Democratic Centre and the Spanish Socialist Workers' Party interpreted institutions in terms of their constitutional and parliamentary traditions, which were inseparable from each other. For instance, José Miguel Ortí Bordás, of the Independent Candidacy of Centre, who one year after the general election of June 1977 became member of Union of Democratic Centre, argued that liberal democracies built on the basis of constitutions "have provided freedom and […] have contributed to the acknowledgement, the proclamation and the possibility to exercise subjective public rights".[6]

[6] "[*H*]*A proporcionado libertad y* […] *ha aportado el reconocimiento, la proclamación y la posibilidad de ejercicio de los derechos públicos subjetivos*" (DSLC, 11 May 1978, Congress: 2166).

To Ortí Bordás democracy was equivalent to the exercise of political freedoms in a constitutional order. A liberal understanding of democracy meant that institutions were aimed at the defence of civil and political freedoms and the safeguarding of individual rights against public powers when necessary. Liberal democracy was not an ideological interpretation of democracy, but a premise to enhance the constitutional freedoms of citizens.

As a token of the conceptual distinction between liberalism and democracy, David Pérez Puga, also senator for Union of Democratic Centre, advised against the dangers of channelling social demands and conflicts between groups inadequately to say: "We all know that a liberal state can exist without democracy, and that democracy can also exist without a liberal state".[7] To Pérez Puga liberalism and democracy should go together, but it was possible that, as a consequence of social and political upheavals, the connection between both ideas would be broken. In that case the transition process to democracy would have failed. No responsible constituent representative could endorse political means endangering the implementation of liberal institutions in the context of a new democratic regime.

In the vocabulary of Union of Democratic Centre the terms 'liberal', 'freedom', 'democracy', 'constitution', and 'coexistence' (*convivencia*) made sense of the transition to democracy. Without a liberal defence of freedoms, democracy would lack its representative function. To build a democratic regime entailed the passing of the Constitution that ensured civil coexistence among Spaniards. Institutions should be directed towards those aims, which were dependent on each other. Political reforms had to comply with each one of those elements.

In a similar vein, Ricardo de la Cierva, senator for Union of Democratic Centre, characterized a strengthened state as an advantage and not as detrimental to build cultural institutions. To him the state "is not an alien shadow, but a common reality".[8] If institutions were indispensable to democracy, then the culture of democracy should contribute to make fair institutions possible. An active state with a moderate intervention in the

[7] "*Todos conocemos que puede existir Estado liberal sin democracia, y que puede existir también democracia sin estado liberal*" (DSLC, 25 September 1978, Senate: 2876).

[8] "[*N*]*O es una sombre ajena, sino una realidad común*" (DSLC, 13 September 1978, Senate: 2624).

economy and more ambitious educational policies was regarded by representatives of Union of Democratic Centre as a condition for undertaking political reforms.

Economic controversies about the degree of state intervention in the economy were lessened due to the prevailing concerns about the structure of the state. The disputed meaning of the Spanish nation clashed two groups of parties against each other. On the one hand, a majority of MPs of Union of Democratic Centre and Popular Alliance argued in favour of considering the Spanish nation the result of regional diversity in a shared cultural tradition; on the other hand, the Democratic Pact for Catalonia, the Basque Nationalist Party, Republican Left of Catalonia, and Euskadi's Left upheld the existence of several nations within Spain with distinctive features.

José Manuel Paredes Grosso, of Union of Democratic Centre, equated the idea of Spain as "nation of nations" with the necessary outcome of Spain's history as "kingdom of kingdoms" (DSLC, 12 May 1978, Congress: 2294–95). Unlike other representatives of Union of Democratic Centre, Paredes Grosso regarded that idea of a grand nation harbouring others as a positive idea. It could be useful to strengthen the Spanish nation and its social diversity. Institutional reforms were openly considered as steps towards a modernized constitutional democracy. To use the medieval history of Spain was both a precaution of realism against the growth of nationalism and a positive drift towards a new historical course of Spain that did not renounce that tradition.

In that regard, Antón Cañellas, of the Catalan group of Union of Democratic Centre, claimed that Spain could be transformed into a quasi-federal state: "It has been said that federalism only makes sense when the unities to federate are still dispersed [...]. I absolutely disagree with this accusation".[9] To Cañellas the process of state decentralization was indispensable to Spain. A decentralized state was interpreted as a conciliatory alternative to a complete federalization of the country and to a centralized state.

Nevertheless, Union of Democratic Centre did not accept Cañellas' stance. In his first speech in the constitutional debate at the Congress of Deputies the constitutional rapporteur José Pedro Pérez-Lorca defended

[9] "*Se ha dicho que el federalismo sólo tiene sentido cuando las unidades a federar se hallan todavía dispersas* [...]. *Discrepo absolutamente de esa acusación*" (DSLC, 8 May 1978, Congress: 2071).

Spain's national unity in terms of a same history of institutions legitimated by a constituent assembly that rejected any form of violence to achieve personal or collective aims against the constitutional text that was to be approved (DSLC, 5 May 1978, Congress: 2106). Accordingly, that political history of the nation was the source of national sovereignty. The issue of the Spanish language was not mentioned in that speech. To Pérez-Llorca the parliamentary and constitutional tradition of Spain was one of the exercise of citizens' freedoms which gave expression to the liberal political tradition in Spain.

Senator and legal scholar Antonio Fernández Galiano, of Union of Democratic Centre, replied to senator Gregorio Monreal, of the Autonomous Front,[10] after his speech. Fernández Galiano said that the name *nationalitas* did not exist as such in the vocabulary of Latin: "in Rome *civitas* is the way of designating the state; [...] the lack in Latin, in the Roman culture, of the name *nationalitas*"[11] was politically revealing. In his speech he aimed to vindicate the importance of civil freedoms and of a sense of political community over a nationalist conception of Spanish regions.

Fernández Galiano reminded that the idea of state did not exist in Roman culture. To join the ideas of state and *nationalities* was a difficult intellectual exercise. To justify institutions in the new Spanish democracy required arguments of contemporary political history and the European constitutionalism formed after World War II. Historical reinterpretations of ancient history, though rhetorically engaging, were barely useful. The link of strengthened democratic institutions with the respect of social pluralism was likely a more effective intellectual recourse.

Luis González Seara, senator for Union of Democratic Centre, warned MPs to be clearer about state competences. They should not be delegated to regional governments because "are transferable those faculties that are not of the exclusive competence of the state, whereas the others, which

[10] The Autonomous Front was the coalition of the Basque Nationalist Party, Euskadi's Socialist Party (*Partido Socialista de Euskadi*), Force for the Unity of Basque Socialists (*Euskal Sozialistak Elkartzeko Indarra*) and independents. They presented a unitary list of candidates for the Senate.

[11] "[*E*]*N Roma la 'civitas' es el modo de designación del Estado;* [...] *la carencia en latín, en la cultura romana, del nombre de 'nationalitas'*" (DSLC, 23 August 1978, Senate: 1764).

are also granted by the Constitution, can be transferred".[12] To González Seara all political parties should agree that there were a series of state competences in the Constitution that exclusively belong to the central administration. Their transfer to regional administrations would hinder the regular functioning of institutions and this would possibly lead to conflicts between administrations, as it finally happened in the following decades.

Statutes of Autonomy formalized the process of state decentralization, but some centrist representatives distrusted abuses and inequalities between Spanish citizens. A differentiated legal treatment of citizens in some regions threatened the equal access to services. Regional institutions in the Autonomous Communities could limit mechanisms of fiscal solidarity if their competences would compete with those of the central administration of the state.

Among members of Union of Democratic Centre there were permanent disagreements that were not only the result of a party that was formed by different minor parties, but that also responded to a highly pluralistic practice of debating (Alonso-Castrillo 1996: 188). For instance, José Pedro Pérez-Llorca understood that violent or revolutionary means jeopardized the success of the constitutional debate and of democracy (Díaz Barrado 2013: 86). Citizens' freedoms and social diversity could be threatened if revolution would prevail over gradual reforms. The Constitution should unleash reformist policies with a broad support from rival ideologies.

2.2 The Spanish Socialist Workers' Party: Between Revolutionary Aims and Reform Policies

In June 1977, two weeks after the general election, Felipe González, leader of the Spanish Socialist Workers' Party, compared the reform of institutions with permanent changes that would transform Spain without risks of backward steps. To him there was no dilemma between reforming institutions and revolution (Del Águila and Montoro 1984: 185). The party kept a simultaneous strategy of vindicating revolutionary changes in

[12] "[*S*]*on transferibles aquellas facultades que no son de competencia exclusiva del Estado, mientras que las otras, que también tiene atribuidas por la Constitución, sí pueden transferirse*" (DSLC, 4 October 1978, Senate: 3278).

the congresses that held between 1977 and 1978, and a more reformist profile, open to negotiate a programme of reforms (Mateos 1996: 225).

Nevertheless, González advocated ambitious reforms in the Constitution to acknowledge self-rule for Catalonia and the Basque Country: "State and autonomous entity cannot oppose each other; what has to be done is to harmonize their functions, to reconcile their functions".[13] His open statement in favour of autonomies was endorsed by his party. Political autonomy, self-rule, was indeed a classic demand that had its roots in the political tradition of the Spanish Socialist Workers' Party during the Second Republic (1931–1939).

Luis Fajardo, of the Spanish Socialist Workers' Party, highlighted that a true democratic representation in any democratic regime should begin from the will of individual citizens. Democratic representation is not of an entelechy of regions, feelings or traditions, but the source of political legitimacy to make possible "that the population is represented and not, as some of my colleagues has said, the cathedrals, or the lands".[14]

With a different goal in mind, Eduardo Martín Toval, of the Spanish Socialist Workers' Party, argued that the new democratic state should not be a "gendarme state". That idea was outdated and belonged to other forms of government during the twentieth century. Martín Toval wanted to discard authoritarian drifts that could be disguised as the result of democratic decisions and liberal institutions. He mentioned that not just the classic liberal states of the nineteenth century were built on the basis of vigilance (DSLC, 9 June 1978, Congress: 3146).

Martín Toval clarified that a programme of reforms to build institutions respecting autonomies was crucial to Spanish democracy, but only if they prevented those autonomies from becoming detrimental to the unity of Spain (DSLC, 16 June 1978, Congress: 3388). Without a strengthened system of institutions democracy would be unsteady. The Constitution should prevail over partial self-rule demands from autonomous regions. The foreseeable consequences of weak institutions were an insufficient state to comply with its redistributive function and in permanent dispute with the Autonomous Communities.

[13] "*No se puede contraponer Estado y entidad autónoma; lo que hay que hacer es armonizar sus funciones, compatibilizar sus funciones*" (DSLC, 16 June 1978, Congress: 4384).

[14] "[*Q*]*ue la población esté representada y no, como ha dicho alguno de mis compañeros, las catedrales, o los terrenos*" (DSLC, 1 June 1978, Congress: 2838).

Martín Toval gave expression to his party's conception of Spain: "A sole limit, a limit that it is convenient to emphasize, [...] a resounding no to the disintegration of the state".[15] Autonomies were to him necessary to modernize Spain and to answer the demands of regions with nationalist parties. However, he repeatedly highlighted that the unity of Spain as a country should not be subordinated to other goals.

Another socialist representative, Enrique Barón Crespo, resumed the argument of a democratic state to enhance citizens' freedoms. He argued that the "gendarme state" had nothing to do with the liberal state of the nineteenth century, characterized by what he considered its insufficient acknowledgement of civil and political freedoms and an invasive vigilance of the press and associations (DSLC, 9 June 1978, Congress: 3148).

That concern of socialist representatives about the functions of political powers and institutions in democracy was expressed by Marta Mata Garriga: "I want to finish by remarking once again our satisfaction for the passing of a text that removes the term 'state' and puts the one of 'public powers'".[16] To socialist MPs, mentioning the state aroused suspicions of authoritarian rule. It was a terminological preference that gave a boost to the idea of public institutions over private interests. From an ideological point of view, the term 'state' had a pejorative image to nationalist parties and the Spanish Socialist Workers' Party aimed to avoid their accusations of authoritarianism.

The speeches of representatives of the Spanish Socialist Workers' Party shed light on the ideological aims of the party. An ambiguous acknowledgement of nations within Spain and the reluctance to use the term 'state' with positive overtones bring them closer to the stances of nationalist parties of Catalonia and the Basque Country. The loyalty to the Spanish Constitution and to the political unity of the country was, however, the baseline shared with Union of Democratic Centre and Popular Alliance.

[15] "*Un único límite, un límite que conviene remarcar,* [...] *es el no rotundo a la desintegración del Estado*" (DSLC, 18 July 1978, Congress: 4366).

[16] "*Quiero terminar remarcando otra vez nuestra satisfacción por la aprobación de un texto que retira el término 'Estado' y sitúa el de 'poderes públicos'*" (DSLC, 7 July 1978, Congress: 4055).

3 A Democratic Regime Shielded by the Constitution

This section deals with how the Communist Party of Spain and Popular Alliance understood the new democratic regime. First, it highlights that Santiago Carrillo, leader of the Communist Party of Spain, was committed to democracy even though that entailed losing electoral support. His respect for the rules of democracy led his party to renounce revolutionary means to imitate instead Western European Communist parties. Second, it surveys the endorsement of democracy by Popular Alliance through its vindication of the historical continuity of the Spanish nation. Its nationalist features were however compatible with a genuine defence of institutions.

*3.1 The Communist Party of Spain (*Partido Comunista de España*) and Its Commitment to Democracy*

The Communist Party of Spain was the most popularly backed left-wing party in exile before the Constituent Assembly. Only after the general election of 15 June 1977 the Spanish Socialist Workers' Party became the left-wing party with more votes and representatives in parliament (Álvarez Borjabad 2014: 800). From the beginning of the Spanish transition to democracy both parties underwent an ideological transformation.

The Spanish Socialist Workers' Party assumed then the principles of social democracy. The Communist Party of Spain renounced its commitment to Marxism and Leninism after its IXth congress in April 1978 and changed its strategy towards more moderate demands (Bell 1983: 70; Andrade Blanco 2015: 33). Carrillo understood that to modernize both his party and the country implied to imitate the communist parties of Western European democracies. Abandoning the ideological ambitions of radically transforming Spain in a short time span was a primary issue.

Santiago Carrillo argued that "social revolution, which the laws of progress impose on the moderate society, concerns the majority of Spaniards".[17] Thus, to Carrillo the term 'revolution' called for a deep sense of change that should be promoted by social movements. His commitment to democratic institutions had pragmatic ends, but also a

[17] "[*E*]*sa revolución social que las leyes del progreso imponen a la sociedad moderada interesa a la inmensa mayoría de los españoles*" (DSLC, 5 May 1978, Congress: 2036–37).

personal sense of political commitment to improve his party to fully accept constitutional rules and political pluralism. The Communist Party of Spain led by Carrillo accepted the legality of Suárez's government as transitional before the general election of June 1977 in exchange for the legalization of the Communist Party of Spain (Colomer 1998: 15).

Among the main reasons that paved the way for democracy, it is widely accepted that the relationship between Adolfo Suárez and Santiago Carrillo was one of them. The leader of Union of Democratic Centre entrusted him to negotiate economic and political measures (Robles-Egea 2016: 89). The fact that they did not compete because their electorates were different was likely an additional reason of the growing confidence between them.

Carrillo advocated to lessen those revolutionary demands that could entail violence (Morán 1979: 338). That can be considered a first pragmatic reason to endorse the constitutional process and the legitimacy of the monarchy. However, there was an additional pragmatic reason, reflected in Carrillo's intuition that his support of a new form of communism, Eurocomunism, was expected to boost his democratic credentials among Spaniards (Sánchez-Terán 2005: 167).

Among the programmatic goals of the Communist Party were a series of reformist policies: first, to build a public space for the exercise of civil and political rights; second, to progressively advance towards socialism through economic and social measures endorsed by a majority of citizens; third, to make compatible autonomous regions and the existence of *nationalities* within Spain; and fourth, to strengthen parliament and the legislative power against the threat of a growing "executive power and the very administration of the state" (Solé Tura 1978: 26–27).

The process to decentralize state competences that Communist leaders had in mind entailed that there should be basic rules to regulate the competences of the autonomous communities defined in the Constitution and not in ordinary laws (DSLC, 15 June 1978, Congress: 3331). Without that capacity of decentralization Jordi Solé Tura, constitutional rapporteur of the Communist Party, thought impossible to attain a certain degree of autonomy for Spanish regions compatible with the territorial unity of the country. That pluralist view about Spain led Carrillo to declare that constituent representatives were "ready to carry out the process of building a state in which all Spaniards, in which all the peoples of Spain, can live united and in peace".[18]

3.2 *Foundations of the State According to Popular Alliance (*Alianza Popular*)*

Manuel Fraga, leader of the conservative Popular Alliance, argued that "states need to ensure at the same time continuity and reform, freedom and its limits, to safeguard freedom".[19] Fraga interpreted the state-building process in terms of reforms. Freedoms and limited reforms went together. His ideological convictions led him to believe that institutions only required small reforms, always gradual changes that can be easily assimilated and fully compatible with the protection of citizens' freedoms.

He insisted on the moderate planning of the economy through limited provisions of a general character: "What we say is that the state shall be able to plan the general economy in certain general points".[20] That vagueness about the role of the state in the economy was intentional. Fraga had just mentioned the economists Pierre Massé and Joseph A. Schumpeter to remind that a centralized organization of the national economy was neither possible nor desirable (DSLC, 13 June 1978, Congress: 3181).

Fraga refused any attempt to strengthen regional powers at the expense of the central administration of the state. He mentioned the French politician Michel Debré to talk about the process of 'political regionalization' that happened in Italy. "The division of essential public services, such as the police" was to him a source of instability that attacked state sovereignty to the extent of exhausting it.[21] To the leader of Popular

[18] "[*D*]*ispuestos a llevar adelante el proceso de construir un Estado en el que todos los españoles, en el que todos los pueblos de España, puedan vivir hermanados y en paz*" (DSLC, 21 July 1978, Congress: 4544).

[19] "*Los Estados necesitan asegurar a la vez la continuidad y la reforma, la libertad y sus límites, para garantizar la libertad*" (DSLC, 5 May 1978, Congress: 2042).

[20] "[*L*]*O que decimos es que el Estado podrá planificar la economía general en ciertos puntos generales*" (DSLC, 13 June 1978, Congress: 3181).

[21] "[*L*]*A división de los servicios públicos esenciales, como la Policía*" (DSLC, 4 July 1978, Congress: 3775).

Alliance "a constitution is not just a set of rules, but a system of institutions that are there, with its own sociological weight".[22]

Accordingly, the national unity of the country did not derive from a parliamentary or a constitutional tradition. To Popular Alliance its source was to be found in medieval times and the early modern times with the Catholic monarchs of Spain. In his view, Spain was established "from a sole and indivisible nation and from a state, also unique and strong, that preserves and does not share its sovereignty".[23]

The historical roots of the Spanish nation had a similar source to that of France. The nation state had its origins in common traditions such as Catholicism and the existence of kingdoms within the Iberian Peninsula. The wide scope of the Hispanic culture in America was also the consequence of a shared cultural and linguistic legacy. That fact, however, did not lead to MPs of Popular Alliance to dismiss the historical relevance of regions in Spain with their own linguistic and cultural particularities (DSLC, 4 July 1978, Congress: 3777).

To the constituent representatives of Popular Alliance the Spanish nation and the state were equivalent to each other. There was no other nation than Spain for them. Nationalism in Catalonia and the Basque Country was interpreted as a phenomenon related to regionalism and not to a proper development of a national identity with historically grounded traditions that distinguished them from the Spanish nation. The building of institutions should be centralized to a certain degree due to the likely rising threat of nationalism in those regions.

4 Nationalist Parties: An Ambiguous Understanding of State Institutions

This section enquires into the views of nationalist parties from the Basque Country and Catalonia that participated in the Constituent Assembly. First, it clarifies the ambiguous strategy of the Democratic Pact for Catalonia and the Basque Nationalist Party, right-wing parties. Their strategy was to attain the greatest possible degree of decentralization of state competences in their respective regions that would be gradually

[22] "[*U*]*na Constitución es, no sólo un conjunto de normas, sino un sistema de instituciones que están ahí, con su propio peso sociológico*" (DSLC, 5 July 1978, Congress: 3880).

[23] "[*P*]*artir de una nación única e indivisible y de un Estado también único y fuerte que conserva y no comparte la soberanía*" (DSLC, 18 July 1978, Congress: 4347).

broaden after the passing of the Constitution. Second, this section surveys the arguments of Euskadi's Left and Republican Left of Catalonia. Their less ambiguous discourse showed that self-determination and not merely self-rule was the main goal to be fulfilled. Their rhetorical criticisms to the Preliminary Draft of the Constitution were aimed to attack institutions discrediting them as unfair to national identities.

4.1 *The Decentralization of State Competences: Basque Nationalist Party (***Partido Nacionalista Vasco***) and Democratic Pact for Catalonia (***Pacte Democràtic per Catalunya***)*

The nationalist parties of Catalonia (Democratic Pact for Catalonia and Republican Left of Catalonia) and of the Basque Country (Basque Nationalist Party and Euskadi's Left) had clear similarities between each other. The Democratic Pact for Catalonia and the Basque Nationalist Party were parties with Catholic roots favourable to market economy that would promote individual initiatives, whereas Republican Left of Catalonia and Euskadi's Left advocated the intervention of public powers in the economy and the greatest possible degree of political autonomy for the so-called historical regions of Catalonia, the Basque Country, and Galicia.

Representatives of the Democratic Pact for Catalonia upheld that the self-rule of autonomies should be gradually broadened even when their real meaning and its consequences were willingly ambiguous (Aguilera de Prat 1990: 115). It was unclear, in 1978, whether or not that demand for autonomy and self-determination was aimed at justifying the secession of Autonomous Communities in the years following the passing of the Constitution. The nationalist vindications of the Democratic Pact for Catalonia were evident, but frequently open to agreements with other parties. Its strategy was pragmatic, focusing on gradualism to satisfy its political demands in advantageous political circumstances.

Miquel Roca, constitutional rapporteur of the Democratic Pact for Catalonia, reproached Union of Democratic Centre and Popular Alliance that the local and provincial administrations of the state had dismissed historically the existence of "realities" (DSLC, 18 July 1978, Congress: 4358). By "realities" he meant the self-rule of Catalonia and the Basque Country.

Marcos Vizcaya, of the Basque Nationalist Party, argued that economic planning was a function in which the Autonomous Communities should take part (DSLC, 13 June 1978, Congress: 3186). He was in favour of a decentralized economic administration that would transfer to the Basque Country several state competences in economy. The Basque Nationalist Party was less ambiguous than the Democratic Pact for Catalonia regarding self-rule. The capacity to decide on economic planning for the Basque Country was interpreted as a step forward to securing self-determination in the long run, though the Constitution did not admit that possibility (Constitution of 1978, art. 2).

Unlike the Democratic Pact for Catalonia, the Basque Nationalist Party clearly endorsed the right to self-determination. Xabier Arzalluz, one of the leaders of the Basque Nationalist Party, claimed that Spain should transfer part of its sovereignty to the so-called historical regions such as the Basque Country: "We see ourselves considered within this state [...] in a sense of original sovereignty, sharing part of that sovereignty".[24] Arzalluz conceived of the state as a sovereign body that resulted from the reciprocal will of different peoples to transfer their original sovereignty: "Because a people is a social body, [sovereign peoples] transfer faculties and form the state transferring all those faculties that are necessary".[25]

Arzalluz interpreted popular sovereignty as a faculty distributed among the so-called historical regions of Spain as if it would be divisible between peoples. Then, the source of sovereignty were the different peoples of Spain, divided according to Autonomous Communities, some of which would enjoy a differential status. As the parliamentary journalist Joaquín Aguirre Bellver highlighted, the strategy of the leader of the Basque Nationalist Party was focused on identifying the Spanish monarchy with a sort of medieval Spain that did not leave room for a strong collaboration between regions (Aguirre Bellver 1978: 20–21).

4.2 *Self-Determination as Argued by Euskadi's Left and Republican Left of Catalonia*

Francisco Letamendía, of Euskadi's Left, argued that the future of Spain was to be transformed into a "*foral state*" (DSLC, 21 July 1978,

[24] "[*N*]*os vemos contemplados dentro de este Estado* [...] *en un sentido de soberanía originaria, con una cesión de parte de esa soberanía*" (DSLC, 11 May 1978, Congress: 2183).

[25] "[*P*]*orque un pueblo es un cuerpo social, ceden facultades y forman el Estado cediendo todas aquellas facultades que son necesarias*" (DSLC, 16 June 1978, Congress: 3381).

Congress: 4568). The *foral* regime was a differentiated fiscal status applied to the Basque Country and Navarre. It roughly entailed that the annual budget of these Autonomous Communities was a proposal of the regional government that the central government could only accept or refuse. From a fiscal perspective, it favoured the Basque Country and Navarre when compared to the rest of Spanish regions in matters of redistribution of public resources.

Democratic reforms of institutions seemed to him just to recognize the incapacity to transform Spain into a plurinational state. The revolutionary aims of Euskadi's Left were identified with a beneficial utopia: "Revolutionary voices that embody utopias of building future societies".[26] In the expectation of building a better society in the future, utopias could be appealing to all reformist ideologies. However, that horizon of expectations, to use Reinhart Koselleck's words, obviates the high risks of revolutionary changes in democratic regimes.

That revolution envisaged by Euskadi's Left was expressed by Letamendía, who stated that according to Title VIII of the Preliminary Draft of the Constitution, Spain "is not a federal, but a regionalized centralist state".[27] A federal state would be the first revolutionary step towards that utopia. Autonomous Communities and a gradual decentralization of state competences were not enough for Euskadi's Left.

Gregorio Monreal, senator for the Autonomous Front, argued that "it has been verified in the debates the inadequacy of the state with regard to assuming all social realities in which it is placed".[28] Spain was called the 'Spanish state' by nationalist parties to despise its institutions as unfair and detrimental to the autonomy of the Basque Country. That strategy was effective because it avoided to criticize Spain as a nation, then preventing nationalist ideologies from disrespecting Spanish citizens.

The strategy of Republican Left of Catalonia was similar to that of Euskadi's Left. Heribert Barrera, one of its most active representatives, interpreted that the state was incomplete if sovereignty was not distributed among the different nations of Spain (DSLC, 8 May 1978,

[26] "[*V*]*oces revolucionarias que encarnan utopías de construcción de sociedades futuras*" (DSLC, 1 June 1978, Congress: 2848).

[27] "[*N*]*O es un estado federal, sino centralista regionalizado*" (DSLC, 14 June 1978, Congress: 3260).

[28] "*Se ha constatado en los debates la insuficiencia del Estado de cara a asumir todas las realidades sociales en que se asienta*" (DSLC, 23 August 1978, Senate: 1773).

Congress: 2076). That plurality of nations was to Barrera an undisputed historical fact deeply rooted in dissimilar institutions from the Middle Ages. That free and distorted interpretation of the history of Spain was a pervasive rhetorical recourse of nationalist parties, intendedly imprecise not to add information that could contravene their arguments.

Lluís Maria Xirinacs, senator for Republican Left of Catalonia, equated Spain to a tyrant state that historically used violence to keep peoples under its control (DSLC, 18 August 1978, Senate: 1554). He did not criticize the authoritarian abuses of dictatorships but took the history of Spanish institutions to caricature current Spain. Xirinacs omitted the fact that political regimes of the nineteenth and twentieth centuries had established the same laws for citizens of all Spanish regions.

Republican Left of Catalonia followed a strategy of broad demands to federalize the country and to enshrine self-determination for the so-called historical regions of Spain. As Euskadi's Left did, its strategy was less ambiguous than the one of right-wing nationalist parties. His conception of institutions was instrumental. To them, institutions could be adapted to strengthen the competences of Autonomous Communities and to give expression to secessionist demands. However, regarding secession, Euskadi's Left was much clearer.

Bibliography

Legal Source

Proceedings of the Constituent Assembly, 1977–1979 [*Diario de Sesiones de la Legislatura Constituyente, 1977–1979*, DSLC]. Available at: https://www.congreso.es/web/guest/indice-de-publicaciones?p_p_id=publicaciones&p_p_lifecycle=0&p_p_state=normal&p_p_mode=view&_publicaciones_selectedLeg=0

Newspaper

La Vanguardia (1881–).

References

Aguilera de Prat, Cesáreo (1990). 'El Estado de la Autonomías en el discurso político de Convergencia Democrática de Catalunya', *Papers. Revista de Sociología*, 34, 115–37.

Aguirre Bellver, Joaquín (1978). *Así se hizo la Constitución*. Valencia: Francisco Manuel Mas.

Alonso-Castrillo, Silvia (1996). 'El apogeo de la UCD', in *La apuesta del centro. Historia de la UCD*. Madrid: Alianza.

Álvarez Borjabad, David (2014). 'Entrevistas personales', in *Periodistas y políticos en la construcción de la democracia española. Estudio de las entrevistas de personalidad en las primeras elecciones de la Transición (1977 y 1979)* (Doctoral Thesis). Madrid: Universidad Complutense.

Andrade Blanco, Juan (2015). *El PCE y el PSOE en (la) transición. La evolución ideológica de la izquierda durante el proceso de cambio político*. Madrid: Siglo XXI.

Bell, David (1983). 'The Spanish Communist Party in the Transition', in *Democratic Politics in Spain: Spanish Politics After Franco*, ed. David Bell. London: Frances Pinter.

Colomer, Josep M. (1998). *La transición a la democracia. El modelo español*. Barcelona: Anagrama.

Del Águila, Rafael & Ricardo Montoro (1984). *El discurso político de la Transición española*. Madrid: Centro de Investigaciones Sociológicas.

Díaz Barrado, Mario P. (2013). 'El discurso político en la Transición democrática. Ideología y expectativas de poder en el debate en torno a la Constitución de 1978', in *Los partidos en la Transición. Las organizaciones políticas en la construcción de la democracia española*, ed. Rafael Quirosa-Cheyrouze y Muñoz. Madrid: Biblioteca Nueva.

Fuentes, Juan Francisco (2008). 'Reforma', in *Diccionario político y social del siglo XX español*, eds. Javier Fernández Sebastián & Juan Francisco Fuentes. Madrid: Alianza.

Hernández Gil, Antonio (1983). 'Facetas de dos procesos constituyentes', *Revista de Estudios Políticos*, 31–32, 11–24.

Mateos, Abdón (1996). 'Una transición dentro de la transición. Auge, unidad y conversión de los socialistas', in *Historia de la transición (1975–1986)*, eds. Javier Tusell & Álvaro Soto. Madrid: Alianza.

Morán, Gregorio (1979). *Adolfo Suárez. Historia de una ambición*. Barcelona: Planeta.

Robles-Egea, Antonio (2016). 'Santiago Carrillo Solares', in *Political Leadership in the Spanish Transition to Democracy (1975–1982)*, eds. José Francisco Jiménez Díaz & Santiago Delgado Fernández. Hauppauge: Nova Science.

Sánchez Agesta, Luis (1978). 'Una revolución a través del derecho. Cómo fue posible la Constitución de 1978', *La Vanguardia*, 20 December, 19.

Sánchez-Terán, Salvador (2005). 'La legalización del Partido Comunista de España', in *La Transición. Síntesis y claves*. Barcelona: Planeta.

Solé Tura, Jordi (1978). 'La Constitución y la lucha por el socialismo', in *La izquierda y la Constitución*, eds. Gregorio Peces-Barba et al. Barcelona: Taula de Canvi.
Zugasti, Ricardo (2012). 'A Forge of Consensus: The Press During the Transition to Democracy in Spain', *Media History*, 18(2), 207–17.

CHAPTER 6

Constitutional State Powers

This chapter surveys how state institutions were envisaged in the debates of the Constituent Assembly held between May and September 1978. The first section analyses the meanings of the ideas of popular and national sovereignty, that were often interpreted as synonyms. The second section sheds light on how the idea of the rule of law was widely accepted among centrist and right-wing representatives. It was considered the guarantor of democratic institutions, which only looked controversial to nationalist parties. The third section clarifies that the Constitution was the cornerstone of institutions and not just an instrument to enhance sovereignty. The last section focuses on the constitutional limits to the executive, the legislative, and the judicial powers. Representatives argued that the legislative power should have mechanisms to counterbalance the executive power. Besides, the independence of the judiciary was deemed unquestionable to maintain democratic institutions.

F. J. Bellido, *Constitutional Debates, Rhetoric, and Political Philosophy in Spain's Parliamentary History*, Rhetoric, Politics and Society,
https://doi.org/10.1007/978-3-031-56894-7_6

1 Public Powers as Guards of National Sovereignty

This section clarifies the meanings of national and popular sovereignty during the constitutional sessions. First, it presents the arguments in favour of a unitary idea of national and popular sovereignty as equivalent concepts raised by Union of Democratic Centre, Popular Alliance, and independent senators. Second, it brings forward the arguments of representatives of the Spanish Socialist Workers' Party and the Communist Party of Spain which make sense on the predominance of popular sovereignty as a unitary concept, source of democratic legitimacy. In the case of the Communist Party of Spain, its leader Santiago Carrillo and the constitutional rapporteur Jordi Solé Tura conceived parliament as an organ of sovereignty beyond its representative function. Third, it suggests that the interpretation of sovereignty by the nationalist parties of the Basque Country and Catalonia left various margins of interpretation of that concept. Sovereignty was often confused with the idea of fiscal autonomy.

1.1 National Sovereignty in a Historical Perspective

During the constitutional sessions, both in the Congress of Deputies and the Senate, representatives agreed on the need to clarifying the meaning of national sovereignty. Controversies that would have jeopardized the legitimacy of the sovereign power were refused by representatives of Union of Democratic Centre, the Spanish Socialist Workers' Party, and Popular Alliance. The history of Europe and, more specifically, the milestone of the Constitution of 1812 illustrated several examples of the changing meanings of that idea.

The French Revolution and its ensuing Constitution of 1791 were identified as the historical changes that altered the idea of national sovereignty. That transformation of sovereignty from a confusing idea with a utopian resounding echo into a modern conception of political unity of a community of equal citizens was regarded as positive. The Constitution of 1978, as the Preliminary Draft of the Constitution sought, would enshrine the political sovereignty of the nation as the source of legitimacy for state institutions.

1.2 The Unitary Conception of National Sovereignty Defended by Union of Democratic Centre, Popular Alliance, and Independent Senators

Óscar Alzaga, of Union of Democratic Centre, reminded that the idea of national sovereignty was already defended by the liberal representative Diego Muñoz-Torrero in the first Constituent Assembly of Spain, in Cadiz (1810–1812). There, he argued that since 1811, the principle of national sovereignty was undisputable from a theoretical perspective because to justify the source of political sovereignty in a different manner would have meant to question the existence of the 'constituent power' (DSLC, 11 May 1978, Congress: 2184).

Alzaga's argument aimed to convene all political parties around a contemporary ideal of national sovereignty. Such ideal had a long history in Europe to which the Spanish parliamentary tradition also contributed. His stance did not mean that national sovereignty was already an undisputed idea in Spain's twentieth century. In fact, the history of the country exemplified a permanent dispute between an organicist idea of national sovereignty and a more sophisticated understanding of political institutions as the result of individual citizens' will expressed through political suffrage. The former was outdated; the latter was improved by the historical development of representative democracy in Spain.

For instance, José Miguel Ortí Bordás, of the Independent Candidacy of Centre, said that in the Constituent Assembly of 1931 representatives decided to enshrine popular instead of national sovereignty to break with the historical distinction between the Spanish people and the "organicist and mythical sense" of national sovereignty (DSLC, 11 May 1978, Congress: 2187). That contrast was regarded as a historical controversy legally solved in twentieth-century democracies. Positive laws of democratic regimes, especially their constitutional texts, should get rid of any holistic understanding of political concepts. If democracy was to be justified as an effective idea of political representation of individual citizens with equal rights, any anti-individualistic understanding of representation should be discarded.

Ortí Bordás seemed to consider that the Constituent Assembly of 1931 had broken with nineteenth-century constitutionalism with the exception of the Cadiz Constitution. Popular sovereignty was the opposite idea of organicist sovereignty because the source of political legitimacy was the Spanish people formed by the union of its individual citizens. It was a well-defined collective body in a political sense, internally diverse and, by that same token, indivisible between sub-categories that were not individual citizens themselves.

To a similar extent, Laureano López Rodó, legal scholar of Popular Alliance, argued that sovereignty was 'indivisible'. Following the theories of the classic political thinkers Jean Bodin and Thomas Hobbes, López Rodó argued that there was no feasible doctrine of sovereignty that would admit the division of that sovereignty among different sources (DSLC, 15 June 1978, Congress: 3340).

The idea of national sovereignty in the Preliminary Draft of the Constitution was equivalent to that of popular sovereignty enshrined in the Constitution of 1931. However, the expression 'national sovereignty' emphasized the unitary character of that sovereignty, incompatible with internal divisions among the peoples of the different Spanish regions. Sovereignty belongs to the Spanish people as a whole in an indivisible manner. The Constitution of 1978 improved the definition of sovereignty from a technical point of view. By clarifying the existence of a national unit, Spain, the Constitution emphasized the historical relevance of the country that plainly justified the Spanish people as sovereign body.

National sovereignty expressed that the source of sovereignty was only the Spanish people and nothing else. Spanish citizens were the source of national sovereignty; other instances were discarded (Varela Suanzes-Carpegna 2014: 815). In that wise, the Constitution clarified the unitary sense of sovereignty. As the constitutional rapporteurs of Union of Democratic Centre Miguel Herrero y Rodríguez de Miñón and José Pedro Pérez Llorca declared during the constitutional sessions, political sovereignty was not "divisible" among the different peoples that formed Spain: the country was a political nation that could not be dependent on a permanent questioning of the source of political sovereignty (DSLC, 5 May 1978, Congress: 2025; DSLC, 4 July 1978, Congress: 3790).

In an interview with the cultural magazine *Cuadernos para el Diálogo*, Pérez-Llorca argued that the Constitution of 1978 categorically enshrined the Spanish nation as a unitary body as "never before has been written in a Constitution" (*Cuadernos para el Diálogo*, 31 December 1978: 16). The Constitution of 1931 should be understood in this sense close to interwar European constitutionalism. It meant a step forward in the history of Spain that the undisputable sovereignty of the Spanish people in the Constitution of 1978 was assumed as a prerequisite for building a lasting democracy.

The concept of popular sovereignty was taken by José Pedro Pérez-Llorca, of Union of Democratic Centre, as part of a modern understanding of a constitutional monarchy, as the safeguard of the unity of the state (DSLC, 11 May 1978, Congress: 2201). Constitutional monarchy was not an impediment to democracy. To a great extent as a result of King Juan Carlos I's endorsement of political changes, the transition to democracy in Spain was possible. For the first time in the history of the country monarchy and democracy were plainly compatible with each other. Sovereignty belonged to the Spanish people and the monarch was the authority that granted the continuity of both the nation and its democratic institutions.

Parliament was not a sovereign power, but the institution in which political representation was exercised. Parliamentary debates contributed to strengthening democracy and its procedures. They were the conditions for the existence of a democratic regime. Even though Manuel Fraga, leader of Popular Alliance, defended parliaments as the only institutions that allow the contrast of ideologies and proposals for the audience, that potential did not mean that parliaments were sovereign organs. Parliaments are the representative institutions of democracy, not sovereign organs.

If national sovereignty was admitted as the expression of the political will of Spanish citizens, then parliament was a crucial democratic institution though not a source of sovereignty. Parliament had political functions that other institutions could not replace. According to his argument, to consider parliament a sovereign institution was a confusing idea. When doing so national sovereignty was undermined. If there was an additional sovereign power different from the Spanish people, it would mean that sovereignty could be shared with other institutions. Fraga refused that idea even when talking in a metaphorical sense. Parliament should be considered as the representative institution of democratic regimes. It was the channel of political sovereignty through representative means, but lacking sovereignty.

For example, to Carlos Ollero, senator by royal designation, the historical reason to distinguish national sovereignty from popular sovereignty was the conflict between, on the one hand, Jean-Jacques Rousseau's theories on popular sovereignty and direct democracy; and on the other hand, Emmanuel-Joseph Sieyès's stance in favour of national sovereignty (DSLC, 18 August 1978, Senate: 1582). National sovereignty was a classic political idea with a historical development that the Constitution should consider.

To Manuel Villar Arregui, of Union of Democratic Centre, the main problem around sovereignty was a conceptual difference regarding the idea of state powers. He argued that "we have to free the whole preliminary title of mandates that the constituent power grants to the constituted power".[1] The constituent power was clearly distinguished from the constituted power by virtue of its importance to understand democracy in its origins. The constituent power is justified because it derives from the will of Spanish citizens expressed through universal suffrage. Instead, the constituted power comes about after the passing of the Constitution, thus paving the way for democratic institutions.

In a nutshell, the concept of sovereignty was undivided to centre-right representatives. The historical development of the idea of sovereignty in the constituent assemblies of Cadiz (1810–1812) and the Spanish Second Republic (1931) were the constitutional texts that inspired constituent representatives. The building of institutions had only a source of sovereignty, the Spanish people. Parliament was considered the institution in which that sovereignty was exercised by political representatives through deliberations.

1.3 Popular Sovereignty According to the Spanish Socialist Workers' Party and the Communist Party of Spain

Gregorio Peces-Barba, constitutional rapporteur of the Spanish Socialist Workers' Party, advocated to "make an agreement [through the Constitution] around a common heritage that is indisputable".[2] The main difference between his speech at the Congress of Deputies on 5 May 1978 and those of representatives of Union of Democratic Centre and Popular Alliance is the ambiguity of Peces-Barba's statements about popular sovereignty. He supported the idea of a shared source of popular sovereignty between the peoples of Spain. At the same time, Peces-Barba maintained that the bearer of sovereignty was the totality of individuals of the different peoples of Spain. That diversity was accepted also

[1] "[*T*]*enemos que liberar a todo el título preliminar de mandatos que el poder constituyente defiere al poder constituido*" (DSLC, 22 August 1978, Congress: 1698).

[2] "[*R*]*ealizan un acuerdo en un acervo común que sea indiscutible*" (DSLC, 5 May 1978, Congress: 2031).

when talking about sovereignty, thus leaving interpretative margins about whether the source of sovereignty was divisible.

Peces-Barba was less ambiguous in his intervention a few days later. The idea of national sovereignty has a long revolutionary tradition in France to mean the representation of the French people. Nevertheless, to him the concept of popular sovereignty was more adequate to Spain in order to avoid a confusion between national and popular sovereignty as two antithetical ideas. He argued that "the acceptable term when sovereignty is to be qualified is that of 'popular sovereignty', a fundamentally personalist concept".[3]

For example, Eduardo Martín Toval, of the Spanish Socialist Workers' Party, distinguished two meanings of sovereignty. The first of them was stated in the Preliminary Draft of the Constitution; the second of them was what he called "the normative sovereignty of the state" (DSLC, 16 June 1978, Congress: 3773). With that expression Martín Toval referred to the capacity of state institutions to distribute competences between the state and the regions without eroding the sovereignty of the Spanish people. To delegate competences was a constitutional instrument that should be applied consistently in order to keep the production of norms by the legislative organs of the Autonomous Communities in accordance with the constitutional principles.

José María Benegas, of the Spanish Socialist Workers' Party, thought that Spain was formed by different peoples, but its sovereignty was one and indivisible (DSLC, 20 June 1978, Congress: 3499). Self-rule for the Basque Country was necessary because it expressed a fair demand with historical roots in Spain's history. His idea of sovereignty was compatible with the existence of regional institutions and the distribution of competences between the state and the regions.

Regarding the foundation of sovereignty, Vicente Sotillo, of the Spanish Socialist Workers' Party, spoke in favour of a unitary meaning of popular sovereignty. He argued that it was unacceptable from a constitutional point of view to divide sovereignty between the regions as if social agreements were just the result of regional pacts (DSLC, 19 July 1978, Congress: 4406). Popular sovereignty was not open to debate. Only one

[3] "[*E*]*L término aceptable cuando se quiere calificar a la soberanía es el de 'soberanía popular', concepto fundamentalmente personalista*" (DSLC, 11 May 1978, Congress: 2189).

bearer of sovereignty was to be acknowledged in the Constitution: the Spanish people.

According to Santiago Carrillo, leader of the Communist Party of Spain, to enshrine 'popular sovereignty' in the Constitution and to consider parliament as the 'receiver' (*depositario*) of that sovereignty was unquestionable (Carrillo 1993: 674). To him the distinction between popular sovereignty and sovereign parliament was not controversial. Parliament had representative functions connected to popular sovereignty, but it was also a sovereign organ with its own competences delimited in the Constitution. To say that the parliament was sovereign meant nothing else than connecting its legitimacy to the Spanish people. The former is the institution that enshrines political sovereignty; the latter is its source.

In that same regard, Jordi Solé Tura, constitutional rapporteur of the Communist Party of Spain, argued in favour of a unitary meaning of popular sovereignty which belonged to Spanish citizens as a whole. Besides, representatives exercise the representative function of popular sovereignty in parliament and never through other institutions (DSLC, 20 June 1978, Congress: 3525). Both Carrillo and Solé Tura regarded parliament as a sovereign institution in a literal sense.

To the Spanish Socialist Workers' Party popular sovereignty should be described as the source of legitimacy of democratic institutions. It was not opposed to the existence of different peoples within Spain, but it kept a unitary sense that could not be divided. To the Communist Party of Spain the unitary sense of popular sovereignty was unquestionable. Despite that fact and unlike centrist and right-wing representatives, Santiago Carrillo and Jordi Solé Tura thought that parliament should be considered a sovereign organ.

1.4 A Divisible Sovereignty: The Position of Nationalist Parties of Catalonia and the Basque Country

To Francisco Letamendía, of Euskadi's Left (*Euskadiko Ezkerra*), "the original powers rest on the peoples and the peoples surrender their sovereignty to the Spanish state".[4] To him sovereignty had its foundation in the so-called historical character of the different nations that would form Spain. According to his words, in its origins sovereignty belongs to

[4] "[*L*]*os poderes originarios residen en los pueblos y los pueblos hacen dejación de soberanía al Estado español*" (DSLC, 11 May 1978, Congress: 2182).

the different peoples of Spain, who delegate that sovereignty to the state. From his conception of sovereignty, the unity of the sovereign power would happen just by voluntary delegation of those peoples. That concept of sovereignty was assumed in a nationalist interpretation of the history of Spain as including nations with original sovereignties. To Letamendía Autonomous Communities would have a participation in that sovereignty together with the state, as if they were equal organs to make economic decisions (DSLC, 13 June 1978, Congress: 3198).

That idea of sovereignty was connected to a demand of fiscal autonomy that distorted the equal sovereignty of Spanish citizens. In that sense, it would entail transforming the idea of sovereignty into a flexible concept sometimes exchangeable with the one of autonomy to mean more economic competences handed to governments of the Autonomous Communities. Letamendía summarized his demands of "fiscal sovereignty" to say that collaboration between Autonomous Communities would be harder to accomplish if their budgetary capacity would be questioned. Economic competences were interpreted as a function of sovereignty that should prevent its control by the central administration of the state (DSLC, 14 June 1978, Congress: 3261).

Letamendía's speeches often seemed to be contradictory with each other regarding his favourable stance to the possibility of secession for the Basque Country, Catalonia, and Galicia. Then, he seemed to disagree with any strong ideal of constitutional loyalty by all state institutions. He was ambiguous when talking about the rights to self-determination in terms of sovereignty of historical regions and at the same time arguing in favour of popular sovereignty in Spain. If the country was a "nation of nations" and the right to self-determination was a fair demand, thus the existence of popular sovereignty was questioned (DSLC, 21 July 1978, Congress: 4568).

Xabier Arzalluz, one of the leaders of the Basque Nationalist Party, was clear about his conception of sovereignty: "We see ourselves considered within this state, or Kingdom, in a sense of original sovereignty".[5] His stance resembled that of Francisco Letamendía: Spain as a nation had just a concession of sovereignty by the different peoples within the country. Among them, Basque citizens would constitute a unitary people. Despite the evident historical difficulties to justify that idea, it was clear that such

[5] "[*N*]*osotros nos vemos contemplados dentro de este Estado, o en su caso Reino, en un sentido de soberanía originaria*" (DSLC, 11 May 1978, Congress: 2183).

conception of sovereignty broke with the constitutional and parliamentary tradition of Spain.

Arzalluz's arguments about the concept of sovereignty aimed at distinguishing his notion of sovereignty from the French tradition initiated with Jean Bodin's *Les Six Livres de la République* (1576) and transformed with the French Revolution. To him France transferred to Spain an inadequate idea of sovereignty that did not fit the territorial features of the country (DSLC, 18 July 1978, Congress: 4369). To Arzalluz popular sovereignty was deemed inadequate because he interpreted it as detrimental to Spain's territorial diversity. Nevertheless, his justification was weak since it failed to distinguish the democratic and individualistic, non-historicist idea, originated in a unitary concept of sovereignty.

Ramón Trías Fargas, of the Democratic Pact for Catalonia, used very similar arguments to those of Francisco Letamendía. To Trías Fargas the economic capacity of Autonomous Communities to distribute resources was more than a way to make autonomy possible, but the condition of political sovereignty (DSLC, 13 June 1978, Congress: 3201–4). That concept of sovereignty was not just a metaphor, it illustrated that sovereignty was conceived by the Democratic Pact of Catalonia far beyond a unitary political body. Sovereignty was to some extent identified with the capacity of broadening economic competences at the expense of the state.

In a more sophisticated way, Miquel Roca Junyent, of the Democratic Pact for Catalonia, regarded the initiative of "derogatory referendums", as he called them, as a function that would make stronger the popular initiative while at the same time not being detrimental to popular sovereignty. To him the mixed mechanisms of representative democracy and popular initiative were complementary. Popular sovereignty was preserved because popular initiative through referendum simply meant a legislative mechanism to abolish some laws in special cases (DSLC, 6 June 1978, Congress: 2941).

Roca Junyent admitted that the connection between popular sovereignty and representative democracy expressed already in the Preliminary Draft of the Constitution was clear. His aim was to settle a series of mechanisms that would allow referendums in some special cases. To him popular sovereignty was not opposed at all to limited mechanisms of direct democracy. His understanding of democracy and self-rule as the expressions of the popular will through mixed mechanisms of representative and direct democracy was evident in his speeches.

Heribert Barrera, of Republican Left of Catalonia, highlighted his nationalism with even clearer overtones. He declared that sovereignty belonged to each one of the nations that formed Spain and not to the Spanish people as a whole. With that argument, Barrera highlighted that the central administration of the state should have very limited competences (DSLC, 15 June 1978, Congress: 3331). Consequently, he thought that limited competences of the central administration of the state would not only benefit the capacity of regional governments, but also improve the quality of those services. Most of state competences could be handed to the regions not just because it was consistent with his idea of sovereignty, but because in his opinion the Autonomous Communities would provide better services to citizens.

To Euskadi's Left and the Basque Nationalist Party there was an original sovereignty of the Basque Country, Catalonia, and Galicia as historical nations within Spain. That idea was aimed to justify a greater degree of decentralization of state competences handed to regional governments, especially fiscal ones. To the Democratic Pact for Catalonia the main concern was to promote mechanisms of direct democracy in the Constitution that would leave open the capacity to use "derogatory referendums". That measure was aimed to dispute the legal capacity of the state to pass laws. Instead, to Republican Left of Catalonia the decentralization of state competences should not be postponed. It was a demand of sovereignty from Autonomous Communities that public powers should fulfil.

2 The Rule of Law as the Mainstay of Representative Democracy

This section examines the stances of deputies and senators about the idea of rule of law. First, it explores how liberal and conservative representatives preferred the expression 'rule of law' to describe the respect for constitutional rules and procedures that protected the stability of democracy. From that view, representatives of Union of Democratic Centre and Popular Alliance argued that freedoms and equality before the law were part of the guarantees that the rule of law enhanced in democratic regimes. Second, this section questions the viability of democracy if the negative view of the rule of law by nationalist parties was assumed. In that case, the very ideas of sovereignty and the rule of law would be distorted.

2.1 *The Rule of Law as Political Concept*

The rule of law (whose closest equivalent was *estado de derecho*, although depending on the context of use this also meant constitutional state) is a political concept and a moral ideal based on the primacy of the legal order to regulate the functioning of public powers. As a token of this, the norms that constitutions recognize set the limits to public powers indicating their functions. Without impartial courts of justice subordinated to the rule of law, democratic institutions would be vulnerable to decisions by government and other authorities, be they public or private. The lack of rule of law leads authorities to contravene the norms and procedures of the legal order.

The rule of law was indispensable to protect state institutions and citizens' freedoms because it raised the constitutional order above any attempt to subordinate state institutions to particularistic ends. By the same token, constituent representatives aimed to prevent arbitrary uses of the political power by creating specific courts of justice as the Supreme Court (*Tribunal Supremo*) and the Constitutional Court (*Tribunal Constitutional*).

Transitions to democracy after World War II made it possible the re-emergence of the idea of rule of law as a distinctive feature ensuring the democratic character of constitutional regimes (Rosenfeld 1998: 1900–1). Constituent representatives emphasized the rule of law (*estado de derecho*) against any authoritarian drift that could use democratic laws to the benefit of rulers (Christiansen 2018: 45). That was a setback that representatives aimed to prevent. The rule of law was part of the definition adopted in the Preliminary Draft of the Constitution regarding the new democratic regime (art. 1). It was so partly because of the prestige of that concept during the Francoism—despite the inadequacy of dictatorships to that ideal—and in the Basic Law (*Grundgesetz*) of the Federal Republic of Germany (Varela Suanzes-Carpegna 2006: 45).

Against the pervasive interferences of public institutions with each other, the Constitution has included mechanisms to limit their action (Aguiar de Luque 1981: 116). Indeed, in a leading article of the monarchic newspaper *ABC* called 'A stable government' the Constitution was interpreted as the resource to control the political power imposing restrictions on public powers (*ABC*, 21 December 1977: 2). Following that argument, political stability and the respect for democracy would rely on the limits that are settled to state powers, institutions, and citizens.

Between 1977 and 1978, as it happened after the transition process to democracy was over, the very idea of democracy was defended with full positive connotations against declining forms of government. Terms such as 'partitocracy', 'oligocracy', or 'technocracy' had pejorative connotations (De Santiago Guervós 1992: 148). To Manuel Fraga, leader of Popular Alliance, one of the greatest dangers of democracy was to become a democracy of parties that would undermine the deliberative function of parliament (Fraga 1978: 108). Legal philosophers and scholars, such as Andrés Ollero Tassara, argued that Western European Constitutions after World War II gave rise to a design of the parliamentary system that strengthened parties to the detriment of single MPs (Ollero Tassara 1994: 10).

The parliamentary deliberations of the Constituent Assembly were undoubtedly embedded in European constitutionalism. As a result of that commitment, the rule of law was the pillar of the building of democratic institutions. Representatives of all parties reflected their own understanding of the rule of law, fertile from a conceptual perspective. Their interpretations make sense of the development of the idea of rule of law in Spain during the 1970s.

2.2 *The Rule of Law in the Constituent Assembly: Limits to Political Powers*

In the beginning of the public deliberations in the Congress of Deputies, Emilio Attard, second speaker (*Presidente*) of the Congress of Deputies of Union of Democratic Centre, connected the existence of the rule of law with the acknowledgement of the rights of citizens and the aspirations "of the peoples, of the regions and of the countries of Spain" (DSLC, 5 May 1978, Congress: 2022).

Unlike that shared understanding of the rule of law, almost irrespective of ideological preferences, Gabriel Cisneros, constitutional rapporteur of Union of Democratic Centre, declared that "conservative liberalism" had a special commitment to the rule of law (DSLC, 11 May 1978, Congress: 2176). Apparently, his speech seemed not just to connect his ideological leaning to the rule of law, but to say that any liberal or conservative party should be committed to the rule of law. His speech clarified it by emphasizing the importance of the legal order to any centre-right political party. However, that conception of the rule of law as closer to his own ideology left out a deeper understanding of the rule of law: a political and moral ideal irrespective of ideological leanings.

Hipólito Gómez de las Roces, of the Aragonese Candidacy of Centre, connected monarchy with the existence of the rule of law: "Monarchy is defined by the whole Constitution, not simply because of the existence of parliament, [but] by the sum of the structures that will constitute the rule of law".[6] In his speech Gómez de las Roces made clear that monarchy was a form of government that fitted with the rule of law. Rather than being inadequate to the rule of law, monarchy had a potential to strengthen the respect for the norms and procedures of the legal order. Monarchy had a permanent character that made it one of the most appropriate instruments to preserve the legal order and the continuity of institutions.

To Miguel Herrero y Rodríguez de Miñón, constitutional rapporteur of Union of Democratic Centre, "a constitutional state is the state that guarantees freedoms and make them to coexist in an order of freedom, and that, even by coercion".[7] The rule of law entailed coercion when freedoms were threatened, but it was not its distinctive feature. The rule of law was better characterized by virtue of its capacity to make political and civil freedoms compatible with each other.

Lluís Maria Xirinacs, of Republican Left of Catalonia, mixed up the ideas of sovereignty and law as if they were almost incompatible with each other. To him sovereignty had an original character connected to the nations of Spain, whereas the rule of law lacked that character and should be an expression of that original sovereignty (DSLC, 18 August 1978, Senate: 1557). It was unclear whether that idea of sovereignty would be valid to a democratic legal order. Xirinacs' approach seemed simply wrong. The unitary character of sovereignty was a prerequisite for the rule of law.

Unlike what senator Xirinacs championed, Luis Olarra, of Popular Alliance, argued that the rule of law was the reason of the existence of equality before the law (DSLC, 29 August 1978, Senate: 2015). Equality among all Spanish citizens was effective because the rule of law existed.

[6] "*La monarquía viene definida por el conjunto de la Constitución, no simplemente por la existencia del Parlamento; por la suma de estructuras que van a constituir el Estado de derecho*" (DSLC, 11 May 1978, Congress: 2214).

[7] "[*U*]*N Estado de Derecho es el Estado que garantiza las libertades y las hace coexistir en un orden de libertad, y ello, incluso, coactivamente*" (DSLC, 18 May 1978, Congress: 2501).

Without the rule of law equality would be just a desideratum or a declaration of principles without real effectiveness. A democratic order required checks and balances that only a rule of law would safeguard.

To most constituent representatives, the rule of law was a basic feature of the new democratic regime. Equality before the law, separation of powers and enforcement of legality were regarded positively by liberal and conservative parties in the Constituent Assembly. Despite that fact, the rule of law, as it was described there, was also endorsed by parties from other ideologies. It was a political and moral ideal to be endorsed by any advocate of constitutional freedoms and democracy.

3 Constitutional Constraints and Constitutional Rights

This section clarifies the meaning of the Constitution as the mainspring to design political institutions. Representatives of Union of Democratic Centre, Popular Alliance, and the Popular Socialist Party conceived of the Constitution as the first step for enhancing popular sovereignty and for applying a design of autonomies that would be compatible with the constitutional text. It expounds that the ideas of constitution, sovereignty, and democracy became intermingled. Together, they reflect the concern of those political parties to harmonize the ideas of a unitary concept of popular sovereignty and a stable democracy in Spain through the Constitution.

3.1 The Unitary Character of the Spanish Nation According to Political Parties

The Constitution of 1978 rests on three political principles: the national unity of Spain, its political plurality, and the protection of autonomous regions (García Morillo 1996: 47). The legitimacy of the Constitution partly derives from its 'internal' structure, legally binding by virtue of its democratic source, the whole Spanish people (Aragón Reyes 1989: 43). Its function is not to eliminate conflicts in a democratic regime, but to provide rules for interpreting those conflicts (Del Águila and Montoro 1984: 241).

Landelino Lavilla, senator by royal designation who would become minister of justice in the government of Union of Democratic Centre, stated that "the political strength of a Constitution is particularly visible through the restrictions imposed upon the action of government by the constitutional declaration of rights".[8] Constraints on government's action were essential in the Constitution insofar as constitutional rights indicated the limits to public powers and made interpretations by courts of justice possible.

By pointing out the potentialities of constitutions, Josep Solé Barberà, Catalan representative of the Spanish Communist Party, declared that constituent representatives were making "a Constitution that we aim that is not just for everyone, but that we aim that has a long validity and a prosperous validity".[9] The democratic aspirations of all Spaniards, irrespective of their ideologies, should be enshrined in the Constitution. Together with it, the Constitution had to be a lasting text that would protect the freedoms of citizens with efficiency, then enhancing democratic institutions and procedures.

To Manuel Fraga, leader of Popular Alliance, the Constitution "has to be an organic collection of fundamental decisions, an orderly and balanced norm of the political community".[10] Thus, the constitutional text would contain not just the basic norms of a democratic regime, but the scope of political decisions that can be taken in compliance with laws. The Constitution of 1978 was thought from its very beginning as a set of rules to regulate a political community. Its norms indicated to public powers, other institutions, and citizens what was legally possible to do and what was not.

For example, to Manuel Villar Arregui, of Union of Democratic Centre, the unitary character of the Spanish nation had a special relevance from a constitutional perspective: "that indissoluble unity is a primary aspect of the Constitution, but I would say that is a primary aspect of a different degree, of a different nature".[11] Accordingly, the Constitution

[8] "*La fuerza política de una Constitución es particularmente visible en relación con las restricciones impuestas a la acción del Gobierno por la declaración constitucional de derechos*" (DSLC, 9 May 1978, Congress: 2101).

[9] "[*U*]*na Constitución que pretendemos que no solamente sea para todos, sino que pretendemos que tenga una vigencia larga y que tenga una vigencia próspera*" (DSLC, 8 June 1978, Congress: 3132).

[10] "[*H*]*A de ser un conjunto orgánico de decisiones fundamentales, una norma ordenada y equilibrada de la comunidad política*" (DSLC, 4 July 1978, Congress: 3775).

[11] "[*E*]*sa indisoluble unidad es un prius de la Constitución, pero yo diría que es un prius de otro grado, de otra naturaleza*" (DSLC, 19 August 1978, Congress: 1622).

raised the unity of the Spanish nation to a higher category than other norms. To Villar Arregui that declaration of the sovereign unity of the Spanish nation was indubitable: it meant that all state institutions should comply with that principle.

Despite the constitutional limits to the functions of the head of government, his capacity was much broader than in other Spanish Constitutions in order to preserve the political stability of governments (Díez-Picazo and Perales 2008: 55–56). In an article titled 'The Constitution and the commitment', journalist Eduardo Haro Tecglen argued that Constitutions should avoid any arbitrary use of the political power (*Triunfo*, 13 May 1978: 19).

A few months before, in another article titled 'Isn't this it?', the intellectual Julián Marías claimed that the organization of Spain as reflected in the Constitution could lead to inequalities among citizens from different regions. He repeated the advice against nationalisms that his mentor, José Ortega y Gasset, had given during the Second Republic (*El País*, 21 January 1978). Representatives of Union of Democratic Centre and Popular Alliance were especially concerned about the mechanisms to regulate the institutions included in the constitutional text. The shielding of popular sovereignty was not a strategy to strengthen democratic institutions, but a principle to design state institutions with full respect for it.

4 Independence of State Powers: A Shared Ideal of National Parties

This section explores how the executive, the legislative, and the judicial powers were envisaged in the Constituent Assembly. First, it points out that the executive and the legislative powers were regarded as intertwined powers in democratic regimes. That circumstance justified tightened procedures to control the executive power to protect legislative's functions. Second, it brings out that the independence of the judicial power and its members was agreed as the best way to safeguard the legitimacy and adequacy of the new democratic regime to the rule of law.

4.1 The Functions of the Executive Power and the Legislative Power

During the Francoist regime administrative law experts developed a legal system of public law inspired by the Italian legal tradition that was completely alien to constitutional law, though remarkable from a doctrinal point of view (Lucas Verdú 1994: 26). The Preliminary Draft of the Constitution imitated the regulation of the executive and the legislative powers from the Italian Constitution of 1947 and the Basic Law (*Grundgesetz*) of the Federal Republic of Germany of 1949.

To Miguel Herrero y Rodríguez de Miñón, constitutional rapporteur of Union of Democratic Centre, it was the authoritarian drift of the executive power and not the legislative power the source of conflicts that could undermine democratic institutions (DSLC, 5 May 1978, Congress: 2028). For that reason, Union of Democratic Centre and the Spanish Socialist Workers' Party agreed on a constitutional regulation that should preserve mechanisms of government stability to avoid giving prevalence to the executive power. The reinforcement of parliamentary democracy was addressed as something to be resolved in the Constitution.

To senator Manuel Villar Arregui, of Union of Democratic Centre, the functions of the executive and the legislative powers were not exactly the same than in the past: "In the regime of a parliamentary monarchy [...] the functions ascribed to those powers are such that neither government is limited to rule nor parliament to legislate".[12] Villar Arregui admitted that the attribution of limited functions to political powers was more an ideal than a reality. The functions of the executive power were beyond the execution of laws. The legislative power was not an isolated political power, but it kept a permanent tension with the rest that was the cause of the balance—though imperfect—of state powers. That tension was part of the historical development of parliamentary democracies.

Gregorio Peces-Barba, of the Spanish Socialist Workers' Party, made clear the basic principles of any Constitution: "In our view all constitutions [...] should fulfil a function of legitimation, a function of security and a function of justice".[13] These three functions were not those of the executive and the legislative powers. Those three axioms should prevail irrespective of the constitutional design of the executive and the legislative powers.

[12] "[*E*]*N el régimen de una Monarquía parlamentaria* [...] *las funciones atribuidas a aquellos poderes es* [sic] *tal que ni el Gobierno se limita a ejecutar ni el Parlamento a legislar*" (DSLC, 7 September 1978, Senate: 2417).

[13] "*A nuestro juicio todas las constituciones* [...] *deben cumplir una función de legitimación, una función de seguridad y una función de justicia*" (DSLC, 5 May 1978, Congress: 2030).

In this regard, in his newspaper article 'About constituents and constitutionalists' legal scholar Francisco Rubio Llorente argued that the legal technique applied to the constitutional debate in parliament was indispensable to the success of the democratic process (*El País*, 26 July 1977). Legal expertise was indispensable to the writing of the Constitution.

In a leading article published in 1978 and titled 'All for one...' there was optimism about the process of state decentralization if equality among citizens of all territories was patent in the Constitution to be passed (*Cambio 16*, 14 May 1978: 64). Nevertheless, the access to the highest degree possible of self-rule by the Spanish regions remained undefined in the Constitution due to the decision to settle it in the ensuing years after 1978 (Alzaga Villaamil 2018: 10–12). The issue of regional autonomy was understood as both part of the executive and the legislative competences to be distributed between the state and the Autonomous Communities.

Besides, the debate about regional autonomy was a discussion about the number of competences that corresponded to the regions and to which extent regional governments could legislate regardless of the central administration of the state. The Constitution was the legal limit to the executive and legislative functions of the Autonomous Communities.

4.2 The Judicial Power in the Constituent Assembly

By the same token, the superior values that the Constitution enshrines allow for legal interpretations of constitutional articles by courts of justice (González Rivas 1988: 140). Those higher values do not entail to identify the constitutional text with the legal order (Merino Merchán 1988: 3415). To Gregorio Peces-Barba, of the Spanish Socialist Workers' Party, there was a reciprocal relationship "between society, power, values, and the legal order" that determined some peculiarities in political and legal issues (Peces-Barba 1988: 24).

The legal control of the constitutionality of ordinary laws by the Constitutional Court (*Tribunal Constitucional*) meant to put Spain on an equal footing with the rest of Western European democracies (Cisneros Laborda et al. 1998: 27). The independence of the judicial power was deemed the cornerstone for the success of democracy. German constitutionalism was widely influential to the systematic design of the sources of law, together with the regulation of the judicial power and its organs (Díez-Picazo and Perales 2008: 57–58).

Juan Antonio Bolea, judge and legal scholar of Union of Democratic Centre, declared his belief in the rule of law and the independence of the judicial power: "We think that any state that is formed as an authentic constitutional state should constitutionally guarantee the independence of the judicial power".[14] The defence of the separation of state powers meant than the judicial power should be a shelter in the Constitution against all those measures that could undermine its legitimacy to enforce the law.

According to José Pedro Pérez-Llorca, of Union of Democratic Centre, "the Constitution that we are making tells about the judicial power and conceives it fundamentally as a sole and independent judicial power".[15] To do that, it was indispensable to create a judicial power with full legal attributions and competences to proceed. The independence of judges was a precondition of democracy that demanded the respect for the personal merits of judges to access their posts.

With a similar goal in mind, Miquel Roca Junyent, of Democratic Pact for Catalonia, argued that to dismiss a better capacity of the General Council of the Judiciary (*Consejo General del Poder Judicial*) was a mistake that denoted the lack of both political and professional confidence in an autonomous judicial power (DSLC, 13 July 1978, Congress: 4267). Roca advocated a strong judicial power with full independence from the executive power. To him a fair consideration of the judicial power implied a full attribution of competences to the General Council of the Judiciary, without reservations.

In a different regard, to Gregorio Peces-Barba, of the Spanish Socialist Workers' Party, a precise interpretation of the coercive capacity in a democratic state made advisable not to identify coercion with state. Since that coercive capacity was a faculty exercised by authorities within the institutional system of democracy, such as for example by police, it was a source of misunderstandings to confuse it with the state (DSLC, 19 July 1978, Congress: 4434). Judicial powers did not have a coercive capacity as such. Coercion was an instrument of the rule of law. Courts of justice were

[14] "*Creemos que todo Estado que se configura como auténtico Estado de Derecho debe garantizar constitucionalmente la independencia del poder judicial*" (DSLC, 8 June 1978, Congress: 3132).

[15] "[*L*]*A Constitución que estamos elaborando habla del Poder judicial y concibe a éste fundamentalmente como un Poder judicial uno e independiente*" (DSLC, 16 June 1978, Congress: 3409).

indispensable to make legitimate coercion possible and efficient through binding decisions that should be the result of the work of qualified courts of justice to make judicial decisions.

During the constitutional sessions representatives did not refer to the relationship between 'constitutional justice' and 'democratic quality' (Garrorena Morales 2011: 60–61). Nevertheless, speeches illustrate how to regulate the judicial power was a serious concern for representatives. Unlike what happened in other debates, Miquel Roca Junyent, of the Democratic Pact for Catalonia, as some representatives of Union of Democratic Centre and the Spanish Socialist Workers' Party did, emphasized the independence of the members of the judicial power to make decisions as a condition for strengthening democracy and shelter state institutions as well as its legitimacy.

Bibliography

Legal Sources

Constitución Española de 1978. Available at: http://www.congreso.es/docu/constituciones/1978/1978_cd.pdf

Preliminary Draft of the Constitution of 1978, [*Anteproyecto de constitución de 1978*]. Available at: http://www.congreso.es/public_oficiales/L0/CONG/BOCG/BOC_044.PDF

Proceedings of the Constituent Assembly, 1977–1979 [*Diario de Sesiones de la Legislatura Constituyente, 1977–1979*, DSLC]. Available at: https://www.congreso.es/web/guest/indice-de-publicaciones?p_p_id=publicaciones&p_p_lifecycle=0&p_p_state=normal&p_p_mode=view&_publicaciones_selectedLeg=0

Spanish Constitution of 1978. Available at: http://www.congreso.es/portal/page/portal/Congreso/Congreso/Hist_Normas/Norm/const_espa_texto_ingles_0.pdf

Newspapers

ABC (1903–).

Cambio 16 (1971–).

Cuadernos para el Diálogo (1963–1978).

El País (1976–).

Triunfo (1946–1982).

References

ABC Editorial (1977). 'Un gobierno estable', *ABC*, 21 December, 2.

Aguiar de Luque, Luis (1981). 'Las garantías constitucionales de los derechos fundamentales en la Constitución española', *Revista de Derecho Político*, 10, 107–29.

Alzaga Villaamil, Óscar (2018). 'El proceso constituyente español visto por uno de sus protagonistas. Entrevista a Óscar Alzaga Villaamil', *Historia Constitucional*, 19, 1–16.

Aragón Reyes, Manuel (1989). *Constitución y democracia.* Madrid: Tecnos.

Cambio 16 Editorial (1978). 'Todos para uno...', *Cambio 16*, 14 May, 64.

Carrillo, Santiago (1993). 'La transición democrática', in *Memorias*. Barcelona: Planeta.

Cuadernos para el Diálogo Interview (1977). 'La unidad de España. Jamás Constitución alguna fue tan tajante', *Cuadernos para el Diálogo*, 31 December, 16.

Christiansen, Eric C. (2018). 'Forty Years from Fascism: Democratic Constitutionalism and the Spanish Model of National Transformation', *Oregon Review of International Law*, 20(1), 1–78.

Cisneros Laborda, Gabriel et al. (1998). *20 años después. La Constitución cara al siglo XXI*. Madrid: Taurus.

Del Águila, Rafael & Ricardo Montoro (1984). *El discurso político de la transición española*. Madrid: Centro de Investigaciones Sociológicas.

De Santiago Guervós, Javier (1992). *El léxico político de la transición española.* Salamanca: Universidad de Salamanca.

Díez-Picazo, Luis María & Ascensión Elvira Perales (2008). *La Constitución de 1978*. Madrid: Iustel.

Fraga, Manuel (1978). *La Constitución y otras cuestiones fundamentales.* Barcelona: Planeta.

García Morillo, Joaquín (1996). *La democracia en España*. Madrid: Alianza.

Garrorena Morales, Ángel (2011). 'El debate justicia constitucional-democracia en los procesos constituyentes de 1931 y 1978', *Revista Española de Derecho Constitucional*, 91, 31–68.

González Rivas, Juan José (1988). 'XI Jornadas de estudio de la Dirección General del Servicio Jurídico del Estado sobre el tema: Título Preliminar de la Constitución', in *Jornadas sobre el Título Preliminar de la Constitución*, vol. I. Madrid: Ministerio de Justicia.

Haro Tecglen, Eduardo (1978). 'La Constitución y el compromiso', *Triunfo*, 13 May.

Lucas Verdú, Pablo (1994). 'Reflexiones en torno y dentro del concepto de constitución. La constitución como norma y como integración política', *Revista de Estudios Políticos*, 83, 9–28.

Marías, Julián (1978). '¿No es esto?', *El País*, 21 January, https://elpais.com/diario/1978/01/21/opinion/254185207_850215.html
Merino Merchán, José Fernando (1988). 'Valores superiores del ordenamiento. Artículo 1.1 de la Constitución', in *Jornadas de estudio sobre el Título Preliminar de la Constitución*, vol. V. Madrid: Ministerio de Justicia.
Ollero Tassara, Andrés (1994). 'El parlamentarismo en el sistema político español', *Revista de las Cortes Generales*, 31, 7–30.
Peces-Barba, Gregorio (1988). 'Los valores superiores', in *Jornadas sobre el Título Preliminar de la Constitución*, vol. I. Madrid: Ministerio de Justicia.
Rosenfeld, Michael (1998). 'Constitution-Making, Identity Building, and Peaceful Transition to Democracy: Theoretical Reflections Inspired by the Spanish Example', *Cardozo Law Review*, 19(6), 1891–920.
Rubio Llorente, Francisco (1977). 'Sobre constituyentes y constitucionalistas', *El País*, 26 July, https://elpais.com/diario/1977/07/26/opinion/238716012_850215.html
Varela Suanzes-Carpegna, Joaquín (2006). 'El Estado en la España del siglo XX', *Revista de Estudios Políticos*, 131, 23–52.
Varela Suanzes-Carpegna, Joaquín (2014). *Política y Constitución en España (1808–1978)*, 2nd ed. Madrid: Centro de Estudios Políticos y Constitucionales.

CHAPTER 7

The Decentralization of Spain as a Political Nation

This chapter presents the arguments of representatives in the Constituent Assembly of 1977–1978 about the structure of the state, the concept of *nationalities*[1] (as opposed to that of regions) and the conflicting understandings of the Spanish nation. First, it explores the interpretations of regional autonomy by right-wing, centrist, and left-wing parties. There, it expounds the differing interpretations by Union of Democratic Centre and Popular Alliance, on the one hand, and left-wing parties, on the other. To the former, the bearer of sovereignty was the Spanish people as a whole; to the latter, it was unclear how the source of democratic powers was envisaged beyond an agreement of what they saw as a plurality of nations or *nationalities* (*nacionalidades*) within Spain.

Second, the chapter clarifies the idea of *nationalities*[2] shedding light on the disagreement between those representatives who considered it substitute for the idea of nation disguising nationalisms (part of Union of Democratic Centre, Popular Alliance, the Aragonese Candidacy of

[1] In the specific Spanish constitutional and political concept, *nationalities* does not refer to the legal status of membership of the state, but to the so-called historical regions of Spain: Catalonia, the Basque Country, and Galicia. That is why, in this book, it is always written in italics.

[2] The term *nationalities* and its singular form, 'historical *nationality*', denoted that ambiguous idea.

F. J. Bellido, *Constitutional Debates, Rhetoric, and Political Philosophy in Spain's Parliamentary History*, Rhetoric, Politics and Society,
https://doi.org/10.1007/978-3-031-56894-7_7

Centre, and independent senators) and those who endorsed it as valid constitutional concept, even though undefined (Spanish Socialist Workers' Party, Communist Party of Spain, and nationalist parties of Catalonia and the Basque Country). Third, it distinguishes the idea of Spain as a political nation from the alternative ethnic interpretation of nations within Spain. By focusing on parliamentary speeches and, as a complement, newspaper articles I argue that the idea of decentralization of state competences was often interpreted as an instrument to weaken Spain as a unitary political nation.

1 Two Ideas of Regional Autonomy: Self-Rule and Self-Determination

This section explores the meanings of regional autonomy to political parties in the Constituent Assembly. On the one hand, it distinguishes the arguments of representatives of Union of Democratic Centre and Popular Alliance, together with those of independent senators; on the other hand, it pays attention to the speeches of the Spanish Socialist Workers' Party, the Communist Party of Spain, and the nationalist parties of Catalonia and the Basque Country. About the first group, I argue that their conceptions of the national unity of Spain aimed to make compatible a certain degree of regional autonomy or self-rule with the safeguard of Spain's sovereignty. About the second group, I highlight that the arguments of nationalist representatives of Catalonia and the Basque Country were beyond the idea of self-government and national pluralism defended by the Spanish Socialist Workers' Party and the Communist Party of Spain.

1.1 Regional Autonomy: An Instrument to Decentralize State Competences According to Centre and Right-Wing Parties

Union of Democratic Centre and Popular Alliance kept a similar stance regarding a moderate state decentralization of competences handed to the autonomous regions of Spain. Representatives of Union of Democratic Centre had in mind a partial decentralization of competences that the Preliminary Constitutional Draft already presented. To them it was key to balance a central administration with capacity to resolve regional disputes that at the same time would protect the capacity of the state to decide on education, health, and the economy without a pervasive interference in regional administrations. Instead, representatives of Popular Alliance thought that the most adequate structure of the state should rest on a regional model that would imitate the French provincial administration in order to secure efficient administrations that would offset the advance of nationalist parties in Catalonia, the Basque Country, and to a lesser extent, Galicia.

Among the representatives of Union of Democratic Centre who had confidence in the positive connotations of the idea of autonomy, José Luis Meilán stood out. He stated that "it is evident that for us autonomy rises above and far exceeds the levels of decentralization".[3] To him autonomy was a fair demand to improve state institutions and to make them adequate to a contemporary democracy in which all Spaniards would enjoy equal rights and self-rule. Self-rule neither hindered the political stability of the country, nor threatened the unity of the Spanish nation.

Meilán mentioned Luis Jiménez de Asúa, socialist leader of the Constitutional Commission that prepared the Constitutional Draft during the Constituent Assembly of 1931. As representative of Union of Democratic Centre, he argued that the 'integral state' adopted, an intermediate design between federal and centralized states, was imitated by constituent representatives in favour of autonomous regions with a certain degree of state decentralization of competences (DSLC, 18 July 1978, Congress: 4378). To improve the design of the structure of the state partly depended on taking as valid some of the constitutional principles of the integral state in the Constituent Assembly of 1931.

With different overtones, Miguel Herrero y Rodríguez de Miñón, constitutional rapporteur of Union of Democratic Centre, distinguished between autonomy and self-determination with a categorical statement: "Autonomy [...] is neither the portico nor the substitute of secessionist self-determination".[4] Self-rule was agreed as a fair demand by Spanish regions; self-determination beyond self-rule was not. The idea of self-rule could not be separated from the life in a shared political community that was Spain. There was a permanent conflict between representative democracy in Spain and how nationalist parties conceived "self-determination" (Linz 1985: 529).

[3] "*Es evidente que para nosotros la autonomía rebasa y excede con mucho los niveles de una descentralización*" (DSLC, 14 June 1978, Congress: 3282).

[4] "*La autonomía* [...] *no es el pórtico ni el sucedáneo de la autodeterminación secesionista*" (DSLC, 21 July 1978, Congress: 4567).

To Manuel Villar Arregui, of Union of Democratic Centre, the concept of autonomy exceeded the meaning of regional autonomy. In his opinion, constituent representatives were exercising a faculty of autonomy, playing with the times of politics and designing institutions "in the realm of civic coexistence" (DSLC, 24 August 1978, Senate: 1815). Autonomy was both a political and social concept, much more complex than other political ideas that were being debated, such as self-determination, that had a clear political meaning.

In that wise, Óscar Alzaga, of Union of Democratic Centre, openly stated in one of his books that to say autonomy was to say "a certain extent of self-rule" (Alzaga Villaamil 1978: 828–29). Then, self-rule and autonomy were inseparable. His interpretation about the issue of the Autonomous Communities and their legal regime was very similar to the one of Herrero y Rodríguez de Miñón and Villar Arregui. Self-rule did not oppose sovereignty but complemented it.

A conflicting interpretation to the one presented by Herrero y Rodríguez de Miñón, though not that far from Alzaga's and Villar Arregui's, was defended by Gabriel Cisneros. This constitutional rapporteur regretted that the territorial organization was not clarified during the Constituent Assembly. To leave the issue open to further development was to him a mistake (Cisneros 2003: 36). Regions could access self-rule but it was unclear when and how that process should finish (Lucas Verdú 1985: 393).

During the Constituent Assembly, but even before it began, representatives of Popular Alliance kept an almost unanimously shared stance with respect to the concept of regional autonomy. To Manuel Fraga, constitutional rapporteur and leader of Popular Alliance, Spain was the only nation that the new Constitution should recognize. Regional autonomy was a useful instrument to enhance state decentralization of competences if improving the services provided to citizens (DSLC, 13 June 1978, Congress: 3185–86). Self-rule was roughly equivalent to a better organization of territories following constitutional rules and with respect to the territorial unity of Spain, unquestionable according to the Preliminary Draft of the Constitution.

In that regard, to Federico Silva Muñoz, of Popular Alliance, the enshrinement of autonomous regions in the constitutional text could endanger the territorial unity of Spain if they were interpreted as members of a confederation with sovereignty: "The region [...] is not equipped with a constituent autonomy, as if it were a state member of a federal state".[5] To him autonomy meant that some rules were a competence of regional governments and not entirely the result of state norms (DSLC, 4 July 1978, Congress: 3798).

Conflicting understandings of laws and unconstitutional procedures by the Autonomous Communities could lead to a disintegration of Spain as a constitutional democracy. Lorenzo Martín-Retortillo, independent senator, stated that "we think that in the future it should be clear that the law acknowledges autonomy"[6]: To him it was a matter of fact that "autonomy consists in self-determination so that the Autonomous Communities [...] which are more formed and more organized assume higher competences, powers and functions".[7]

To explain the issue around autonomies Luis Sánchez Agesta, senator by royal designation, distinguished three forms of autonomy, roughly responding to the different speeds that make the process impossible to resolve once and for all: "small autonomies", "grand autonomies", and "expandable autonomies" with capacity to broaden their competences (DSLC, 13 September 1978, Senate: 2644). To him it was clear that the demands for autonomy of some regions largely differed from others. That asymmetry between almost incompatible conceptions of state institutions provoked heated speeches during the constitutional sessions around autonomy and self-rule in the Congress of Deputies and the Senate from the very beginning of parliamentary debates.

Although it is roughly correct to assume that the idea of territorial autonomy gained prominence as the result of the advance of democracy in Spain after 1975, it was an incomplete explanation for the vindications of regional autonomy. It did not have into account that the historical controversy of Spain regarding autonomies was associated to the country's own regional features. Some citizens perceived that to extend a higher degree of autonomy to Spanish regions would provoke a rising threat of nationalist movements. Others, especially in Catalonia and the Basque Country, demanded autonomy and self-rule in ambiguous terms,

[5] "*La región* [...] *no está dotada de una autonomía constituyente, como el Estado miembro de un Estado federal*" (DSLC, 4 July 1978, Congress: 3798).

[6] "[*C*]*reemos que en el futuro debe quedar muy claro que es la ley la que reconoce la autonomía*" (DSLC, 25 August 1978, Senate: 1935).

[7] "*La autonomía consiste en la autodeterminación para que las Comunidades Autónomas* [...] *que están más trabadas y más organizadas, asuman mayores competencias, mayores poderes y mayores funciones*" (DSLC, 12 September 1978, Senate: 2562).

sometimes closer to a nationalist vindication; sometimes related to a better functioning—understood as a decentralized functioning—of institutions to make democratic reforms effective with scepticism about the idea of Spain as a unitary nation for all citizens.

The constitutional debate in both the Congress of Deputies and the Senate gave expression to the polysemy of the idea of autonomy. To representatives of Union of Democratic Centre the idea of autonomy was closely linked to self-rule, the capacity of autonomous regions to benefit from the delegation of state competences to enhance public services for citizens. Despite that commitment, there were representatives of the party in Navarre and Catalonia who defended an idea of autonomy closer to original sovereignty of the so-called historical territories, then affecting the cohesion of Union of Democratic Centre around the issue of regional autonomy.

Unlike Union of Democratic Centre, members of Popular Alliance were better coordinated to refuse the idea of a strong autonomy that would undermine the unity of the Spanish nation. They were instead in favour of a minimum degree of regional autonomy under the premise of protecting state institutions from the rise of economic conflicts and disputes around sovereignty. In that vein, independent senators did not hesitate to point out the difficulties that the process of autonomy entailed in a country where regional longings largely varied to the point of being incompatible with each other in practice.

1.2 Regional Autonomy to Enhance Territorial Self-Government

Demands for regional autonomy had different meanings for the Spanish Socialist Workers' Party, the Communist Party of Spain, the Democratic Pact for Catalonia, Republican Left of Catalonia, the Basque Nationalist Party, and Euskadi's Left (*Euskadiko Ezkerra*). However, to any of these parties the idea of regional autonomy entailed to assume that national diversity within Spain was a social fact. The unity of Spain as a territory was backed by the Spanish Socialist Workers' Party and the Communist Party of Spain; its unity as a nation with historical features that all Spanish territories shared was not, or at least only in an incomplete manner.

To José María Benegas, of the Spanish Socialist Workers' Party, political autonomy for the territories of Spain was a fair demand that should improve democracy in Spain: "We socialists value autonomies not just as a right that peoples have to their self- government, but as a huge step to deepening democracy".[8] Self-rule was interpreted as self-government. Both concepts were exchangeable to Benegas. The capacity of citizens to be represented in autonomous institutions for regions was a way to gain self-government, plainly compatible with state institutions. Self-rule was regarded as an instrument to incorporate the particular features of some territories of Spain with their own peculiarities, though there was a lack of clarity about how that would be accomplished.

Eduardo Martín Toval, also representative of the Spanish Socialist Workers' Party, enumerated four ideas that were to his party fundamental to clarify "the issue of autonomies". First, there was a problem regarding how the process to obtain regional autonomy should begin; second, the competences that each one of the Autonomous Communities had should be clarified; third, it was needed to prepare and to improve from a formal point of view the norms that would safeguard autonomy for the regions; fourth, it was indispensable to agree on the norms that best organize such autonomy (DSLC, 18 July 1978, Congress: 4366).

Unlike the more detailed account of the implications of regional autonomy by Martín Toval, Santiago Carrillo, leader of the Communist Party of Spain, was more schematic. He argued that the existence of autonomous regions in Spain was indispensable to build lasting institutions and to ensure the territorial unity of the country: "It is not true that autonomies endanger the unity of Spain, but just the other way around, they are the only way to strengthen them".[9] Carrillo supported that regional autonomies would result in a stronger state, though he did not fully explain how that was possible.

Jordi Solé Tura, constitutional rapporteur of the Communist Party of Spain, clarified the relationship between self-rule and autonomy, to him two ideas that were joint both from a doctrinal and a practical point of view: "[This] is not just about a simple administrative decentralization, but really about a process of self-rule, which is the exact meaning that the

[8] "*Los socialistas valoramos las autonomías no sólo como un derecho que tienen los pueblos a su autogobierno, sino como un paso enorme en la profundización de la democracia*" (DSLC, 18 July 1978, Congress: 4356).

[9] "*No es cierto que las autonomías pongan en peligro la unidad de España, sino al contrario, son el único camino para lograr su fortalecimiento*" (DSLC, 5 May 1978, Congress: 2038–39).

concession of autonomy acquires".[10] As representatives of the Spanish Socialist Workers' did, to Solé Tura the concept of self-rule was mainly a political concept that should be applied to a fast process of state decentralization of competences that benefited the interests of the territories that demanded it.

With more scholarly details, Miquel Roca Junyent, constitutional rapporteur of the Democratic Pact for Catalonia, called attention to the doctrinal agreement by authors such as the legal scholars Guido Zanobini from Italy and Juan Ferrando Badía in Spain on the close meanings of the ideas of autonomy and self-rule. Roca opposed Manuel Fraga in a speech to remind him that self-rule was inseparable from the autonomy of some territories of Spain such as Catalonia (DSLC, 14 June 1978, Congress: 3273).

Miquel Roca Junyent upheld the same idea that had already defended in his speech on 14 June to emphasize that the demands of self-rule and autonomy were two conditions, indistinguishable from each other, to make democracy in Spain possible: "Without democracy, the exercise of autonomy, the right to autonomy of the different nationalities and regions that form Spain is not possible".[11] Democracy and regional autonomy were not independent concepts. The additional aspect that characterized the political position of Roca was his demand of *nationality* (*nacionalidad*) as something typical of some Spanish territories such as Catalonia, the Basque Country, and Galicia.

Republican Left of Catalonia kept a less ambiguous position. One of its leaders, Heribert Barrera, argued against Manuel Fraga's arguments about the relationship between the ideas of nation and regional autonomy as the necessary base for the success of democracy in Spain. Barrera challenged Fraga to state "I say unity of the state and autonomy of the nations" (DSLC, 8 May 1978, Congress: 2081). The idea of different *nationalities* within Spain was deemed insufficient. Barrera expressed an overreaching demand of a national character of Catalonia and the Basque Country that equated Spain with a state that was not properly a nation.

[10] "[*Esto*] *se trata no sólo de una simple descentralización administrativa, sino realmente de un proceso de autogobierno, que es el sentido exacto que adquiere la concesión de la autonomía*" (DSLC, 14 June 1978, Congress: 3290).

[11] "[*S*]*in democracia, el ejercicio de la autonomía, del derecho a la autonomía de las diferentes nacionalidades y regiones que integran España no es posible*" (DSLC, 16 June 1978, Congress: 3382).

Lluís Maria Xirinacs, independent senator from Catalonia with nationalist leanings, was more demanding about the extension of autonomy for territories. His speech in the Senate on 18 August 1978 denoted that self-rule was secondary to him. The keystone of his argument was that many territories of Spain were sovereign lands because they enjoyed a different historical status. His justification of inequalities between territories was that Catalonia, as other territories within Spain, were nations historically subordinated to a tyrant state identified with Spain: "Only to sovereign peoples is the right to autonomy recognized. The machine of crushing nations is indissoluble, indivisible, unremovable".[12]

Autonomy was expressed in terms that had a loose connection to political self-rule for all territories. It was mostly a way to emphasize particular demands that were unsustainable if applied to all territories. Mitxel Unzueta, senator for the Basque Nationalist Party, argued that political autonomy was a means to give expression to a historical demand of economic autonomy by Basque citizens: "We believe that any Autonomy should have also financial autonomy".[13] Self-government and autonomy were described in economic terms aiming to obtain fiscal benefits for the Basque Country, even though that economic regime could not be extended to other regions.

Unlike the Basque Nationalist Party, regional autonomy was understood as self-determination in a secessionist sense by Francisco Letamendía, leader of Euskadi's Left. He criticized other parties referring to representatives of Union of Democratic Centre and Popular Alliance in these terms: "You [that] have defined the right to self-determination as the possibility to accept or to refuse autonomy are doing word games that do not mislead anyone and, least of all, us".[14] To him autonomy did not meant just self-rule, but self-determination as the right to referendum in the Basque Country that could lead to the secession of territories from Spain.

12 "*Sólo se les reconoce el derecho a la autonomía a los pueblos soberanos. La máquina de triturar naciones es indisoluble, indivisible, indesmontable*" (DSLC, 18 August 1978, Senate: 1560).

13 "*Nosotros creemos que toda Autonomía tiene que tener también su contrapartida en la autonomía financiera*" (DSLC, 13 September 1978, Senate: 2693).

14 "[*V*]*osotros* [*que*] *habéis definido el derecho de autodeterminación como la posibilidad de aceptar o rechazar la autonomía estáis haciendo juegos de palabras que no engañan a nadie, y menos a nosotros*" (DSLC, 8 May 1978, Congress: 2085).

The design of regional autonomy for all territories was a secondary issue to Euskadi's Left. Senator Juan María Bandrés spoke frankly to say that the distribution of competences among autonomous regions should allow legal asymmetries between regions. To him it was plainly legitimate that there were some regions with self-rule from the very beginning and some others that would have that degree of autonomy in a later phase. Thus, the design of Autonomous Communities was easier to justify as partly developed after the Constitution was passed and not before (DSLC, 12 September 1978, Senate: 2561). The consequences for those territories that would assume a minor degree of decentralization was intendedly left aside by Bandrés.

Regional newspapers with nationalist affinities like *Avui* in Catalonia and *Egin* in the Basque Country endorsed the position of Catalan and Basque parties regarding the decentralization of state competences handed to the regions. Among national media *El País* and the cultural journal *Cuadernos para el Diálogo* did so. *El País* was in favour of the process of decentralization of competences to a similar extent to the vindications of Catalan and Basque nationalist parties (Sanmartí 2017: 202–3).

In a nutshell, the Spanish Socialist Workers' Party and the Communist Party of Spain defended a decentralized state with respect to the cultural plurality of Spain that entailed to partly renounce an idea of Spain as the unique political nation of citizens. That stance was exploited by the nationalist parties of Catalonia and the Basque Country to increase their demands of self-government to the extent of jeopardizing the political and economic stability of Spain in the long run. Those parties ranged from advocating self-rule as a growing process of decentralization that should be accomplished after the passing of the Constitution (Democratic Pact for Catalonia and Basque Nationalist Party) to the possibility of admitting the secession of territories from Spain (Republican Left of Catalonia and Euskadi's Left).

2 *Nationalities* (*Nacionalidades*) According to Political Parties

This section is made of four parts each one addressing the meanings that political groups gave to the idea of *nationalities* (*nacionalidades*). First, it takes into account the parliamentary speeches of Union of Democratic Centre and some independent senators. The issue of *nationalities* was the only one that led to a strong disagreement between the centrist party and senators by royal designation. The former endorsed the idea of *nationality* as a necessary concession that did not mean the existence of nations within Spain, with the exception of the constitutional rapporteur Miguel Herrero Rodríguez de Miñón and some representatives of the party in Catalonia and the Basque Country. The latter rejected the concept of *nationalities* as detrimental to building democratic institutions under the principle of equality for all citizens.

Second, it presents the most salient speeches about *nationalities* by Popular Alliance and the Aragonese Candidacy of Centre to show how their demands were plainly compatible with regional autonomy as a principle of efficiency. The idea of *nationality* was to them a trump card that concealed the idea of nations within Spain beyond the decentralization of state competences. Third, it examines the favourable stances of the Spanish Socialist Workers' Party about the idea of *nationalities*, partly explained as a consequence of pragmatic agreements between those parties and nationalist parties of Catalonia and the Basque Country. Finally, the last section focuses on the contradictions of nationalist parties shaping an ethnic ideal of *nationality* that conflicted with a democratic understanding of the Spanish nation.

2.1 Nationalities*: Disagreements Between Union of Democratic Centre and Independent Senators*

Rafael Arias-Salgado, of Union of Democratic Centre regarded the "concept of nationalities [*nacionalidades*]" as an idea that reflected the historical development of some territories and that responded to "a principle of self-identification and [to] the acknowledgment of socio-historical formations".[15] In his view, Spain's diversity was both cultural and linguistic. That social fact was to be admitted as a circumstance conditioning the structure of the state that fitted better the peculiarities of the country.

In a different light, Miguel Herrero y Rodríguez de Miñón, constitutional rapporteur of Union of Democratic Centre, contrasted the terms *nationality* and 'citizenship' with each other to assert that they were not the same at all (DSLC, 6 July 1978, Congress: 3914). In his opinion,

[15] "[*U*]*N principio de autoidentificación y el reconocimiento de formaciones socio-históricas*" (DSLC, 12 May 1978, Congress: 2281).

the notion of *nationality* referred to the status that some territories enjoyed by the fact of language and traditions. It was, by its very historical features, an idea opposed to the civic, legal, and political implications of citizenship that, however, Herrero y Rodríguez de Miñón accepted.

Unlike the aforementioned speeches, Torcuato Fernández-Miranda, senator by royal designation with a prominent role in the transition to democracy, refused the idea of *nationality* as an inadequate political label: "Nationality refers to the principle of sovereignty, it is argued in terms of sovereignty".[16] Fernández-Miranda was convinced that the term 'nationality' was and would be used to vindicate a sort of original sovereignty in some regions of Spain. It was to him detrimental to the unity of the country because it selfishly led to mistake decentralization of state competences with the internal division of Spain into small nations with sovereign power.

2.2 *The Refusal of* Nationalities*: Popular Alliance and Aragonese Candidacy of Centre*

In general, the negative arguments of independent senators by royal designation regarding the acknowledgement of *nationalities* were much closer to Popular Alliance than to Union of Democratic Centre. Manuel Fraga, constitutional rapporteur and leader of Popular Alliance, fully agreed with the remark of senator Torcuato Fernández-Miranda: "And it is not the moment to come back to the indisputable fact that nation and nationality are the same".[17]

Fraga deemed a mistake to promote the distinction of several *nationalities* within Spain. He argued at different moments between May and July 1978 in the Congress of Deputies that doing so meant to challenge democratic institutions. Pervasive consequences for the rising process of growing nationalist demands in Catalonia and the Basque Country were expectable if the idea of *nationality* worked as a hinge ideal to unite different nationalist movements. As him, Francisco Cacharro, senator for

[16] "*Nacionalidad hace referencia al principio de soberanía, se plantea en términos de soberanía*" (DSLC, 19 August 1978, Senate: 1604).

[17] "*Y no es el momento de volver sobre el hecho indiscutible de que nación y nacionalidad es lo mismo*" (DSLC, 5 May 1978, Congress: 2044).

Popular Alliance, had no doubts: "Nationality and nation mean the same in practice and so think many Spaniards".[18]

Hipólito Gómez de las Roces, of the Aragonese Candidacy of Centre, distrusted the idea of *nationalities*. He considered it as detrimental to those regions without that recognition in the Preliminary Draft of the Constitution (DSLC, 9 May 1978, Congress: 2098). It was evident to him that such distinction between regions would lead to territorial inequalities. Gómez de las Roces understood that those territories that were considered *nationalities* would enjoy 'privileges' that others had not (DSLC, 12 May 1978, Congress: 2285). To him the enshrinement of *nationalities* would have as a consequence the federalization of the country at different speeds. Admitting *nationalities* with federal overtones would necessarily lead to an unequal treatment of territories: richer regions would have a better position to negotiate its status with the state (DSLC, 12 May 1978, Congress: 2288).

The term *nationality* was often deemed by representatives a confused term, harmful to the territorial unity of the country (Belmonte 1979: 72). The disagreements about the idea of *nationalities* became one of the hardest obstacles to the constitutional process since much before the parliamentary debate in the Congress of Deputies, in the private meetings held during the second half of 1977 (Conversi 2002: 237). Besides, there was an additional problem, to distinguish *nationalities* from regions led to ambiguities that were not resolved in the Constitution (López Rodó 1984: 48).

2.3 Spanish Socialist Workers' Party, Popular Socialist Party, and Communist Party of Spain

Enrique Tierno Galván, leader of the Popular Socialist Party, argued that the term *nationalities* was applied to those regions where a different language to Spanish was used (DSLC, 5 May 1978, Congress: 2061). Those linguistic differences that were particular to some regions provoked that nationalist parties in Catalonia and the Basque Country vindicated the constitutional acknowledgement of their respective regions as *nationalities*, but it was a reason among others. That the different languages of Spain deserved institutional protection was not denied. Representatives

[18] "*Nacionalidad y nación vienen a significar lo mismo en la práctica y así lo consideran muchos españoles*" (DSLC, 19 August 1978, Congres 1615).

agreed on that. The difficulties were to establish whether linguistic differences would be a reasonable aspect to justify a particular status to some territories of Spain. Tierno Galván thought that the idea of *nationalities* responded to the coexistence of more than a language in some territories, as it was the case in Catalonia, the Basque Country, and Galicia.

Gregorio Peces-Barba, constitutional rapporteur of the Spanish Socialist Workers' Party, upheld the existence of *nationalities* within Spain with a very similar meaning to cultural nations. He aimed to distinguish those *nationalities* from the assumption "formulated by the liberals in the nineteenth century, that any nation should be an independent state".[19] The distinction that Peces-Barba sought to clarify was between the equivalence of nations and state in the nineteenth century and the liberal tradition of twentieth-century democracies. In the former, any nation was thought to have a state; in the latter, he interpreted that different nations should coexist within a same state.

José María Benegas, also representative of the Spanish Socialist Workers' Party, admitted that some nations could be distinguished in Spain, but always in the context of a grand nation-state that was Spain sheltering culturally diverse territories: "We use the word 'nationality' in the right sense in which it was used in the nineteenth century to conceptualize small nations, that are not found at the bosom of grand nation-states or plurinational states".[20] The sovereignty of the Spanish nation excluded self-determination of any of its parts, though that was not incompatible with the existence of nations within Spain (García Escudero and García Martínez 1998: 76).

With similar implications, Jordi Solé Tura, constitutional rapporteur of the Communist Party of Spain, assumed a more abstract position: "Nationality is, fundamentally, a collective state of conscience, but a state of conscience that is founded [...] on a certain way of conceiving its own reality as regards the others".[21] The abstract meaning of the idea

[19] "[C]*omo se formuló por los liberales en el siglo XIX, de que cada nación debe ser un Estado independiente*" (DSLC, 11 May 1978, Congress: 2170).

[20] "[U]*tilizamos la palabra nacionalidad en el correcto sentido en que se utilizó en el siglo XIX para conceptuar naciones pequeñas, que no se encuentran en el seno de grandes Estados-Nación o de Estados-Plurinacionales*" (DSLC, 18 July 1978, Congress: 4354).

[21] "*Nacionalidad es, fundamentalmente, un estado de conciencia colectivo, pero un estado de conciencia colectivo que se fundamenta* [...] *en una forma determinada de concebir su propia realidad frente a las otras*" (DSLC, 4 July 1978, Congress: 3806).

of *nationality* according to Solé Tura was difficult to understand in strict political terms. Thus, a nationalist interpretation assumed that if a number of citizens in a given territory considered themselves members of a nation, that was enough to validate the existence of a differentiated political nation irrespective of centuries-old shared political institutions with other fellow citizens.

As an illustrative consequence, the parliamentary reporter and writer Joaquín Aguirre Bellver disapproved of Enrique Tierno Galván's speech on 5 July 1978. The leader of the Popular Socialist Party considered that the term *nationalities* was the result of what it was agreed between socialist representatives and nationalist parties (Aguirre Bellver 1978: 94). It is fair to indicate that those agreements were made since much before the Constituent Assembly was established.

Negotiations between left-wing political groups in exile entailed that the Spanish Socialist Workers' Party, the Communist Party of Spain, and other left-wing minority sectors were open to the idea of *nationalities*. Speeches between 1977 and 1978 of leaders such as Felipe González, of the Spanish Socialist Workers' Party, Santiago Carrillo, of the Communist Party of Spain, and Enrique Tierno Galván were very clear on that subject. The idea of *nationalities* or nations within Spain was accepted in exchange for the respect of nationalist parties towards the unity of Spain, even though there were no guarantees about it once the Constitution would be passed.

2.4 Nationalist Parties of Catalonia and the Basque Country

As a token of the visible nationalist demands of parties from Catalonia and the Basque Country, Francisco Letamendía, of Euskadi's Left, stated that "in the last century, on the objective base of a Basque nationality, a nation has emerged. A nationality becomes a nation when it is presented with a political project".[22] To him the Basque Country was the nation of Euskadi, built in the last century, between the nineteenth century and the twentieth century. Nation and *nationality* were synonymous to Letamendía.

[22] "[*E*]*N este último siglo, sobre la base objetiva de una nacionalidad vasca, ha surgido una nación. Pues una nacionalidad se convierte en nación cuando se alza sobre ella un proyecto político*" (DSLC, 12 May 1978, Congress: 2264).

However, there was a basic conceptual misunderstanding there. If the Basque *nationality* was formed in the nineteenth century, how was it possible the existence of previous national rights (the so-called historical rights of *nationalities*) rooted in the medieval tradition of Spain? Even further, would it make sense to talk about ancestral historical rights and modern *nationalities* to vindicate equal political rights for citizens?

Following similar arguments to those of Letamendía, though with more pragmatism, Miquel Roca Junyent, constitutional rapporteur of the Democratic Pact for Catalonia, equated political stability with the acknowledgement of *nationalities* in the Constitution (DSLC, 12 May 1978, Congress: 2276). To him, any attempt to dismiss the national feelings of the citizens of some territories meant to deny not just cultural diversity of Spain, but its own history.

Miquel Roca Junyent advocated that it was senseless to distinguish in the Constitution two meanings for the term *nationalities* (DSLC, 6 July 1978, Congress: 3913). Roca regarded the idea of *nationalities* with full positive connotations, compatible with the idea of a unitary state in Spain. However, to him to enshrine *nationalities* in the constitutional text was a step towards the full attribution to historical territories of Spain of their own historical identity. In that regard, to Roca nationalist feelings in Catalonia and the Basque Country justified the recognition of *nationalities*.

Lluís Maria Xirinacs, independent senator, argued that the right to secession of some territories of Spain was justified using the idea of *nationality* as an exclusive category: "Each nationality has the right to [form] a state and, therefore, to the official character of its own language in its own territory, without competing with other official languages".[23] His speech was a clear example of how a nationalist understanding of democracy was opposed to the territorial unity of Spain. Basque and Catalan nationalists challenged the idea of Spain as political nation for everyone. Their particular demands regarding the idea of *nationality* justified a different treatment to the citizens of certain territories.

[23] "[C]*ada nacionalidad tiene derecho a* [*formar*] un *Estado y, por tanto, a la oficialidad de su propia lengua en su propio territorio, sin competencias con otras lenguas oficiales*" (DSLC, 18 August 1978, Senate: 1560).

3 Nation: A Contested Concept with Ethnic and Civic Overtones

This section aims to shed light on how the idea of Spain as a nation was interpreted by representatives and, to a lesser extent, by journalists and newspaper articles written by scholars. It presents those speeches that make clear two ideas of nation. First, it highlights how right-wing and centre parties interpreted the idea of Spain as a political nation dispensing with an ethnic interpretation of Spain. Second, it emphasizes the opposed interpretation of the idea of nation by nationalist parties. Culture and tradition were used to justify an ethnic view of Catalonia and the Basque Country as nations disregarding democratic institutions and legality as two essential bonds of a political nation in a democratic sense.

3.1 The Spanish Nation as a Political Nation

Ranging from conservatism to socialism, the interpretations of representatives about the features of Spain as a nation largely differed from each other. To conservative representatives such as Manuel Fraga, of Popular Alliance, any feasible concept of nation demanded a shared historical tradition, a certain economic system beyond "linguistic, ethnic or administrative particularities" (DSLC, 5 May 1978, Congress: 2044). Fraga's account on the Spanish nation combined a liberal understanding of the nation as the result of historical bounds of citizenship and state institutions with the existence of a peculiar history to which ethnic features were secondary.

Miguel Herrero y Rodríguez de Miñón, of Union of Democratic Centre, drew attention to the will of citizens to live together as the main characteristic of a nation: "A nation, in our opinion, is above all, the will to live together".[24] Following that idea as the only necessary condition to a nation, a political nation could be easily dissolved when a number of citizens there would agree to do so. It was incomplete insofar as it undermined the functions of shared political institutions and a parliamentary tradition as key elements of a political nation in a contemporary sense.

In a more elaborated way, Rafael Arias-Salgado, of Union of Democratic Centre, explained Max Weber's definition of a nation to say that

[24] "*Una nación, a nuestro juicio, es, ante y sobre todo, la voluntad de vivir juntos*" (DSLC, 5 May 1978, Congress: 2080).

he connected it with the political organization of a 'community' that already existed. To Arias-Salgado that definition was 'empirical', though incomplete (DSLC, 12 May 1978, Congress: 2268).

For instance, Licinio de la Fuente, of Popular Alliance, was convinced about some unintendedly negative effects of the so-called consensus. Despite its potentialities consensus brought in contradictions: "The eagerness of consensus had hitherto led us to [...] say, for example, that Spain is a nation and that at the same time there are many nations in Spain".[25] His understanding of political nations meant that the Spanish nation was incompatible with the existence of several nations within Spain precisely because a political reading of the institutions of the country rested on a unitary conception of sovereignty. If there were several nations in Spain, there was no political nation possible for all citizens, but a group of confederate states.

Manuel Fraga, of Popular Alliance, argued that regional autonomy and a certain degree of decentralization, when compatible with a strong state and with the unity of the country, were always acceptable. Spain was a nation with a distinctive status in Europe, capable to shelter all Spaniards and to improve the country by means of territorial autonomy (DSLC, 13 June 1978, Congress: 3186). Fraga argued that the main goal of constituent representatives should be to prepare a constitutional text to build democracy in Spain based on a unique sovereignty and a united people as its indisputable source (DSLC, 14 June 1978, Congress: 3271).

In that wise, Emilio Gastón Sanz, of the Socialist Party of Aragon, disagreed with nationalist parties by defending autonomy in terms of equality (DSLC, 12 July 1978, Congress: 4194). He thought that many regions hurried to demand autonomy for their territories without taking into consideration its political consequences. To him an accelerated process of decentralization could benefit those regions with nationalist parties. They could obtain bigger privileges than other territories. If the process was imitated by many regions the consequence would be the weakening of the state.

Instead, Laureano López Rodó explained the unity of the nation through a classic metaphor that reminded of Ernst H. Kantorowicz's book on the medieval theme of the king's two bodies, though he did not

[25] "*El afán de consenso nos había llevado hasta ahora a* [...] *decir, por ejemplo, que España es una nación y que al mismo tiempo hay muchas naciones en España*" (DSLC, 23 May 1978, Congress: 2618).

mention it. The crown of Spain was the permanent guarantor of both the state and the Spanish nation. It was so because, following parliamentary monarchies in Europe, the crown functioned as the head of state that safeguarded its institutions and its unity (DSLC, 12 July 1978, Congress: 4159).

The principle of autonomy applied to the Autonomous Communities entailed, above other meanings, the access to legislative autonomy (Aparicio Pérez 1988: 969). Carlos Ollero, senator by royal designation, admitted that. Nevertheless, he stated that "the Spanish nation is a historical-sociological reality to which in the legal-political realm befits a state".[26] Regional autonomy was needed for a better organization of Spain, but always under the condition of respecting the legal and political dimensions of Spain, a political nation with historical features from medieval times towards the liberal tradition that began with the Cadiz Constitution of 1812, and to the present.

Regional autonomy was conceived, at least, as an agreement for civil coexistence enshrined in a constitutional text, impossible to modify without a constitutional amendment (Ariño Ortiz 1985: 282). To say regional autonomy was to say that the structure of the state in Spain was based on a distribution of competences between the state and the Autonomous Communities. Through that commitment the Spanish nation broadened the capacity of citizens of all regions to enjoy self-rule, not as a means to oppose the state, but as an aspect that was thought to unite all Spanish citizens around a same political project.

The agreement between parties during the Constituent Assembly was about the need of decentralizing state competences, but not about the shared design for each one of the Autonomous Communities of the country (Ortega Álvarez 2003: 2). That fact explains a high degree of inequality in the fiscal and political treatment regarding negotiations between the central administration and some Autonomous Communities such as the Basque Country and Catalonia.

In a later paper, Gregorio Peces-Barba argued that both José Pedro Pérez-Llorca and Gabriel Cisneros were in favour of regional autonomy, whereas Miguel Herrero y Rodríguez de Miñón expressed a different opinion that was closer to the demands to decentralize political competences in Catalonia, the Basque Country, and Galicia (Peces-Barba 2002:

[26] "[*L*]*A nación española es una realidad histórica-sociológica a la que en el plano jurídico-político corresponde un Estado*" (DSLC, 12 September 1978, Senate: 2547).

69). Regarding the design of autonomous regions constitutional rapporteurs deemed indispensable to achieve gradual agreements from the beginning without imposing any particular state model (Rebollo Delgado 2018: 484).

The Preliminary Draft of the Constitution debated in parliament already included the basic plan of the Autonomous Communities (Martín Oviedo 1988: 6). The design of Autonomous Communities, unlike federalism, entailed to recognize that the bearer of sovereignty was the nation that from the constituent moment acknowledged the access to a certain degree of autonomy to their regions (Sánchez Agesta 1979: 17). However, from a technical point of view, the Autonomous Communities of Spain have similarities with federal states (Trujillo Fernández 1994: 35).

In the newspaper article 'The last constitutional dinner', the journalists Soledad Gallego Díaz and José Luis Martínez García drew attention to the distinction between "delegating and transferring" competences: the first ones were just to develop a function already acknowledged; the second ones meant to bestow or to renounce a certain faculty (*Cuadernos para el Diálogo*, 29 July 1978: 12). That distinction was not highlighted with clarity by representatives, though it was relevant to adopt a system of distributed competences between the state and the regions to reinforce the Spanish nation from an institutional point of view.

The legal scholar Juan Ferrando Badía was especially disappointed with the lack of clarity to define the ideas of regions and *nationalities*. In his newspaper article 'Federal state or regional state?' he stated that not to clarify those terms would lead to "serious legal-political consequences" (*El País*, 11 December 1977). Tomás Ramón Fernández, also legal scholar, wrote another newspaper article titled the 'The regional autonomies'. There he argued that the existence of autonomous regions necessarily entailed to adapt the provincial administration of the country (*Triunfo*, 18 February 1978, 29). The state should be modernized in order to strengthen the bonds between territories.

Cambio 16 showed the enthusiasm of all political parties but the Basque Nationalist Party in a lead article titled 'Long live the consensual (*consentida*)' to play on words with the last term, that in Spanish also means 'spoiled' (*Cambio 16*, 12 November 1978: 22–24). Other newspapers, like the Galician newspaper *La Voz de Galicia*, included a number of articles written by politicians. One of them was the chronicle of a symposium in which José Luis Meilán, representative of Union of Democratic Centre, had declared that there was a limit to regional autonomy and state decentralization of competences, that is to say, the privilege for some regions at the expense of others (*La Voz de Galicia*, 27 June 1978: 21). A privileged situation for some territories was necessarily detrimental to build the Spanish nation.

Both parliamentary speeches and the newspaper articles selected in this subsection showed the agreement around the need to limit the extent of decentralization to enhance the acceptance of Spain as a unitary nation. Their ideas reflected the understanding of Spain as a political nation that discarded ethnic elements. Institutions were regarded as the best alternative to unite democracy and political nation. Spain as a nation forms a political community in which *nationalities* and regions coexist requiring a commitment of integration from within by nationalisms (Aragón Reyes 1995: 194–95). As a political community Spain had its birth not just in medieval kingdoms but, more recently, in the parliamentary and constitutional history since the General and Extraordinary Cortes (*Cortes Generales y Extraordinarias*) of Cadiz.

3.2 Nationalist Understandings of Spain

Against the political defence of Spain as a nation, Heribert Barrera, of Republican Left of Catalonia, considered that Spain was an alien state that contravened the feelings of Catalan people due to historical aggressive measures (DSLC, 8 May 1978, Congress: 2080). His concept of Spain left out the constitutional and parliamentary tradition of the country, to which Catalonia always belonged. It was a nationalist understanding of Spain because he equated Spain as nation with an invasive state, as if Catalonia was a colony and not a historical territory within Spain. Barrera made even clearer his nationalism when he stated that "our nation is only Catalonia and we cannot have another".[27]

Rosendo Audet, independent representative from Catalonia, regarded Catalonia as a nation because many Catalan citizens thought that. Consequently, it should be acknowledged that Spain had different nations within (DSLC, 18 August 1978, Congress: 1581). His nationalist concept of Spain was patent: "We the Catalan people generally consider that the existence of Spain as a state does not imply that of Spain as a nation".

[27] "*Nuestra nación es sólo Cataluña y no podemos tener otra*" (DSLC, 4 July 1978, Congress: 3761).

In that sense, Audet did not want to say that Spain was a nation, so he named it as "Spanish state".[28]

Surprisingly, even Gregorio Peces-Barba, constitutional rapporteur of the Spanish Socialist Workers' Party, thought that Spain was a motherland with ethnic overtones, a moral reality that covered a certain political and cultural community. His view reproduced the arguments of nationalist representatives to a great extent: "The nation is, in our opinion, a human community founded in the fact of birth and heritage, but with all the moral connotations of these terms".[29]

Turning around the argument of Peces-Barba, Mitxel Unzueta, senator for the Basque Nationalist Party, distinguished different perceptions about Spain by citizens of some regions. He intentionally called Spaniards only those citizens who have the national feeling of belonging to Spain, excluding other Spanish citizens: "Spain is a state for all Spaniards, a nation-state for a large part of the population and only a state, but not a nation for important minorities".[30]

In the newspaper article titled 'Still about the term "nationalities"', Josep Benet, independent Catalan senator, declared that the term *nationalities* had been mentioned by Catalan politicians such as Tomàs Bertran i Soler in 1847 and Josep Baptista Guardiola in 1851 (*El País*, 21 June 1978). He sought to demonstrate that the term *nationality* had a long history in Spain and was originally envisioned in Catalonia to improve the structure of the state in Spain. Further, *nationality* was presented as an idea with roots in the second half of the nineteenth century. To Benet the idea of *nationalities* was perfectly adequate to the political vocabulary, even though when its meaning could be contested.

For nationalist representatives as a unitary country Spain was deemed either a tyrannical state or an insufficient political community. Nationalist views precluded the idea of Spain as a political nation. Ethnic aspects were highlighted against democratic institutions, such as parliament and

[28] "*Los catalanes, en general, consideramos que la existencia de España como Estado no implica la de España como nación*" (DSLC, 19 August 1978, Congress: 1605).

[29] "*La nación es, a nuestro juicio, una comunidad humana fundada en el hecho del nacimiento y de la herencia, pero con todas las connotaciones morales de estos términos*" (DSLC, 4 July 1978, Congress: 3801).

[30] "*España es un Estado para todos los españoles, una nación-Estado para una gran parte de la población y solamente un Estado, pero no una nación para minorías importantes*" (DSLC, 19 August 1978: 1608).

the Constitution to be passed, as the key elements of a nation. That understanding of Spain did not respond to the aims of the Constituent Assembly and included an anti-liberal outline of the concept of nation.

Bibliography

Legal Sources

Constitución Española de 1978. Available at: http://www.congreso.es/docu/constituciones/1978/1978_cd.pdf

Preliminary Draft of the Constitution of 1978 [*Anteproyecto de constitución de 1978*]. Available at: http://www.congreso.es/public_oficiales/L0/CONG/BOCG/BOC_044.PDF

Proceedings of the Constituent Assembly, 1977–1979 [*Diario de Sesiones de la Legislatura Constituyente, 1977–1979*, DSLC]. Available at: https://www.congreso.es/web/guest/indice-de-publicaciones?p_p_id=publicaciones&p_p_lifecycle=0&p_p_state=normal&p_p_mode=view&_publicaciones_selectedLeg=0

Spanish Constitution of 1978. Available at: http://www.congreso.es/portal/page/portal/Congreso/Congreso/Hist_Normas/Norm/const_espa_texto_ingles_0.pdf

Newspapers

Avui (1976–2011).

Cambio 16 (1971–).

Cuadernos para el Diálogo (1963–1978).

Egin (1977–1998).

El País (1976–).

La Voz de Galicia (1882–).

Triunfo (1946–1982).

References

Aguirre Bellver, Joaquín (1978). *Así se hizo la Constitución*. Valencia: Francisco Manuel Mas.

Alzaga Villaamil, Óscar (1978). *Comentario sistemático a la Constitución española de 1978*. Madrid: Foro.

Aparicio Pérez, Antonio (1988). 'La nueva estructura del Estado español. Especial consideración al principio de autonomía', in *Jornadas de estudio sobre el Título Preliminar de la Constitución*, vol. II. Madrid: Ministerio de Justicia.

Aragón Reyes, Manuel (1995). 'El Estado autonómico. ¿Modelo indefinido o modelo inacabado?', *Autonomies*, 20, 187–98.

Ariño Ortiz, Gaspar (1985). 'El Estado de las autonomías', in *La España de las autonomías*, ed. Fernando Fernández Rodríguez. Madrid: Ministerio de Administración Territorial.

Belmonte, José (1979). *La Constitución. Texto y Contexto*. Madrid: Prensa Española.

Benet, Josep (1978). 'Todavía sobre el término nacionalidades', *El País*, 21 June, https://elpais.com/diario/1978/06/30/opinion/268005605_850215.html

Cambio 16 Editorial (1978). 'Viva la consentida', *Cambio 16*, 12 November, 22–24.

Cisneros, Gabriel (2003). 'Historia de un éxito incompleto', in *Reflexiones de los ponentes de la Constitución española (1978–2003)*, eds. Gabriel Cisneros et al. Pamplona: Aranzadi.

Conversi, Daniele (2002). 'The Smooth Transition: Spain's 1978 Constitution and the Nationalities Question', *National Identities*, 4(3), 223–44.

Ferrando Badía, Juan (1977). '¿Estado federal o Estado regional?', *El País*, 11 December, https://elpais.com/diario/1977/12/11/opinion/250642808_850215.html

Gallego Díaz, Soledad & José Luis Martínez García (1978). 'La última cena constitucional', *Cuadernos para el Diálogo*, 29 July, 12.

García Escudero, José María & María Asunción García Martínez (1998). *La Constitución día a día. Los grandes temas de la Constitución de 1978 en el debate parlamentario*. Madrid: Congreso de los Diputados.

La Voz de Galicia Reportage (1978). 'Simposio sobre administración, economía y autonomía en Galicia', *La Voz de Galicia*, 27 June, 21.

Linz, Juan José (1985). 'De la crisis de un estado unitario al estado de las autonomías', in *La España de las autonomías*, ed. Fernando Fernández Rodríguez. Madrid: Ministerio de Administración Territorial.

López Rodó, Laureano (1984). *Estado y Comunidades Autónomas*. Madrid: Abella.

Lucas Verdú, Pablo (1985). 'El Estado autonómico como pluralidad institucional integrada', in *Comentarios a las leyes políticas*, vol. X, ed. Óscar Alzaga Villaamil. Madrid: Edersa.

Martín Oviedo, José María (1988). 'De las Comunidades Autónomas', in *Comentarios a las leyes políticas*, vol. XI, ed. Óscar Alzaga Villaamil. Madrid: Edersa.

Ortega Álvarez, Luis (2003). 'El modelo español de control sobre las autonomías territoriales', *Revista General de Derecho Administrativo*, 2, 1–11.

Peces-Barba, Gregorio (2002). 'Una lectura de la Constitución española', in *La organización territorial del Estado*, eds. Alfonso Cucó, Joan Romero & Joaquín Farinós. Valencia: Universitat de València.

Ramón Fernández, Tomás (1978). 'Las autonomías regionales', *Triunfo*, 18 February, 29.

Rebollo Delgado, Lucrecio (2018). 'Antecedentes, surgimiento y conformación del Estado autonómico en la Constitución de 1978', *Revista de Derecho Político*, 101, 461–502.

Sánchez Agesta, Luis (1979). 'Algunos caracteres generales de la Constitución de 1978', *Revista de Derecho Público*, 74, 5–21.

Sanmartí, Josep Maria (2017). 'La influencia de *El País*', in *La transición de la prensa. El comportamiento político de diarios y periodistas*, ed. Jaume Guillamet. Valencia: Universitat de València.

Trujillo Fernández, Gumersindo (1994). 'Principio federal y estado autonómico', in *Parlamento y consolidación democrática*, eds. Juan Cano Bueso & Antonio Porras Nadales. Madrid: Tecnos.

CHAPTER 8

Liberalism and Democracy in Contemporary Spain

This chapter explores the legacy of liberalism and democracy in Spain. It aims to identify present challenges to its constitutional legacy by resorting to its constitutional foundations. The chapter is organized around four sections. First, it deals with how constitutional liberalism consolidated in Spain during the nineteenth century. Second, it outlines the parallelisms and differences between the Spanish, the Portuguese, and the Greek transitions to democracy. To compare them is helpful to understand that the establishment of constitutional democracies is always uncertain and necessarily relies on the acceptance of political and social pluralism. Third, the chapter surveys the influence of the European Economic Community, later named as European Union, on Spanish democracy since the early 1970s. Fourth, it looks into the consequences of the economic crash of 2008 for the stability of democratic institutions. Additionally, it enquires into the subsequent debasement of constitutionalism and democratic liberalism that populist and anti-liberal rhetoric have brought into play.

F. J. Bellido, *Constitutional Debates, Rhetoric, and Political Philosophy in Spain's Parliamentary History*, Rhetoric, Politics and Society, https://doi.org/10.1007/978-3-031-56894-7_8

1 Spain's Parliamentary History Before 1977: Liberal Constitutionalism and Autocratic Interludes

The parliamentary constitutional tradition which began with the *Cortes* of Cadiz has been regarded as one of the milestones of Spain's history as a political nation. "Spaniards, here you have your fatherland" were the words attributed to the liberal representative Agustín de Argüelles in the oratorio San Felipe Neri of Cadiz on 19 March 1812, after the passing of the Constitution. His words have been often interpreted as if Argüelles had made patent the lack of a nation in Spain. On the contrary, he affirmed the existence of one political nation united through laws that made all citizens equal and bound to comply with corresponding duties.

Spain's parliamentary history remained one of the most enduring in Europe. After Fernando VII death in 1833, the country's absolutist monarchy was transformed into a constitutional monarchy. In that process constitutional freedoms were gradually acknowledged (Luis 2021: 32). Liberalism became the dominant ideology of the monarchy. Spain was neither a political exception nor a latecomer constitutional monarchy compared to other European nations. As newspapers, pamphlets, and legal documents evince, Spanish parliamentarism was connected to the success of liberal constitutionalism.

Spanish liberalism was a far-reaching ideology encompassing both gradual and immediate reforms. Furthermore, the reformist language of liberalism pervaded all spheres of the social and the political life in Europe and America (Rosales 2013: 67–82). Constitutional debates during the nineteenth century were the scenario of the existing tensions in Europe between liberalism and absolutism during the first third of the century, and between the so-called moderate and progressive liberalisms during the last two thirds. As the nineteenth century moved forward, families within liberalism competed against each other.

Despite military uprisings and civil wars between liberals in favour of the legitimate queen, Isabel II of Spain, and the followers of the absolutist candidate, Carlos María Isidro, Isabel II's uncle, Spain parliamentary tradition did withstand. The fact that the name *Cortes* was reminiscent of medieval institutions that legitimized the crown's power was rhetorically appealing to join the loyalties of diverse political groups. That included moderate liberals related to Hispanic Scholastic theories on the undivided legitimacy of royal power and the so-called internal, unwritten constitution of Spain. Even for groups against intensive social reforms, constitutions were synonymous with civil peace. There was no political sector in the Spanish parliament after 1845 that seriously aimed to dispense with parliamentary institutions. Even when republican groups started to rise during the 1860s, monarchy, and not parliamentarism, was questioned.

In the twentieth century, after the demise of the Bourbon Restoration (29 December 1874–14 April 1931), the corporativist dictatorship established in 1923 and led by general Miguel Primo de Rivera kept the name of National Assembly for his corporativist consultative institution. The loss of prestige that parliamentary politics underwent unleashed antiparliamentarism vindications in the middle of the 1930s, when adversaries of the Spanish Second Republic multiplied. By that time many of them deemed it a partisan regime that hindered agreements between left-wing and right-wing parties.

The triumph of the dictator Francisco Franco in 1939, after a bloody Civil War of three years, did not eliminate the prestige of the word '*Cortes*'. That was the name for the corporativist consultative body during dictatorship. Political parties were forbidden, and national Catholicism became the official ideology of the regime for 36 years. After the dictator's death in 1975, a gradual transition to democracy was the best choice for Spain's future.

2 Democratic Transitions in Spain, Portugal, and Greece

Like the Portuguese and the Greek cases, Spain's smoother path to democracy was full of difficulties. Terrorism and the military's ambiguous loyalties put at risk the establishment of democracy. The contrast between constitutionalism and liberal democracy, on the one hand, and autocratic anti-liberalism, on the other hand, was resolved in favour of the former. The latter became residual, just endorsed by dictatorship's *nostálgicos*.

Portugal was an impoverished country with a limited peninsular population. In September 1973 Guinea-Bissau declared its independence (Teixeira 2008: 76). But Portugal also faced colonial insurmountable uprisings in Angola and Mozambique. In April 1974 the military's *coup d'état* ended the autocratic period. Nevertheless, opposition's democratic groups were divided and poorly articulated to stabilize the country (Costa

Pinto 2006: 176). There was no political or social group able to take back the control of the country without the army's support.

António de Oliveira Salazar's (1933–1968) and Marcelo das Neves Alves Caetano's (1968–1974) autocratic regimes were equated with each other. The need of a complete break with the past precluded negotiations and led to a relatively slow path towards democracy (Costa Pinto 2006: 175). Portugal dealt with revolutionary political demands beyond reformism. On 25 April 1974, during the Carnation Revolution, a military group, the Armed Forces Movement (*Movimento das Forças Armadas*, MFA), dissolved Caetano's regime. The conservative general António de Spínola became the new head of government. Between 1974 and 1976 Portugal was in a weak economic position. Authoritarian state elites undertook detrimental international policies and colonial warfare, opposed to an active civil society formed by middle classes (Magone 2013: 7). In the aftermath of the Carnation Revolution most citizens were reluctant to support parties and groups "perceived to be right-wing" (Marchi and Azevedo Alves 2023: 104). However, the clashing political cultures within the Portuguese society hampered democratization.

Portugal's path towards democracy started from similar standpoints when compared to Spain. The sort of 'semi-opposition' put into practice in Portugal by organizations such as Social Development Study Group (*Sociedade para o Desenvolvimento Económico e Social*, SEDES) was determinant to break with Caetano's regime (Bermeo 1987: 224). In Spain semi-opposition was also exercised by tempered personalities with liberal affinities that were not regime insiders within the Francoist regime, such as the constitutional rapporteur José Pedro Pérez-Llorca.

Portugal's social revolution resulted in a stronger nationalization of economic sectors and a decreasing political influence of part of the previous dominant elites (Fishman and Lizardo 2013: 216). Unlike the vast changes of civil society in Portugal, Spanish society changed gradually without dismantling the existing social and economic centres of the country's effective power (Fishman 2017: 392). Spanish economic elites became part of the democratic process and, with few exceptions, did not aim to torpedo the efforts of politicians in favour of democracy. Elites, broadly understood, ranged from regime insiders in favour of democracy to coordinated opposition leaders in exile (Threlfall 2008: 936). Instead, in Portugal Caetano's elites lacked minimum democratic credentials to partake of democracy.

As indicated by Tiago Fernandes, the robustness of civil society in Portugal and Spain before and after the democratic period is "not positively correlated" (Fernandes 2015: 1079). Higher levels of affiliation to political and social organizations were neither synonym with broader public endorsement of democracy nor an indicator of more political stability. However, Fernandes denies that part of the elites during dictatorships must take part in the negotiations leading to a new democratic regime (See Fernandes 2015: 1080). Whether democratization can be channelled through completely new elites and an organized civil society or not remains a contested issue.

Greece's transition to democracy was also intricate. The Polytechnic's students revolt of 17 November 1973 ended tragically after being stifled by Colonels' armed forces. That momentum became a someway mystified symbol of later democratic success (Kornetis 2019: 514). Whatever the case is, the Greek transition to democracy faced additional problems. The high risk of war against Turkey was a worrying menace increased over years. Greece needed a government capable to bring civil peace, to avoid military rule, and to overcome the country's economic *impasse*.

The path to democratization opened in 1974 after the conservative leader Constantinos Karamanlis came back from exile and was endorsed by the military, part of the right and the centre. His main task was to make compatible democratic pluralism, military loyalty and peace with Turkey (Kaloudis 2000: 46). Like Spain's transition to democracy, the Greek one was a top-down process in which political and economic elites contributed to make it possible (Karamouzi 2015: 2). A substantial difference was the prominence of the military in Greece, which hindered the establishment of democracy. On 1 August 1974 the democratic Constitution of 1952 replaced the fundamental norms of the dictatorship. Soon afterwards Greece re-entered the Council of Europe, triggering subsequent steps to enhance democratization (Karamouzi 2015: 6–7). That process of democratization in Greece was equated with better integration within Europe.

Ex post facto analyses have too often taken advantage of analytical instruments and selective information that leaves aside other possible causes or factors as irrelevant to clarify processes of democratization. Spanish, Portuguese, and Greek transitions to democracy took place in dissimilar political, social, and economic contexts. Despite sharing some conditions such as predominant agrarian economies, lower levels of industrialization as compared to northern European countries, strong dependence of foreign investments and high risk of military rebellion, the Spanish case had other features. A salient circumstance is that Spain coped with regional nationalisms that neither Portugal nor Greece faced (Papadogiannis and Ramos Pinto 2023: 13). Another circumstance is that the legal transition from dictatorship to democracy in Spain was possible through regime insiders' initiative in favour of democracy.

King Juan Carlos I understood that the continuity of monarchy depended on his endorsement of democracy. With the support of insider politicians such as Torcuato Fernández-Miranda, Juan Carlos I favoured the interests of Adolfo Suárez, who sought to democratize the regime. That difference is crucial as regards to Portugal and Greece. King Juan Carlos I worked as a 'catalytic' of different platforms and groups whose legitimacy unified around a step-by-step strategy in favour of democracy (Martínez Roda and Rezola 2016: 135).Fernández-Miranda's political concerns led him to defend a representative system and the rule of law as the future mainstay of Spanish society. He meant to build a constitutional state and a liberal democracy (Ponce-Alberca 2016: 33). Portugal lacked a fundamental source of legitimacy to give guidance to ideologically and strategically divided democratic supporters (Martínez Roda and Rezola 2016: 140).Karamanlis in Greece confronted similar difficulties.

One of the most salient facts of the democratization processes underwent in Spain and Portugal during the 1970s was the victory of a centre-left party in Portugal, the Socialist Party, and the victory of a centre-right party in Spain, the Union of Democratic Centre. As suggested by Nancy Bermeo, the distinctive rhetorical and procedural paths of break (Portugal) and reform (Spain) can partly explain the electoral victories of those parties (Bermeo 1987: 214). However, colonial warfare in Portugal, the subsequent weakening of its economy and clashing ideologies within the military made it unlikely to improve the country's poor economic and political performance in the medium run (Bermeo 2007: 391–92). That situation resulted in a more uncertain and irregular process of democratization.

In Spain, political platforms and parties in favour of reforms towards democracy, such as Democratic Coordination (*Coordinación Democrática*), often relinquished to comply with their party maxims to achieve beneficial agreements for the country. Widespread social fear of possible backward steps and civil violence among Spaniards boosted the chances of the centrist leader Adolfo Suárez among the emerging middle class. Suárez inspired confidence in both moderate right-wing and moderate left-wing citizens. With the help of an efficient political team, he succeeded in becoming the leader of most Spaniards during critical years. His party, Union of Democratic Centre, was a platform specifically designed to integrate prominent legal and economic experts.

3 Spain and the European Economic Community

During dictatorship countries within the Council of Europe avoided any rapprochement with the Francoist regime, blocking the access of Spain to the Council (Salm 2021: 99–100). That situation changed as Suárez's government put into practice diplomatic strategies and legal measures of unequivocal democratic character. When democracy was no longer a promise, but a reality, Spain joined the Council of Europe. 24 November 1977 was the official date.

To explain the European Economic Community's efforts to supervise and to foster steps towards democracy in Spain requires to pay attention to their mutual interests. The European Economic Community refused to accept Spain as a member during Franco's dictatorship. For instance, by impeding its access better trade conditions with the British market were impossible (Powell 1996: 296–97). The regime's search for diplomatic and economic support in Europe was hampered. That was thought an efficient way of forcing Spanish political elites to gradually pave the way for democracy.

In December 1973 Luis Carrero Blanco, head of government, was killed by ETA. Since then, the most reformist wing of the regime, the so-called technocrats, strived for improving their status within it. They carried out economic reforms to make Spain closer to other European countries. It was clear that without international support, the country would jeopardize its future changes. Democracy was the only possible alternative to autocracy.

The Spanish government led by Adolfo Suárez since 1976 increased an open international profile in line with the reformist efforts of the previous minister of foreign affairs, José María de Areilza. After Suárez's endeavours to meet opposition platforms and to include legal changes, his democratic credentials among European leaders began to be recognized. They knew that the success of Spain's democratization depended on the reciprocal interest of European countries such as Germany, the United Kingdom, and France to allow Spain to become a member of the European Economic Community.

The German government led by Helmud Schmidt understood that it should endorse Spanish democratic groups in favour of democracy. Suárez's party seemed the best choice for Spain's democratic future. The economic crisis during the transition to democracy was an additional reason to prevent the country from becoming an unstable country with deficient democratic institutions. By 1976 the public endorsement of the German social-democratic chancellor Schmidt in favour of Spain's steady changes towards democracy bolstered them up (Blanco Sío-López, 2019). The German endorsement was crucial to join the support of other European countries such as France and Italy.

Spanish executive power, led by civilians appointed by Suárez and the field marshal (*capitán general*) Manuel Gutiérrez Mellado, revamped the intelligence agency to create the Higher Centre of Defence Information (*Centro Superior de Información de la Defensa*, CESID) in 1977 (Matei et al. 2018: 772). Other political measures increased media pluralism and lifted censorship. Between 1976 and 1977 Spain faced a fast process of modernization. Political, economic, and social freedoms were widespread and European leaders welcomed those changes.

Members of the European Economic Community thought that Spain's democratic advent could strengthen the international position of Western Europe against the Soviet Union. To obtain the support of Spain meant to ensure that a new democratic country would be responsive to the interests of the rest of liberal democracies. Economic investments from Europe were welcomed by moderate Spanish democratic platforms, strengthened from a diplomatic point of view. Spain became member of the North Atlantic Treaty Organization (NATO) in 1982 and of the European Economic Community in 1986. These achievements were determinant to give a boost to the positive international image of the country.

Despite the high costs in terms of deindustrialization for Spain, agreements for the distribution of European resources helped the country to reduce the economic gap with the richest European countries. A large majority of Spanish citizens were pro-European Union. Democracy, economic prosperity, and European Union are correlated ideas to many Spanish citizens. Despite the inrush of the economic crisis of 2008, neither the democratic foundations of the European Union nor pro-European policies to include new countries within the Union were seriously questioned in Spain.

4 Challenges Against Liberal Democracy

The challenges that the Spanish democracy faced after the failed military *coup d'état* on 23 February 1981 were to consolidate a pluralist democracy by keeping constitutional loyalty of all political parties, to keep a steady process of economic growth and to strengthen diplomatic bonds with the rest of European democracies and the United States. That autocratic failed *coup d'état* paradoxically precluded outdated military uprisings in Spain (Fuentes 2020: 203). It made clear that one of the unwanted results of anti-parliamentary politics by the early 1980s was authoritarian backsliding.

Since the 1980s conservative nationalist parties of Catalonia and the Basque Country retain their respective regional power through agreements with the party in the national government. As José Pedro Pérez-Llorca—one of the constitutional rapporteurs of Union of Democratic Centre—acknowledged in an interview in 2012, the democratic transition prevented autocratic reversals at the expense of nurturing future destabilizing issues (Pérez López and Lafuente del Cano 2014: 116–17). Pérez-Llorca had in mind the unsettled process of state decentralization that the Constitution of 1978 left open.

Not to delimit the state competences which could be transferred to regions (later named as Autonomous Communities) together with increasing nationalist demands in Catalonia and the Basque Country have provoked a decreasing, now residual presence, of state institutions in those regions. Further, decentralizing demands have gradually undermined the economic and administrative capacity of the state to fairly distribute public resources between regions since the early 1980s. Fiscal imbalances and increasing regional debts have grown (Utrilla de la Hoz 2020: 329). This situation imperils the Spanish economy.

Felipe González, socialist head of government in Spain between 1982 and 1996, combined a rhetoric of social reforms in domestic politics with a strategy of visibility in the international context. As a setback, the Spanish economy went through three basic problems during his mandate: high rates of unemployment, deindustrialization, and scarce productivity. Felipe González succeeded in retaining power until the general election of 1996, when the Popular Party led by José María Aznar won after becoming the leader of a refunded union of conservatives and liberals.[1] The right-wing nationalist Catalan leader Jordi Pujol strengthened his position after agreements with Aznar's government. Pujol kept his nationalist policies in Catalonia and forced a higher degree of state decentralization of competences that compromised the fiscal equality of Spanish citizens. Three days after the terrible terrorist massacre perpetrated on 11 March 2004, José Luis Rodríguez Zapatero, leader of the Spanish Socialist Workers' Party, became the new head of government.

On 15 March 2011 *indignados*' massive protests were mostly the consequence of economic impoverishment and political uneasiness. The *indignados* claimed that Spain was a flawed democratic regime, not truly representative. Besides, they raised strong criticisms against "evictions, inequality and corruption" (De Nadal 2021: 41). Their aspirations of radical reforms came together with the questioning of the Spanish transition to democracy (Kornetis 2019: 513–14). Upset by what they regarded as insufficient political reforms, an irresponsive political elite and high rates of unemployment, they called for revolutionary unarticulated reforms.

Those groups deemed Spanish democracy an unfair regime by means of a powerful populist rhetoric. They were opposed to representative democracy and called for citizens' informal assemblies and direct democracy. The *indignados* portrayed the Spanish transition as a betrayal to forget the past and to not repair the injustices committed against the losers of the Spanish Civil War, namely, dead and exiled pro-republicans of the 1930s. In their view, the democratic transition was blurred because Francoist elites retained power and remained unpunished by the crimes committed.

That narrative was against the empirical evidence that the democratic transition was a never equated success in Spain's history despite its shortcomings. The so-called politics of consensus made it possible the reconciliation of all Spaniards without resort to violence. The populist rhetoric that emerged after the economic crash of 2008 concealed a basic fact: ETA's terrorism, and not the men who welcomed democracy despite their participation in the Francoist regime, were the actual challenge to the democratic transition.

Reconciliation among Spaniards did not imply to forget the past bloody civil war and its consequences after a brutal dictatorship. In fact, that tragedy was the main reason not to use the past as a political weapon

[1] A less accurate though widespread translation for the party is People's Party.

among Spaniards. The foundations of a liberal democracy and a constitutional state were established under the premise of forgiveness, not of amnesia. Authoritarianism was no longer an alternative for Spain.

After losing the confidence of many Spaniards because of his inability to deal with the economic crisis of 2008, Zapatero lost the general election held on 20 November 2011. The electoral results gave a majority of seats in parliament to the conservative leader of the Popular Party, Mariano Rajoy. One month before that same year ETA announced their cessation of violence. During Rajoy's term in office (2011–2018) the country fought against unsurmountable rates of unemployment and poverty. The head of government's orthodox policies to reduce public expenses, to improve exports, and to take advantage of positive incomes led to a gradual though incomplete recovery of the economy.

In parallel with the economic crisis Catalan nationalist parties got involved in the so-called *procés*, a plan to force an illegal referendum of independence in Catalonia against the constitutional legality. On 1 October 2017 an illegal unilateral referendum of independence for Catalonia was held with the approval of the autonomous government led by Carles Puigdemont. Seven days later he declared the independence of Catalonia to immediately suspend it.[2] For the first time since 23 February 1981 Spain faced a rebellion against its constitutional order. Rajoy's government activated Article number 155 of the Constitution with the endorsement of the Spanish Socialist Workers' Party to reestablish the legal and social order in Catalonia. Eight months later Rajoy had to face a vote of no confidence (*moción de censura*) through which Pedro Sánchez, leader of the Spanish Socialist Workers' Party, became head of government.

Between 2018 and 2023 Spain has undergone definite changes that seriously question the integrity of its constitutional order. In 2018 the Spanish Socialist Workers' Party formed an alliance with the far-left party Podemos, which in 2019 was renamed as United We Can (*Unidas Podemos*), with the support of nationalist parties from Catalonia, the Basque Country, and Galicia, besides the endorsement of the regionalist party New Canarias. Since then, there has been a major division between two blocs.

[2] It is statistically relevant that richer citizens of Catalonia are more prone to support its independence from Spain than poorer citizens (Oller et al. 2020: 15).

On the one hand, the Spanish Socialist Workers' Party, the far-left and nationalist parties. On the other hand, the Popular Party, Citizens (until its downfall between 2019 and 2023) and, since 2019, the far-right Vox. Within the former bloc, United We Can experienced a significant loss of prestige in favour of another far-left platform, *Sumar*, led by Yolanda Díaz. That heterogenous platform consists of the confluence of twenty minor parties and presented its candidacy in the general election of July 2023. Within the later bloc, the Popular Party was the most voted party. The electoral rise of Vox is largely correlated with the electoral decline of Citizens and a heightened contrast with the adversarial bloc.

The Spanish Socialist Workers' Party and the Popular Party have been incapable to defend together the constitutional order against populist and nationalist parties of Catalonia and the Basque Country, *Sumar* and Vox. But more importantly, with different degrees of political responsibility, they have failed to slow down the transformation of Spain into a confederal-like state in which the Basque Country and Catalonia enjoy fiscal advantages that citizens of poorer regions do not. Decentralization of state competences has risen above the limits of a federal state.

It is possible to distinguish three phases of regionalization: the first one in 1978 with the passing of the Constitution; the second one between 1978 and 1981 with the drafting and passing of autonomy statutes for Catalonia and the Basque Country; and the third one when Autonomous Communities such as Andalusia, as early as 1981, prompted autonomy statutes for other Spanish regions (Jaroszyk 2020: 34–36). As argued by Mora-Sanguinetti and Spruk, autonomy statutes accomplished after the Spanish transition to democracy had positive economic consequences for peripheral poorer regions, such as Andalusia and Extremadura; whereas those autonomy statutes passed in the 2000s were significantly correlated with higher regulatory complexity and negative economic performance (Mora-Sanguinetti and Spruk 2023: 58–59). In fact, the increased territorial tensions within Spain have paved the way for the electoral growth of *Podemos* and Vox (Vampa 2020: 313). Their incompatible answers of self-determination with secessionist overtones in the case of *Podemos* and of centralization of state competences in the case of Vox have engendered additional problems for the country's governability.

After the general election on 23 July 2023, the Popular Party was the most voted party. As a setback to its electoral prospects, the party could not reach the majority of 176 seats in parliament together with Vox. The socialist leader, Pedro Sánchez, aimed to secure the support of Catalonian,

Basque, and Galician nationalist parties for his investiture and subsequent government. The affirmative vote of the seven representatives obtained by Together for Catalonia (*Junts per Catalunya*) were essential. In exchange for them, Carles Puigdemont has demanded an amnesty law for all those prosecuted due to their alleged involvement in the illegal referendum of 1 October 2017. Further, he has successfully requested international mediation between his own party and the Spanish Socialist Workers' Party to negotiate outside Spain.

The amnesty law has been legally and morally questioned. It will be likely passed in parliament, although an appeal of unconstitutionality should be settled by the Spanish Constitutional Court (*Tribunal Constitucional*). Its announcement has provoked protests in many Spanish cities, since November 2023, and the opposition of the judiciary's organizations, as well as other civil society organizations. From a constitutional point of view, the likely passing of that amnesty law is the beginning of a new political period. The Amnesty Law of 15 October 1977, officially named as Law 46/1977, of 15 October, of Amnesty (*Ley 46/1977, de 15 de octubre, de Amnistía*) was pre-constitutional and meant that all crimes for political reasons, including those of convicted republicans, Francoists, and ETA, were exonerated from punishment due to the anti-democratic character of the dictatorship.

Instead, the proposal of an amnesty law presented by the socialist group in parliament in November 2023, Proposal for an Organic Law of amnesty for institutional, political, and social normalization in Catalonia (*Proposición de Ley Orgánica de amnistía para la normalización institucional, política y social en Cataluña*), would entail that crimes under judicial investigation did not take place. From a legal and a political perspective, impossible to separate from each other, a new amnesty law would mean, at least, two things. First, it would entail that equality before the law of all Spaniards is broken. Unlike the case of legal pardon, alleged crimes against the constitutional order—not only punishments—would be cancelled. Second, it would lead to reinterpret the rules of game of the constitutional order, not following the amendment procedures in the Constitution to include amnesty laws as prerogatives of parliament. If the amnesty law is passed by parliament and the ruling of the Constitutional Court is favourable, it would set a precedent implying that the executive power is able to discretionarily pass future amnesties.

Liberalism and democracy are struggling against growing international hostility (Galston 2020: 8–9). Spanish pluralist democracy is not an exception. The Constitution of 1978 channels ideological disagreements through legal means. It sets the legal limits to public powers. A culture of legality is not at odds with a democratic culture, but it is its precondition. That means to vindicate the constitutional legacy that constituent representatives during the nineteenth and the twentieth centuries strived for against authoritarianism. To give up Spain's constitutional and parliamentary legacy in favour of projects of social division among citizens means to feed anti-liberal trends and to weaken the foundations of liberal democracy.

Bibliography

Legal Sources

Law 46/1977, of 15 October, of Amnesty [Ley 46/1977, de 15 de octubre, de Amnistía]. Available at: https://www.boe.es/buscar/pdf/1977/BOE-A-1977-24937-consolidado.pdf

Proposal for an Organic Law of amnesty for institutional, political and social normalization in Catalonia [*Proposición de Ley Orgánica de amnistía para la normalización institucional, política y social en Cataluña*]. Available at: https://www.congreso.es/public_oficiales/L15/CONG/BOCG/B/BOCG-15-B-32-1.PDF

References

Bermeo, Nancy (1987). 'Redemocratization and Transition Elections: A Comparison of Spain and Portugal', *Comparative Politics*, 19(2), 213–31.

Bermeo, Nancy (2007). 'War and Democratization: Lessons from the Portuguese Experience', *Democratization*, 14(3), 388–406.

Blanco Sío-López, Cristina (2019). 'Transitional Margins to Re-join the West', in *Spain's Dual Strategy of Democratisation and Europeanisation*. London & New York: Routledge.

Costa Pinto, António (2006). 'Authoritarian Legacies, Transitional Justice and State Crisis in Portugal's Democratization', *Democratization*, 13(2), 173–204.

De Nadal, Luis (2021). 'On Populism and Social Movements: From the Indignados to Podemos', *Social Movement Studies*, 20(1), 36–56.

Fernandes, Tiago (2015). 'Rethinking Pathways to Democracy: Civil Society in Portugal and Spain, 1960s–2000s', *Democratization*, 22(6), 1074–104.

Fishman, Robert M. (2017). 'How Civil Society Matters in Democratization: Setting the Boundaries of Post-transition Political Inclusion', *Comparative Politics*, 49(3), 391–409.

Fishman, Robert M. & Omar Lizardo (2013). 'How Macro-Historical Change Shapes Cultural Taste: Legacies of Democratization in Spain and Portugal', *American Sociological Review*, 78(2), 213–39.

Fuentes, Juan Francisco (2020). *23 febrero 1981. El golpe que acabó con todos los golpes*. Barcelona: Taurus.

Galston, William A. (2020). 'The Enduring Vulnerability of Constitutional Democracy', *The Journal of Democracy*, 31(3), 8–24.

Jaroszyk, Joanna (2020). 'Spain as the State of Autonomies: Principles Behind the Territorial Organization Between 1978 and 1983', *Humanities and Social Sciences*, 27(4), 29–38.

Kaloudis, George (2000). 'Transitional Democratic Politics in Greece', *International Journal on World Pace*, 17(1), 35–59.

Karamouzi, Eirini (2015). 'A Strategy for Greece: Democratization and European Integration, 1974–75', *Cahiers de la Méditerranée*, 90, 11–24.

Kornetis, Kostis (2019). 'Projections Onto the Past: Memories of Democratization in Spain, Greece, and Portugal During the Great Recession', *Mobilization: An International Quarterly*, 24(4), 511–24.

Luis, Jean-Philippe (2021). 'The Mutations of the Spanish Monarchy', in *Monarchy and Liberalism in Spain: The Building of the Nation State, 1780–1931*, eds. David San Narciso, Margarita Barral-Martínez & Carolina Armenteros. New York: Routledge.

Magone, Jose M. (2013). *Politics in Contemporary Portugal: Democracy Evolving*. Bouldon: Lynne Rienner.

Marchi, Riccardo & André Azevedo Alves (2023). 'The Right and Far-Right in the Portuguese Democracy (1974–2022)', in *The Oxford Handbook to Portuguese Politics*, eds. Jorge M. Fernandes, Pedro C. Magalhães & António Costa Pinto. Oxford: Oxford University Press.

Martínez Roda, Federico & Maria Inácia Rezola (2016). 'Spanish Monarchy and the Portuguese Republic: Two Routes of Democratization', *Portuguese Journal of Social Science*, 15(1), 129–43.

Matei, Florina Cristiana, Andrés de Castro García & Carolyn C. Halladay (2018). 'On Balance: Intelligence Democratization in Post-Franco Spain', *International Journal of Intelligence and Counterintelligence*, 31(4), 769–804.

Mora-Sanguinetti, Juan S. & Rok Spruk (2023). 'Economic Effects of Recent Experiences of Federalism: Analysis of the Regionalization Process in Spain', *Journal of Regional Science*, 63(1), 30–63.

Oller, Josep M., Albert Satorra & Adolf Tobeña (2020). 'Privileged Rebels: A Longitudinal Analysis of Distinctive Economic Traits of Catalonian Secessionism', *Genealogy*, 4(19), 1–17.

Papadogiannis, Nikolaos & Pedro Ramos Pinto (2023). 'Social Change, Protest and Participation in Greece, Portugal and Spain', *Mélanges de la Casa de Velázquez*, 53(1), 1–23.

Pérez López, Pablo & Jorge Lafuente del Cano (2014). 'Diversity and Decentralization in the Democratization Process in Spain', *International Relations and Diplomacy*, 2(2), 111–19.

Ponce-Alberca, Julio (2016). 'Torcuato Fernández-Miranda', in *Political Leadership in the Spanish Transition to Democracy*, eds. José Francisco Jiménez Díaz & Santiago Delgado. New York: Nova Publishers.

Powell, Charles (1996). 'International Aspects of Democratization: The Case of Spain', in *The International Dimensions of Democratisation*, ed. Laurence Whitehead. Oxford: Oxford University Press.

Rosales, José María (2013). 'Liberalism's Historical Diversity: A Comparative Conceptual Exploration', *Contributions to the History of Concepts*, 8(2), 67–82.

Salm, Christian (2021). 'Diffusing Democracy in Europe: The European Parliament and European Community Enlargement Policy, 1974–79', *Journal of European Integration History*, 27(1), 99–119.

Teixeira, Nuno Severiano (2008). 'Portugal: Democratization and Foreign Policy', in *The International Politics of Democratization: Comparative Perspectives*. London & New York: Routledge.

Threlfall, Monica (2008). 'Reassessing the Role of Civil Society Organizations in the Transition to Democracy in Spain', *Democratization*, 15(5), 930–51.

Utrilla de la Hoz, Alfonso (2020). *Cuatro décadas de descentralización fiscal en España: Luces y sombras del Estado de las autonomías*. Logroño: Genueve.

Vampa, Davide (2020). 'Competing Forms of Populism and Territorial Politics: The Cases of Vox and Podemos in Spain', *Journal of Contemporary European Studies*, 28(3), 304–21.

CHAPTER 9

Conclusions

This book has explored the Spanish constitutional debates of the nineteenth and twentieth centuries from the perspectives of political philosophy, conceptual history and parliamentary history. From the first one, parliamentary speeches of constituent assemblies bring in controversies which contain arguments of political philosophy about the legitimacy of a constitutional state, the structure of the state, and the acknowledgment and scope of fundamental rights. From the second one, political concepts receive rival meanings from diverse ideological standpoints in connection with those controversies. Thus, constituent assemblies prompt new connotations for classic political concepts. From the third one, parliamentary speeches reflect how political concepts differ over time, albeit very often keeping part of their classic meanings.

This study has aimed to answer how political philosophy arguments in the parliamentary deliberations inspired conceptual changes and informed the design of state institutions. Consequently, this research has surveyed to which extent the arguments raised by representatives led to conceptual innovations and institutional changes. Throughout its different chapters, this study has presented the arguments that justify why constitutional debates have played a determinant role in understanding the renewal of the political vocabulary of Spain. Especially, that process has affected concepts such as 'sovereignty', 'constituent power', 'constituted power',

F. J. Bellido, *Constitutional Debates, Rhetoric, and Political Philosophy in Spain's Parliamentary History*, Rhetoric, Politics and Society,
https://doi.org/10.1007/978-3-031-56894-7_9

'freedom', 'equality', 'sovereignty', 'reform', 'autonomy', 'self-rule', 'self-determination', 'nation', and 'nationalities' (*nacionalidades*).

During the nineteenth-century constitutional debates entailed successive renewals of both the political vocabulary and the country's existing regimes. From the defence of constitutional monarchy in the *Cortes* of Cadiz of 1810–1812 to the passing of the 89-articles-long Constitution of 1876, constitutional debates reflected the modernization of institutions and ideological changes, translated into the political languages of liberalism and republicanism.

In the constitutional debate of 1931, after the Spanish Second Republic was proclaimed, intellectuals and ideologues engaged in the constitutional deliberations. Intellectuals elected as representatives, from José Ortega y Gasset and Miguel de Unamuno to Gregorio Marañón and Ramón Pérez de Ayala, contributed to revamping the political language of different political traditions. Liberalism, republicanism, and democracy were connected to the necessity of political, social, and economic reforms.

As this book has presented, between 1977 and 1978 constituent representatives contributed to establishing the democratic institutions of Spain following the parliamentary and constitutional models of Germany, the United Kingdom, France, and Italy to varying degrees. 'Reform', 'self-rule', 'self-determination', 'nation', and 'nationalities' became key political terms. Over the next decades, the decentralized state enshrined in the Constitution of 1978 ushered in a never-ending process of transfer of competences from the central administration of the state to the autonomous communities.

The constitutional debates that resulted in the Constitutions of 1812, 1837, 1845, 1869, 1876, 1931, and 1978 served to appraise unsettled issues and old controversies. Ideological premises and intellectual contributions were intermingled in the course of parliamentary argumentations. As a consequence, political, economic, and social concepts and topics were successively revised.

1 Parliamentary and Constitutional Rhetoric in Spain: A Panoramic Perspective

By clarifying parliamentary speeches, the abovementioned political concepts have been reviewed from an argumentative perspective in the framework of constituent assemblies. Conceptual controversies raised by constituent representatives have been examined when devising new political institutions through arguments and concepts that largely relied on political philosophy ideas and contributions to political thought. By doing so, the blend of political traditions, ideologies, and intellectual affinities of parties and representatives are brought into light.

In that regard, this research has attended not just to the ideological and theoretical backgrounds that gave rise to some of the political concepts and debates. It has connected the analysis of political concepts to argumentations of political philosophy by integrating the methodological potentialities of an interdisciplinary approach in a clearer way. Moreover, this study has sought to provide a different approach to parliamentary speeches that attends to their argumentative potential when designing the new institutions of parliamentary regimes. It has contrasted their analysis with historically founded interpretations of them in the light of the clash between nationalist and liberal understandings of state institutions.

There are two argumentative axes for distributing the chapters' contents. The first refers to the division of chapters according to the constitutional debates, issues, and political concepts examined. The second axis has entailed classifying the parliamentary speeches of constitutional debates according to partisan affinities and ideologies.

The relationship between ideologies and parties does not always completely elucidate the connotations provided to the concepts. Nevertheless, the ideological preferences of representatives and parties help to primarily illustrate how ideological disagreements sustained the debate. It makes possible to identify the more contested concepts and how they were used during argumentations.

With that previous goal in mind, this book has been organized into seven chapters. They have aimed to show that the speeches selected usually relied on the rhetorical usage of resources from the history of political thought, legal theory, and parliamentary history. Taking into consideration this theoretical background it has been possible to identify argumentative links between ideologies and the diverse meanings of political concepts. However, it also has highlighted how constituent representatives resorted to ideas of political philosophy to justify their positions.

The first chapter, 'Examining Political Rhetoric in Spanish Constitutional Debates', of an introductory character, has argued that constitutional debates are a fertile realm to investigate the development of political concepts in the course of parliamentary argumentations. It has delved into the conflicting meanings that basic political concepts acquire when they are rhetorically used, as in this case, to defend the purpose, contents, and structure of a new constitution. The analysis of parliamentary speeches of constituent assemblies allows us to further explore the controversies affecting every political issue about how to build institutions and enshrine constitutional freedoms.

'A Survey of Constitutional Debates in Spain's Nineteenth Century', the second chapter, has presented the constitutional debates of the nineteenth century focusing on the conceptual disagreements around the ideas of sovereignty, constituent power, constituted power and nation that shaped liberal constitutions. Political philosophy ideas were thoroughly debated when applied to the writing of the Spanish constitutions that came into force in that century: those of 1812, 1837, 1845, 1869, and 1876. But they were so also regarding the acknowledgement of constitutional freedoms.

In 1812 liberal representatives gave expression to a new language of individual freedoms and constitutional rights. Ideological and intellectual disagreements between the so-called moderate and progressive liberals explain the historical development of constitutionalism, liberalism, and republicanism during the second half of that century, making sense of the complexities and diversity of the liberal tradition.

Chapter 3, 'The Historical Framework of Spain's Twentieth-Century Constitutional Debates', has contextualized the features of democracy that representatives highlighted in their speeches during the Constituent Assemblies of 1931 and 1977–1978. First, it has presented the ideological groups that had a prominent role in the Constituent Assembly, from traditionalism to classic liberalism, democratic socialism and Jacobin radicalism of French roots. Second, it has pointed out how 1931 and 1977–1978 were the two benchmarks of democratization in Spain's history. Third, the chapter has argued that terrorism was the looming threat against democracy that jeopardized the politics of consensus, gradual and open to disagreements. Fourth, it has remarked that the Constitution of 1978 took inspiration from the post-World War II democratic experiences and constitutions of Germany, Italy, and France.

Chapter 4, 'Understanding Democracy in the Constitutional Debates of 1931 and 1977–1978', pays attention to the contrast between the model of 'integral state' envisaged in 1931 and the decentralized state of Autonomous Communities agreed in 1977–1978. Both designs of the structure of the state relied on similar grounds. First, they sought to strengthen the new democratic state by decentralizing state competences handed to regions and Autonomous Communities respectively. Second, they intended to lessen nationalist demands with secessionist pretensions. And third, a partial decentralization of competences, so it was argued, could have the potential to improve the administration by obtaining higher levels of efficiency in providing public services.

The chapter has argued that it is valuable from a methodological point of view to distinguish two models of federalism in agreement with each one of the constitutional debates of Spain. In 1931 the integral state enhanced a modern understanding of institutions and self-rule to foster political stability by clarifying the distribution of competences between the state and the regions. That clarification was left out in the constitutional debate held between May and October 1978, after being decided that the distribution of competences between the state and the Autonomous Communities should be specified through ordinary laws in a later phase. Autonomy statutes for some territories such as Catalonia and the Basque Country seemed a more feasible alternative to better distribute competences. In that sense, regional autonomy and self-rule were interpreted as connected to the respect for the capacity of the state and public powers to intervene in economic and social matters by means of ordinary legislation.

Chapter 5, 'Competing Meanings of the New Democratic State', explains how Union of Democratic Centre standardized the idea of reform as closely linked to the very idea of parliamentary democracy. Democracy was conceived of as a regime of gradual reforms based on political and social pluralism and the respect for minority rights and majority rule. Then, representative democracy necessarily opposed revolution. To the Spanish Socialist Workers' Party the ideas of revolution and reform did not exclude each other. Revolutionary aims worked as a rhetorical hinge appealing to deep political reforms that benefited workers and would make the decentralization of state competences possible. Despite that fact, the party did not refuse the idea of reform, also useful to demand political changes that could be more or less gradual and that should be included in the Constitution.

The sixth chapter, 'Constitutional State Powers', has reviewed the meanings of sovereignty and the rule of law. There, it has examined the meanings of the ideas of popular and national sovereignty to outline that both of them were generally understood as synonyms. Union of Democratic Centre, the Spanish Socialist Workers' Party, the Communist Party of Spain, and Popular Alliance upheld that the bearer of sovereignty was the Spanish people as a whole, though there were discrepancies about the national features of the country.

To the majority of representatives of the Union of Democratic Centre and the conservative Popular Alliance national sovereignty was not divisible. The whole Spanish nation was the source of democratic legitimacy. To the Spanish Socialist Workers' Party and the Communist Party of Spain there were different nations within Spain that in no case justify the division of sovereignty between different peoples.

Instead, the nationalist parties of Catalonia and the Basque Country, the Democratic Pact for Catalonia, Republican Left of Catalonia, the Basque Nationalist Party and Euskadi's Left (*Euskadiko Ezkerra*) argued that each one of the historical regions of the so-called 'Spanish state', namely, Catalonia, the Basque Country and Galicia, enjoyed original sovereignty. They criticized that the bearer of sovereignty was a unitary source, to rather claim that each one of the peoples within Spain had an original sovereignty that sustained not the right to self-rule, but to self-determination or secession. That position was rejected by Union of Democratic Centre, the Spanish Socialist Workers' Party and Popular Alliance as detrimental to democratic institutions and to the very idea of Spain as a country.

Chapter 6 has explored the debates around the division of state powers and the rule of law. In that case, the Democratic Pact for Catalonia agreed with national parties that the independence of the judiciary from the rest of the powers by reinforcing the General Council of the Judiciary (*Consejo General del Poder Judicial*) was positive. Despite the parliamentary defence by a majority of parties of the separation and clear constitutional limits to the executive and the legislative powers, some mechanisms to ensure political stability for governments made it possible for the executive power to appoint some of the members of the Supreme Court (*Tribunal Supremo*). However, the independence of the judiciary was regarded as indispensable to shelter democratic institutions.

Chapter 7, 'The Decentralization of Spain as a Political Nation', has surveyed the two general interpretations of the idea of regional autonomy advanced by political parties and representatives. In a nutshell, that idea received either an interpretation in terms of self-rule as self-government for territories or a meaning that made it closer to self-determination. The chapter has highlighted the clashes between, on the one hand, the Union of Democratic Centre, Popular Alliance, a number of independent senators and, on the other hand, the nationalist parties of Catalonia and the Basque Country.

To the former, the Spanish Constitution should imitate the design of provincial decentralization of France, even though the degree of state decentralization of competences handed to regions could be much higher in Spain. The latter presented a completely decentralized state not based on self-rule but in the idea of a vague understanding of self-determination. Thus, self-determination worked as a trump card to vindicate a higher level of decentralization than the one defended by centrist and right-wing national parties. But it also could mean that referenda were a valid mechanism to make it possible the secession of some regions from Spain. Union of Democratic Centre, Popular Alliance and some independent senators clearly precluded that possibility, as it was finally enshrined in the Constitution.

In addition, the idea of original sovereignty for Catalonia and the Basque Country was used as an argument to answer for secession from a legal point of view, though that possibility was finally rejected in the Constitution. For instance, the idea of 'nationalities' (*nacionalidades*) led to disagreements between Union of Democratic Centre and some independent senators. To representatives of Popular Alliance, and to some independent senators, the idea of 'nationalities' was just a euphemism of nation to which every party gave the connotations that better fitted their interests.

Unlike Popular Alliance and some independent senators, national left-wing parties and nationalist parties of Catalonia and the Basque Country defended that Spain consisted of several nations with differentiated cultural aspects. That view meant a specific treatment in the Constitution and a high degree of self-rule, when not self-determination in secessionist terms to nationalist parties. In that wise, to Catalan and Basque nationalist parties, the idea of a single political nation derived from shared institutions vanished as a valid political project of nation.

The seventh chapter has presented the conflicting interpretations of Spain as a nation. The Union of Democratic Centre and Popular Alliance imagined Spain as a political nation culturally diverse. To them the several languages of Spain were the patrimony of all Spaniards, though this should not advocate an ethnic understanding of territories. The source of the Spanish nation could be to some extent historically founded on Christian medieval kingdoms. But that point of view about the Spanish nation was incomplete or simply wrong if it would leave out the parliamentary and constitutional history of Spain that began with the General and Extraordinary *Cortes* (Cortes Generales y Extraordinarias) of Cadiz between 1810 and 1812.

The nationalist parties of Catalonia and the Basque Country argued for an ethnic understanding of their territories and political institutions. In order to maintain that Catalonia and the Basque Country were nations, these parties referred to either so-called historical rights such as the *foral* regime or to linguistic particularities. Their idea of nation openly rejected the parliamentary and constitutional tradition of all territories of Spain founded on the equal rights of a political community.

Chapter 8, 'Liberalism and Democracy in Contemporary Spain', has surveyed current challenges to liberal democracy in Spain. The transitions to democracy that other southern European countries such as Portugal and Greece underwent in the 1970s shows that political pluralism is not merely a choice, but the cornerstone to building responsive public powers. Individual freedoms within a constitutional state are the source of democratic legitimacy that the checks and balances of liberal constitutionalism protect against arbitrariness. No democracy can dispense with the baseline of liberal constitutionalism without eroding its legitimate foundations and transmuting itself into a different sort of regime.

2 The Potentialities of Parliamentary Argumentation in a Constituent Assembly

The findings of this research have emphasized the potentialities of arguments of political philosophy to identify how political concepts were used during the constitutional debates. Those arguments shaped the institutions of each parliamentary regime, from 1812 to 1978. In addition, this study has aimed to advance towards a more accurate understanding of the conceptual controversies in constituent assemblies. Thus, it has facilitated both to compare constitutional debates in the analysis and to survey the conceptual innovations produced during those debates.

This research has shown how in their deliberation representatives often provided innovative interpretations for classic political concepts and controversies. Their pervasive concern about the structure of the state led them to foresee some of the practical effects that could come about after the passing of each constitutional article. In that sense, this study has shed light on the potentialities of parliamentary speeches of constituent assemblies to identify rival meanings of political concepts. Representatives' speeches often relied on political philosophy arguments when pondering over the conceptual and institutional solutions argued.

Finally, the analysis of the parliamentary speeches in the Constituent Assembly of 1977–1978 has highlighted innovative conceptual and institutional changes when compared to the Constituent Assembly of 1931 and to nineteenth-century constitutional debates. That contrast is possible because of the parliamentary practices of constituent assemblies. There, the political vocabulary is updated, and parliamentary democratic institutions are gradually refined. In that wise, this research can arguably provide a methodological path for further research to analyse conceptual controversies through the lens of political philosophy, conceptual history and parliamentary history in other constituent assemblies.

As this book has set forth, the argumentative character of constituent assemblies accentuates the rapid increase of new meanings given to classic or traditional political concepts. By the same token, it strengthens legal and historical expertise as two empowering conditions for representatives to discuss constitutional issues with competence. Drawing on authors such as Kari Palonen, it can be argued that the rhetorical rationale of speaking *pro et contra* means to understand constituent assemblies through the lens of the necessarily conflicting views about each issue at stake. Those assemblies are characterized by the need to discuss the items of the agenda, in this case, a constitutional draft, from opposite points of view.

Spanish constituent assemblies provide a deliberative framework to compare diverse and rival political ideas argued by the intervening representatives. That is interpreted as an essential condition of politics to understand parliamentary debates in their rhetorical dimension, addressed to different audiences, ranging from fellow representatives to journalists and citizens. The outlook that constitutional debates offers to pinpoint the ups and downs of national institutions and their changing language is irreplaceable. Viewing constituent assemblies as settings of political innovation leads to research findings that would be impossible to achieve otherwise.

Bibliography

Legal Sources

Constitución Española de 1978. Available at: http://www.congreso.es/docu/constituciones/1978/1978_cd.pdf

Law 46/1977, of 15 October, of Amnesty [Ley 46/1977, de 15 de octubre, de Amnistía]. Available at: https://www.boe.es/buscar/pdf/1977/BOE-A-1977-24937-consolidado.pdf

Preliminary Draft of the Constitution of 1978 [*Anteproyecto de constitución de 1978*]. Available at: http://www.congreso.es/public_oficiales/L0/CONG/BOCG/BOC_044.PDF

Proceedings of the Constituent Assembly, 1977–1979. [*Diario de Sesiones de la Legislatura Constituyente, 1977–1979*, DSLC]. Available at: https://www.congreso.es/web/guest/indice-de-publicaciones?p_p_id=publicaciones&p_p_lifecycle=0&p_p_state=normal&p_p_mode=view&_publicaciones_selectedLeg=0

Proceedings of the Constituent Assembly of the Spanish Second Republic [*Diario de Sesiones de las Cortes Constituyentes de la República Española*, DSCCRE]. Available at: https://app.congreso.es/est_sesiones/

Proposal for an Organic Law of amnesty for Institutional, Political and Social Normalization in Catalonia [*Proposición de Ley Orgánica de amnistía para la normalización institucional, política y social en Cataluña*]. Available at: https://www.congreso.es/public_oficiales/L15/CONG/BOCG/B/BOCG-15-B-32-1.PDF

F. J. Bellido, *Constitutional Debates, Rhetoric, and Political Philosophy in Spain's Parliamentary History*, Rhetoric, Politics and Society,
https://doi.org/10.1007/978-3-031-56894-7

Provisional Standing Orders of the Congress of Deputies [*Reglamento provisional del Congreso de los Diputados*], 13 October 1977. Available at: https://www.boe.es/buscar/doc.php?id=BOE-A-1977-25701
Provisional Standing Orders of the Senate [*Reglamento provisional del Senado*], 14 October 1977. Available at: https://www.boe.es/buscar/doc.php?id=BOE-A-1977-25702
Spanish Constitution of 1978. Available at: http://www.congreso.es/portal/page/portal/Congreso/Congreso/Hist_Normas/Norm/const_espa_texto_ingles_0.pdf

Newspapers

ABC (1903–).
Avui (1976–2011).
Cambio 16 (1971–).
Cuadernos para el Diálogo (1963–1978).
El País (1976–).
Egin (1977–1998).
El Socialista (1886–).
La Vanguardia (1881–).
La Voz de Galicia (1882–).
Triunfo (1946–1982).

References

ABC Editorial (1977). 'Un gobierno estable', *ABC*, 21 December, 2.
Abella, Carlos (2006). 'El primer gobierno de UCD', in *Adolfo Suárez. El hombre clave de la Transición*. Madrid: Espasa.
Aguiar de Luque, Luis (1981). 'Las garantías constitucionales de los derechos fundamentales en la Constitución española', *Revista de Derecho Político*, 10, 107–29.
Aguilar, Paloma (2002). 'The Memory of War and the Lessons of Peace in the Democratic Transition', in *Memory and Amnesia: The Role of the Spanish Civil War in the Transition to Democracy*, trans. Mark Oakley. New York: Berghahn.
Aguilera de Prat, Cesáreo (1990). 'El Estado de la Autonomías en el discurso político de Convergencia Democrática de Catalunya', *Papers. Revista de Sociología*, 34, 115–37.
Aguirre Bellver, Joaquín (1978). *Así se hizo la Constitución*. Valencia: Francisco Manuel Mas.
Aja, Eliseo (1989). 'La distribución de competencias entre el Estado y Comunidades Autónomas en España. Balance y perspectivas', *Revista del Centro de Estudios Constitucionales*, 4, 233–54.

Albadalejo, Tomás (2011). 'Los discursos del conflicto y los conflictos del discurso. Análisis interdiscursivo y retórica cultural', in *Vozes, Discursos e Identidades em Conflito*, eds. Ana Gabriela Macedo, Carlos Mendes de Sousa & Vítor Moura. Braga: Húmus.

Albadalejo, Tomás (2013). 'The Cortes of Cadiz: Discourses for the Constitution and for the Everyday Life', in *1812 Echoes: The Cadiz Constitution in Hispanic History, Culture and Politics*, eds. Stephen G. H. Roberts & Adam Sharman. Newcastle upon Tyne: Cambridge Scholars Publishing.

Alonso-Castrillo, Silvia (1996). 'El apogeo de la UCD', in *La apuesta del centro. Historia de la UCD*. Madrid: Alianza.

Álvarez Borjabad, David (2014). 'Entrevistas personales', in *Periodistas y políticos en la construcción de la democracia española. Estudio de las entrevistas de personalidad en las primeras elecciones de la Transición (1977 y 1979)* (Doctoral Thesis). Madrid: Universidad Complutense.

Álvarez Conde, Enrique (1978). 'La Constitución española de 30 de junio de 1876. Cuestiones previas', *Revista de Estudios Políticos*, 3, 79–100.

Alzaga Villaamil, Óscar (1978). *Comentario sistemático a la Constitución española de 1978*. Madrid: Foro.

Alzaga Villaamil, Óscar (2018). 'El proceso constituyente español visto por uno de sus protagonistas. Entrevista a Óscar Alzaga Villaamil', *Historia Constitucional*, 19, 1–16.

Andrade Blanco, Juan (2015). *El PCE y el PSOE en (la) transición. La evolución ideológica de la izquierda durante el proceso de cambio político*. Madrid: Siglo XXI.

Aparicio Pérez, Antonio (1988). 'La nueva estructura del Estado español. Especial consideración al principio de autonomía', in *Jornadas de estudio sobre el Título Preliminar de la Constitución*, vol. II. Madrid: Ministerio de Justicia.

Aquillué Domínguez, Daniel (2015). 'La Constitución de 1837, ¿una Constitución transaccional?', *Revista Historia Autónoma*, 6, 45–49.

Aragón, María Aurora (1989). 'Traducciones de obras francesas en la "Gaceta de Madrid" entre 1790 y 1799', in *Imágenes de Francia en las letras hispánicas*: [Symposium held at the University of Barcelona, 15 to 18 November 1988], 261–70. Barcelona: Promociones y Publicaciones Universitarias.

Aragón Reyes, Manuel (1989). *Constitución y democracia*. Madrid: Tecnos.

Ariño Ortiz, Gaspar (1985). 'El Estado de las autonomías', in *La España de las autonomías*, ed. Fernando Fernández Rodríguez. Madrid: Ministerio de Administración Territorial.

Artola, Miguel (1973). 'Guerra y revolución', in *La burguesía revolucionaria (1808–1874)*. Madrid: Alianza.

Balaguer Callejón, Francisco (1988). 'Soberanía popular y democracia en la Constitución española de 1978', in *Jornadas de estudio sobre el Título Preliminar de la Constitución*, vol. II. Madrid: Ministerio de Justicia.

Baro Pazos, Juan (1987). 'Hacia la consolidación del régimen parlamentario en España. El Congreso de los Diputados en la Constitución de 1837', *Revista de Estudios Políticos*, 57, 55–106.

Bell, David (1983). 'The Spanish Communist Party in the Transition', in *Democratic Politics in Spain: Spanish Politics After Franco*, ed. David Bell. London: Frances Pinter.

Belmonte, José (1979). *La Constitución. Texto y Contexto.* Madrid: Prensa Española.

Ben-Ami, Shlomo (1978). *The Origins of the Second Republic in Spain.* Oxford: Oxford University Press.

Benet, Josep (1978). 'Todavía sobre el término nacionalidades', *El País*, 21 June, https://elpais.com/diario/1978/06/30/opinion/268005605_850215.html

Bermeo, Nancy (1987). 'Redemocratization and Transition Elections: A Comparison of Spain and Portugal', *Comparative Politics*, 19(2), 213–31.

Bermeo, Nancy (1997). 'Myths of Moderation: Confrontation and Conflict During Democratic Transitions', *Comparative Politics*, 29(3), 305–22.

Bermeo, Nancy (2007). 'War and Democratization: Lessons from the Portuguese Experience', *Democratization*, 14(3), 388–406.

Blanco Sío-López, Cristina (2019). 'Transitional Margins to Re-join the West', in *Spain's Dual Strategy of Democratisation and Europeanisation.* London & New York: Routledge.

Bolaños Mejías, Carmen (1998). 'Soberanía nacional y soberanía compartida en la estructura política de la Constitución española de 1869', *Boletín de la Facultad de Derecho*, 13, 183–99.

Cambio 16 Editorial (1978). 'Todos para uno…', *Cambio 16*, 14 May, 64.

Cambio 16 Editorial (1978). 'Viva la consentida', *Cambio 16*, 12 November, 22–24.

Camus García, Estela (2015). *En torno al liberalismo de Agustín Argüelles. Una aproximación a la construcción política e intelectual de la idea de España* (Doctoral Thesis). Dir. Jesús M. Rodés. Barcelona: Universidad Autónoma de Barcelona.

Canosa Usera, Raúl (1992). *Legitimación autonómica en el proceso constitucional.* Madrid: Trivium.

Capellán de Miguel, Gonzalo (2002). 'Representación', in *Diccionario político y social del siglo XIX español*, eds. Javier Fernández Sebastián & Juan Francisco Fuentes. Madrid: Alianza.

Carrillo, Santiago (1993). 'La transición democrática', in *Memorias.* Barcelona: Planeta.

Christiansen, Eric C. (2018). 'Forty Years from Fascism: Democratic Constitutionalism and the Spanish Model of National Transformation', *Oregon Review of International Law*, 20(1), 1–78.

Chueca, Fernando (1977). 'Centralismo o pluricentralismo', *El País*, 23 August, https://elpais.com/diario/1977/08/23/opinion/241135209_850215.html

Cisneros, Gabriel (2003). 'Historia de un éxito incompleto', in *Reflexiones de los ponentes de la Constitución española (1978–2003)*, ed. Gabriel Cisneros et al. Pamplona: Aranzadi.

Cisneros Laborda, Gabriel et al. (1998). *20 años después. La Constitución cara al siglo XXI*. Madrid: Taurus.

Colomer, Josep M. (1995). *Game Theory and the Transition to Democracy: The Spanish Model*. Aldershot & Brookfield: Edward Elgar Publishing.

Colomer, Josep M. (1998). *La transición a la democracia. El modelo español*. Barcelona: Anagrama.

Conversi, Daniele (2002). 'The Smooth Transition: Spain's 1978 Constitution and the Nationalities Question', *National Identities*, 4(3), 223–44.

Corcuera Atienza, Francisco Javier (1991). 'El constitucionalismo de entreguerras y la Constitución española de 1931', *Historia Contemporánea*, 6, 15–46.

Costa Pinto, António (2006). 'Authoritarian Legacies, Transitional Justice and State Crisis in Portugal's Democratization', *Democratization*, 13(2), 173–204.

Cotarelo, Ramón (1992). *Transición política y consolidación democrática, España (1975–1986)*. Madrid: Centro de Investigaciones Sociológicas.

Crawley, Charles W. (1939). 'French and English Influences in the Cortes of Cadiz, 1810–1814', *The Cambridge Historical Journal*, 6(2), 176–208.

Cuadernos para el Diálogo Reportage (1977). 'Esta es la Constitución', *Cuadernos para el Diálogo*, 26 November, 14.

Cuadernos para el Diálogo Interview (1977). 'La unidad de España. Jamás Constitución alguna fue tan tajante', *Cuadernos para el Diálogo*, 31 December, 16.

Del Águila, Rafael (1982). 'La Transición a la democracia en España. Reforma, ruptura y consenso', *Revista de Estudios Políticos*, 25, 101–27.

Del Águila, Rafael & Ricardo Montoro (1984). *El discurso político de la transición española*. Madrid: Centro de Investigaciones Sociológicas.

Demarchi, Giacomo (2016). *Provincia y territorio en la Constituyente española de 1931. Las raíces europeas del Estado integral*. Madrid: Universidad Carlos III de Madrid.

De Nadal, Luis (2021). 'On Populism and Social Movements: From the Indignados to Podemos', *Social Movement Studies*, 20(1), 36–56.

De Santiago Guervós, Javier (1992). *El léxico político de la transición española*. Salamanca: Universidad de Salamanca.

Díaz Barrado, Mario P. (2013). 'El discurso político en la Transición democrática. Ideología y expectativas de poder en el debate en torno a la Constitución de 1978', in *Los partidos en la Transición. Las organizaciones políticas en la construcción de la democracia española*, ed. Rafael Quirosa-Cheyrouze y Muñoz. Madrid: Biblioteca Nueva.

Díaz Fernández, Paloma (2006). 'La Constitución de 1837. ¿Qué tipo de Monarquía queremos?', *Historia Contemporánea*, 18, 73–89.

Díez-Picazo, Luis María & Ascensión Elvira Perales (2008). *La Constitución de 1978*. Madrid: Iustel.

Duso, Giuseppe (2007). 'Politica e filosofia', in *La logica del potere. Storia concettuale come filosofia politica*. Milan: Polimetrica.

Elkins, Zachary, Tom Ginsburg & James Melton eds. (2009). 'What Makes Constitution Endure?', in *The Endurance of National Constitutions*. Cambridge: Cambridge University Press.

El País Editorial (1977). 'Las nacionalidades, primera piedra de toque para el debate de la Constitución', *El País*, 27 December, https://elpais.com/diario/1977/12/27/espana/252025202_850215.html

Elster, Jon (1995). 'Forces and Mechanisms in the Constitution-Making Process', *Duke Law Journal*, 45, 364–96.

El Socialista Editorial (1977). 'Por la senda constitucional', *El Socialista*, 7 May, 8, http://archivo.fpabloiglesias.es/files/Hemeroteca/ElSocialista/1977/5-1977/3.pdf

Escobar Fornos, Iván (2012). 'La Constitución de Cádiz. Modelo de constitucionalismo', *Anuario Iberoamericano de Justicia Constitucional*, 16, 165–89.

Fernandes, Tiago (2015). 'Rethinking Pathways to Democracy: Civil Society in Portugal and Spain, 1960s–2000s', *Democratization*, 22(6), 1074–104.

Fernández Sarasola, Ignacio (2002). *La función de gobierno en la Constitución española de 1978*. Oviedo: Universidad de Oviedo.

Fernández Sarasola, Ignacio (2009). *Los partidos políticos en el pensamiento español. De la Ilustración a nuestros días*. Madrid: Marcial Pons.

Fernández Sarasola, Ignacio (2010). 'La opinión pública. De la Ilustración a las Cortes de Cádiz', *Ayer. Revista de Historia Contemporánea*, 80(4), 53–81.

Fernández Sarasola, Ignacio (2016). ''So, You Want Us to Be Englishmen…': Jovellanos and British Influence on Spain's First Modern Parliament (1808–1810)', *Comparative Legal History*, 4(1), 51–81.

Fernández-Sebastián, Javier & José María Rosales (2018). 'A Conceptual History of Democracy in Spain Since 1800', in *Democracy in Modern Europe: A Conceptual History*, eds. Jussi Kurunmäki, Jeppe Nevers & Henk te Velde. New York & Oxford: Berghahn.

Fernández Segado, Francisco (1983). 'Pragmatismo jurídico y concertación política. Dos ideas-clave en la obra de los constituyentes de 1837', *Revista de Derecho Político*, 20, 33–65.

Ferrando Badía, Juan (1977). '¿Estado federal o Estado regional?', *El País*, 11 December, https://elpais.com/diario/1977/12/11/opinion/250642808_850215.html

Finlayson, Alan (2017). 'What Is the Point of Parliamentary Debate? Deliberation, Oratory, Opposition and Spectacle in the British House of Commons',

Redescriptions: Political Thought, Conceptual History, and Feminist Theory, 20(1), 11–31.

Fishman, Robert M. (2017). 'How Civil Society Matters in Democratization: Setting the Boundaries of Post-transition Political Inclusion', *Comparative Politics*, 49(3), 391–409.

Fishman, Robert M. & Omar Lizardo (2013). 'How Macro-Historical Change Shapes Cultural Taste: Legacies of Democratization in Spain and Portugal', *American Sociological Review*, 78(2), 213–39.

Fraga, Manuel (1978). *La Constitución y otras cuestiones fundamentales.* Barcelona: Planeta.

Freeden, Michael (2017). 'Conceptual History, Ideology and Language', in *Conceptual History in the European Space*, eds. William Steinmetz, Michael Freeden & Javier Fernández-Sebastián. New York: Berghahn.

Freixes Sanjuán, María Teresa (1984). 'Crónica de una Constitución consensuada', *Revista de Estudios Políticos*, 40, 101–22.

Fuentes, Juan Francisco (2008). 'Reforma', in *Diccionario político y social del siglo XX español*, eds. Javier Fernández Sebastián & Juan Francisco Fuentes. Madrid: Alianza.

Fuentes, Juan Francisco (2010). 'Las Cortes de Cádiz: Nación, soberanía y territorio', *Cuadernos de Historia Contemporánea*, 32, 17–35.

Fuentes, Juan Francisco (2020). *23 febrero 1981. El golpe que acabó con todos los golpes*. Barcelona: Taurus.

Fusi, Juan Pablo (2017). 'De la dictadura a la democracia', in *Espacios de libertad. La cultura española bajo el franquismo y la reinvención de la democracia en España (1960–1990).* Barcelona: Galaxia Gutenberg.

Gallego Díaz, Soledad & José Luis Martínez García (1978). 'La última cena constitucional', *Cuadernos para el Diálogo*, 29 July, 12.

Galston, William A. (2020). 'The Enduring Vulnerability of Constitutional Democracy', *The Journal of Democracy*, 31(3), 8–24.

García Atance, María Victoria (1983). 'Crónica parlamentaria de la Constitución de 1837', *Revista de Derecho Político*, 20, 171–83.

García Canales, Mariano (1977). *La teoría de la representación en la España del siglo XX*. Murcia: Universidad de Murcia.

García Escudero, José María & María Asunción García Martínez (1998). *La Constitución día a día. Los grandes temas de la Constitución de 1978 en el debate parlamentario.* Madrid: Congreso de los Diputados.

García Morillo, Joaquín (1996). *La democracia en España.* Madrid: Alianza.

Garrorena Morales, Ángel (2011). 'El debate justicia constitucional-democracia en los procesos constituyentes de 1931 y 1978', *Revista Española de Derecho Constitucional*, 91, 31–68.

González Rivas, Juan José (1988). 'XI Jornadas de estudio de la Dirección General del Servicio Jurídico del Estado sobre el tema: Título Preliminar de la

Constitución', in *Jornadas sobre el Título Preliminar de la Constitución*, vol. I. Madrid: Ministerio de Justicia.
González Rodríguez, Hortensia (2002). 'La forma de gobierno en el debate constituyente de 1869', *Revista de Derecho Político*, 55–56, 365–410.
Gunther, Richard (1986). 'El proceso constituyente español', *Revista de Estudios Políticos*, 49, 33–61.
Gurpegui, José Antonio (2018) 'Historical Determinism in the Constitutions of the United States and the Spanish of 1812', *Complutense Journal of English Studies*, 26, 9–25.
Haro Tecglen, Eduardo (1978). 'La Constitución y el compromiso', *Triunfo*, 13 May.
Hernández Gil, Antonio (1983). 'Facetas de dos procesos constituyentes', *Revista de Estudios Políticos*, 31–32, 11–24.
Hijano Pérez, Ángeles (2016). 'Las claves de la monarquía en las Cortes de Cádiz', *Rúbrica Contemporánea*, 5(9), 123–44.
Ihalainen, Pasi, Cornelia Ilie & Kari Palonen eds. (2016). *Parliaments and Parliamentarism: A Comparative History of Disputes on a European Concept*. New York: Berghahn.
Ilie, Cornelia (2022). 'How to Argue with Questions and Answers: Argumentation Strategies in Parliamentary Deliberation', *Languages*, 7(205), 1–19.
Iñesta, Emilia (2010). 'The Spanish Parliament and Legislative Delegation (1844–1849)', *Parliaments, Estates & Representation*, 30(1), 41–56.
Jaroszyk, Joanna (2020). 'Spain as the State of Autonomies: Principles Behind the Territorial Organization Between 1978 and 1983', *Humanities and Social Sciences*, 27(4), 29–38.
Kaloudis, George (2000). 'Transitional Democratic Politics in Greece', *International Journal on World Pace*, 17(1), 35–59.
Karamouzi, Eirini (2015). 'A Strategy for Greece: Democratization and European Integration, 1974–75', *Cahiers de la Méditerranée*, 90, 11–24.
Kornetis, Kostis (2019). 'Projections Onto the Past: Memories of Democratization in Spain, Greece, and Portugal During the Great Recession', *Mobilization: An International Quarterly*, 24(4), 511–24.
Lario, Ángeles (2021). 'The Consolidation of the Constitutional Monarchic System (1874–1902)', in *Monarchy and Liberalism in Spain: The Building of the Nation-State, 1780–1931*, eds. David San Narciso, Margarita Barral-Martínez & Carolina Armenteros. London & New York: Routledge.
Lavilla Rubira, Juan José (1998). 'El problema regional en tiempos de la II República', in *Terceras Jornadas Niceto Alcalá-Zamora y su época*, ed. José Manuel Cuenca Toribio. Córdoba: Patronato Niceto Alcalá-Zamora.
La Voz de Galicia Reportage (1978). 'Simposio sobre administración, economía y autonomía en Galicia', *La Voz de Galicia*, 27 June, 21.

Linz, Juan José (1985). 'De la crisis de un estado unitario al estado de las autonomías', in *La España de las autonomías*, ed. Fernando Fernández Rodríguez. Madrid: Ministerio de Administración Territorial.

López Rodó, Laureano (1984). *Estado y Comunidades Autónomas*. Madrid: Abella.

López Sánchez, Carmina (2014). 'La soberanía compartida de 1876 frente a la soberanía nacional de 1812', *Revista de Historiografía*, 20, 189–98.

Lucas Verdú, Pablo (1978). 'La singularidad del proceso constituyente español', *Revista de Estudios Políticos*, 1, 9–27.

Lucas Verdú, Pablo (1985). 'El Estado autonómico como pluralidad institucional integrada', in *Comentarios a las leyes políticas*, vol. X, ed. Óscar Alzaga Villaamil. Madrid: Edersa.

Lucas Verdú, Pablo (1994). 'Reflexiones en torno y dentro del concepto de constitución. La constitución como norma y como integración política', *Revista de Estudios Políticos*, 83, 9–28.

Luengo, Jorge & Paul Dalmau (2018). 'Writing Spanish History in the Global Age: Connections and Entanglements in the Nineteenth Century', *Journal of Global History*, 13, 425–45.

Luis, Jean-Philippe (2021). 'The Mutations of the Spanish Monarchy', in *Monarchy and Liberalism in Spain: The Building of the Nation State, 1780–1931*, eds. David San Narciso, Margarita Barral-Martínez & Carolina Armenteros. New York: Routledge.

Luna-Fabritius, Adriana (2012). 'Defining the Borders for an Interpretation of the Concept of Liberalism in Cádiz's Constitutional Moment 1810–1812', Working Paper, Centro de Investigación y Docencia Económicas (CIDE), 78, 1–22.

Magone, Jose M. (2013). *Politics in Contemporary Portugal: Democracy Evolving*. Bouldon: Lynne Rienner.

Marchi, Riccardo & André Azevedo Alves (2023). 'The Right and Far-Right in the Portuguese Democracy (1974–2022)', in *The Oxford Handbook to Portuguese Politics*, eds. Jorge M. Fernandes, Pedro C. Magalhães & António Costa Pinto. Oxford: Oxford University Press.

Marías, Julián (1978). '¿No es esto?', *El País*, 21 January, https://elpais.com/diario/1978/01/21/opinion/254185207_850215.html

Marichal, Carlos (1980). *La revolución liberal y los primeros partidos políticos en España: 1834–1844*. Madrid: Cátedra.

Martín Oviedo, José María (1988). 'De las Comunidades Autónomas', in *Comentarios a las leyes políticas*, vol. XI, ed. Óscar Alzaga Villaamil. Madrid: Edersa.

Martínez Roda, Federico & Maria Inácia Rezola (2016). 'Spanish Monarchy and the Portuguese Republic: Two Routes of Democratization', *Portuguese Journal of Social Science*, 15(1), 129–43.

Martínez Sospedra, Manuel (1981). 'Las fuentes de la Constitución de 1876. Continuidad y cambio en el constitucionalismo español del siglo XIX', *Revista de Derecho Político*, 8, 71–96.

Matei, Florina Cristiana, Andrés de Castro García & Carolyn C. Halladay (2018). 'On Balance: Intelligence Democratization in Post-Franco Spain', *International Journal of Intelligence and Counterintelligence*, 31(4), 769–804.

Mateos, Abdón (1996). 'Una transición dentro de la transición. Auge, unidad y conversión de los socialistas', in *Historia de la transición (1975–1986)*, ed. Javier Tusell & Álvaro Soto. Madrid: Alianza.

Medina Muñoz, Miguel Ángel (1976). 'Las Cortes en la Constitución de 1845', *Revista de Estudios Políticos*, 208–209, 131–48.

Merino Merchán, José Fernando (1988). 'Valores superiores del ordenamiento. Artículo 1.1 de la Constitución', in *Jornadas de estudio sobre el Título Preliminar de la Constitución*, vol. V. Madrid: Ministerio de Justicia.

Mirow, Matthew C. (2010). 'Visions of Cadiz: The Constitution of 1812 in Historical and Constitutional Thought', *Studies in Law, Politics and Society*, 53, 59–88.

Montero, José Ramón (1981). 'Partidos y participación política. Algunas notas sobre la afiliación política en la etapa inicial de la transición española', *Revista de Estudios Políticos*, 23, 33–72.

Morán, Gregorio (1979). *Adolfo Suárez. Historia de una ambición*. Barcelona: Planeta.

Morán, Gregorio ([1991] 2015). *El precio de la transición*, 2nd ed. Madrid: Akal.

Mora-Sanguinetti, Juan S. & Rok Spruk (2023). 'Economic Effects of Recent Experiences of Federalism: Analysis of the Regionalization Process in Spain', *Journal of Regional Science*, 63(1), 30–63.

Morodo, Raúl (1984). *La transición política*. Madrid: Tecnos.

Müßig, Ulrike ed. (2016). *Reconsidering Constitutional Formation: National Sovereignty. A Comparative Analysis of the Juridification by Constitution*. New York: Springer.

Müller, Marius (2016). 'The Notion of Sovereignty in the Constitutional Process of Cádiz', *Ivs Fvgit. Revista de Cultura Jurídica*, 19, 177–208.

Muñoz Machado, Santiago (2004). 'La configuración histórica de las principales características de la Constitución como norma jurídica', in *Constitución*. Madrid: Iustel.

Muñoz Sánchez, Antonio (2017). 'Un padrino en Europa. La República Federal de Alemania y España durante la presidencia de Adolfo Suárez', in *Adolfo Suárez y la transición política*, ed. Manuel Redero San Román. Salamanca: Universidad de Salamanca.

Nieto Sánchez, Carlos (2017). 'Soberanía nacional y monarquía. La oposición republicana a la opción monárquica en la Constitución de 1869', *Fides et Ratio*, 2, 65–78.

Núñez Rivero, José María Cayetano (1983). 'Inviolabilidad e inmunidad en la Constitución de 1837', *Revista de Derecho Político*, 20, 151–59.

Oller, Josep M., Albert Satorra & Adolf Tobeña (2020). 'Privileged Rebels: A Longitudinal Analysis of Distinctive Economic Traits of Catalonian Secessionism', *Genealogy*, 4(19), 1–17.

Ollero Tassara, Andrés (1994). 'El parlamentarismo en el sistema político español', *Revista de las Cortes Generales*, 31, 7–30.

Ortega Álvarez, Luis (2003). 'El modelo español de control sobre las autonomías territoriales', *Revista General de Derecho Administrativo*, 2, 1–11.

Palonen, Kari (2008). *The Politics of Limited Times: The Rhetoric of Temporal Judgment in Parliamentary Democracies*. Baden-Baden: Nomos.

Palonen, Kari (2012). 'Parliamentary Procedure as an Inventory of Disputes. A Comparison Between Jeremy Bentham and Thomas Erskine May', *Res Publica. Revista de Filosofía Política*, 27, 13–25.

Palonen, Kari (2014). *The Politics of Parliamentary Procedure: The Formation of the Westminster Procedure as a Parliamentary Ideal Type*. Opladen, Berlin, & Toronto: Barbara Budrich Publishers.

Palonen, Kari (2019). *Parliamentary Thinking: Procedure, Rhetoric and Time*. Cham: Palgrave Macmillan.

Palonen, Kari & José María Rosales eds. (2015). *Parliamentarism and Democratic Theory: Historical and Contemporary Perspectives*. Opladen, Berlin, & Toronto: Barbara Budrich Publishers.

Papadogiannis, Nikolaos & Pedro Ramos Pinto (2023). 'Social Change, Protest and Participation in Greece, Portugal and Spain', *Mélanges de la Casa de Velázquez*, 53(1), 1–23.

Pascual Sastre, Isabel María (2020). 'Teoría y práctica de la monarquía nacional y democrática. La Constitución de 1869 y su forma de gobierno', *Bulletin d'Histoire Contemporaine de l'Espagne*, 55, 1–18.

Peces-Barba, Gregorio (1988a). *La elaboración de la Constitución de 1978*. Madrid: Centro de Estudios Constitucionales.

Peces-Barba, Gregorio (1988b). 'Los valores superiores', in *Jornadas sobre el Título Preliminar de la Constitución*, vol. I. Madrid: Ministerio de Justicia.

Peces-Barba, Gregorio (2002). 'Una lectura de la Constitución española', in *La organización territorial del Estado*, ed. Alfonso Cucó, Joan Romero & Joaquín Farinós. Valencia: Universitat de València.

Peces-Barba, Gregorio et al. (1978). *La izquierda y la Constitución*. Barcelona: Taula de Canvi.

Pereira, Juan Carlos (2008). 'The International Dimension of the Spanish Transition', in *The International Politics of Democratization: Comparative Perspectives*, ed. Nuno Severiano Teixeira. New York & Abingdon: Routledge.
Pérez Herrera, Gema (2020). *José Pedro Pérez-Llorca. Una biografía política.* Madrid: Centro de Estudios Políticos y Constitucionales.
Pérez Ledesma, Manuel (1991). 'Las Cortes de Cádiz y la sociedad española', *Ayer*, 1, 167–206.
Pérez-Llorca, José Pedro (1998). 'Veinte años después. Reflexiones de los padres constituyentes', in *La Constitución Española de 1978. 20 años de democracia.* Madrid: Centro de Estudios Políticos y Constitucionales.
Pérez-Llorca, José Pedro (2003). '¿Balance o liquidación?', in *Reflexiones de los ponentes de la Constitución española (1978–2003)*, ed. Gabriel Cisneros Laborda. Pamplona: Aranzadi.
Pérez-Llorca, José Pedro (2018). 'Reflexiones de un ponente constitucional', *Revista de las Cortes Generales*, 103, 637–51.
Pérez López, Pablo & Jorge Lafuente del Cano (2014). 'Diversity and Decentralization in the Democratization Process in Spain', *International Relations and Diplomacy*, 2(2), 111–19.
Pérez-Prendes, José Manuel (1981). 'Continuidad y discontinuidad en la Constitución de 1876', *Revista de Estudios Políticos*, 8, 21–32.
Ponce-Alberca, Julio (2016). 'Torcuato Fernández-Miranda', in *Political Leadership in the Spanish Transition to Democracy*, eds. José Francisco Jiménez Díaz & Santiago Delgado. New York: Nova Publishers.
Porras Nadales, Antonio (1981). 'Notas sobre la teoría del poder constituyente y la experiencia española', *Revista de Estudios Políticos*, 24, 175–200.
Powell, Charles (1996). 'International Aspects of Democratization: The Case of Spain', in *The International Dimensions of Democratisation*, ed. Laurence Whitehead. Oxford: Oxford University Press.
Ramírez, Manuel (1989). *Partidos políticos y Constitución. Un estudio de las actitudes parlamentarias durante el proceso de creación constitucional.* Madrid: Centro de Estudios Constitucionales.
Ramón Fernández, Tomás (1978). 'Las autonomías regionales', *Triunfo*, 18 February, 29.
Ramos Rovi, María José (2000). 'La Constitución de 1876 a través de los discursos parlamentarios', *Revista de Historia Contemporánea*, 9–10(1), 85–100.
Ramos Silgado, Héctor (2022). 'El clero en las Cortes constituyentes de 1836–1837', *Anuario de Historia de la Iglesia Andaluza*, 15, 259–96.
Rebollo Delgado, Lucrecio (2018). 'Antecedentes, surgimiento y conformación del Estado autonómico en la Constitución de 1978', *Revista de Derecho Político*, 101, 461–502.

Robles-Egea, Antonio (2016). 'Santiago Carrillo Solares', in *Political Leadership in the Spanish Transition to Democracy (1975–1982)*, eds. José Francisco Jiménez Díaz & Santiago Delgado Fernández. Hauppauge: Nova Science.

Romeo Mateo, María Cruz (1998). 'Lenguaje y política del nuevo liberalismo moderado y progresista, 1834–1845', *Ayer*, 29, 37–62.

Rosales, José María (2013). 'Liberalism's Historical Diversity: A Comparative Conceptual Exploration', *Contributions to the History of Concepts*, 8(2), 67–82.

Rosales, José María (2014). 'On the Irrelevant Place of Parliamentarism in Democratic Theory: Antecedents', in *The Politics of Dissensus: Parliament in Debate*, eds. Kari Palonen, José María Rosales & Tapani Turkka. Santander & Madrid: Cantabria University Press & McGraw-Hill.

Rosales, José María (2016a). 'Parliamentarism in Spanish Politics in the Nineteenth and Twentieth Centuries: From Constitutional Liberalism to Democratic Parliamentarism', in *Parliaments and Parliamentarism: A Comparative History of Disputes on a European Concept*, ed. Pasi Ihalainen, Cornelia Ilie & Kari Palonen. New York: Berghahn.

Rosales, José María (2016b). 'From Partisan to Pluralist Ideology: The Changing Practices of Democracy Through Spain's 20th-Century Constitutional Moments', *Journal of Political Ideologies*, 21(3), 225–41.

Rosales, José María (2018). 'Parliamentarism in Spanish Politics in the Nineteenth and Twentieth Centuries: From Constitutional Liberalism to Democratic Parliamentarism', in *Parliament and Parliamentarism: A Comparative History of a European Concept*, eds. Pasi Ihalainen, Cornelia Ilie & Kari Palonen. New York: Berghahn.

Rosenfeld, Michael (1998). 'Constitution-Making, Identity Building, and Peaceful Transition to Democracy: Theoretical Reflections Inspired by the Spanish Example', *Cardozo Law Review*, 19 (6), 1891–1920.

Rubio Llorente, Francisco (1977). 'Sobre constituyentes y constitucionalistas', *El País*, 26 July, https://elpais.com/diario/1977/07/26/opinion/238716012_850215.html

Rubio Llorente, Francisco (1997). *La forma del poder. Estudios sobre la Constitución*. Madrid: Centro de Estudios Constitucionales.

Saiz Valdivieso, Alfonso Carlos (1999). 'Don Emilio Castelar en las Cortes Constituyentes de 1869 (Apuntes para conmemorar un centenario olvidado)', *Estudios de Deusto*, 47(2), 171–84.

Salm, Christian (2021). 'Diffusing Democracy in Europe: The European Parliament and European Community Enlargement Policy, 1974–79', *Journal of European Integration History*, 27(1), 99–119.

Sánchez Agesta, Luis (1978). 'Una revolución a través del derecho. Cómo fue posible la Constitución de 1978', *La Vanguardia*, 20 December, 19.

Sánchez Agesta, Luis (1979). 'Algunos caracteres generales de la Constitución de 1978', *Revista de Derecho Público*, 74, 5–21.

Sánchez Ferriz, Remedio (1979). 'Aproximación al concepto de soberanía en el pensamiento de Cánovas y su consideración en las Cortes de 1876', *Estudis. Revista de Historia Moderna*, 8, 177–91.

Sánchez Ferriz, Remedio (1998). 'Cánovas y la Constitución de 1876', *Revista de Estudios Políticos*, 101, 9–44.

Sánchez-Terán, Salvador (2005). 'La legalización del Partido Comunista de España', in *La Transición. Síntesis y claves*. Barcelona: Planeta.

Sanmartí, Josep Maria (2017). 'La influencia de *El País*', in *La transición de la prensa. El comportamiento político de diarios y periodistas*, ed. Jaume Guillamet. Valencia: Universitat de València.

Sierra, María, Rafael Zurita & María Antonia Peña (2006). 'La representación política en el discurso del liberalismo español (1845–1874)', *Ayer*, 61, 15–45.

Simón Tobalina, Juan Luis (1981). *El Estado autonómico y sus matices federales*. Madrid: Instituto de Estudios de la Administración Local y Autonómica.

Smith, Angel (2016). 'The Rise and Fall of 'Respectable' Spanish Liberalism, 1808–1923: An Explanatory Framework', *Journal of Iberian and Latin American Studies*, 22(1), 55–73.

Solozábal, Juan José (1992). 'Sobre el Estado autonómico español', *Revista de Estudios Políticos*, 78, 105–29.

Souto Paz, José Antonio (2002). 'Las libertades públicas en la Constitución de 1869', *Revista de Derecho Político*, 55–56, 107–58.

Tajadura Tejada, Javier (2012). 'La problemática de los límites del poder de reforma constitucional en la Constitución de Cádiz. Límites materiales y limitación temporal', *Historia Constitucional*, 13, 257–70.

Teixeira, Nuno Severiano (2008). 'Portugal: Democratization and Foreign Policy', in *The International Politics of Democratization: Comparative Perspectives*. London & New York: Routledge.

Threlfall, Monica (2008). 'Reassessing the Role of Civil Society Organizations in the Transition to Democracy in Spain', *Democratization*, 15(5), 930–51.

Timmermann, Andreas & Ulrike Müßig (2017). 'Sovereignty Doctrines in the Constitutional Debates Around the Cadiz Cortes: Transition of Monarchical Sovereignty to National Sovereignty', *Giornale di Storia Costituzionale*, 34, 105–35.

Tomás Villarroya, Joaquín (1979). 'Proceso constituyente y nueva Constitución. Un análisis crítico', *Revista de Estudios Políticos*, 10, 59–86.

Tomás Villarroya, Joaquín (1983). 'La publicación de la Constitución de 1837', *Revista de Derecho Político*, 20, 15–31.

Trujillo Fernández, Gumersindo (1994). 'Principio federal y estado autonómico', in *Parlamento y consolidación democrática*, eds. Juan Cano Bueso & Antonio Porras Nadales. Madrid: Tecnos.

Tusell, Javier (2007). *La transición a la democracia (España, 1975–1982)*. Madrid: Espasa.
Urdánoz, Jorge (2019). 'El origen del modelo representativo de la Constitución de 1978', *Revista de Estudios Políticos*, 186, 13–44.
Utrilla de la Hoz, Alfonso (2020). *Cuatro décadas de descentralización fiscal en España: Luces y sombras del Estado de las autonomías*. Logroño: Genueve.
Vallejo Fernández de la Reguera, Jesús (1993). 'Ortografía y heterografía constitucionales (1869)', *Anuario de historia del derecho español*, 63–64, 615–700.
Vampa, Davide (2020). 'Competing Forms of Populism and Territorial Politics: The Cases of Vox and Podemos in Spain', *Journal of Contemporary European Studies*, 28(3), 304–21.
Varela Suanzes-Carpegna, Joaquín (1983). 'La Constitución española de 1837. Una Constitución transaccional', *Revista de Derecho Político*, 20, 95–106.
Varela Suanzes-Carpegna, Joaquín (2005). 'Propiedad, ciudadanía y sufragio en el constitucionalismo español (1810–1845)', *Historia Constitucional*, 6, 105–23.
Varela Suanzes-Carpegna, Joaquín (2006a). 'El Estado en la España del siglo XX', *Revista de Estudios Políticos*, 131, 23–52.
Varela Suanzes-Carpegna, Joaquín (2006b). 'La monarquía en las Cortes y en la Constitución de 1869', *Historia Constitucional*, 7, 209–28.
Varela Suanzes-Carpegna, Joaquín (2013). 'La Constitución de 1876 y la organización territorial del Estado', *Iura Vasconiae*, 10, 11–37.
Varela Suanzes-Carpegna, Joaquín (2014). *Política y Constitución en España (1808–1978)*, 2nd ed. Madrid: Centro de Estudios Políticos y Constitucionales.
Varela Suanzes-Carpegna, Joaquín (2020). *Historia constitucional de España*, ed. Ignacio Fernández Sarasola. Madrid: Marcial Pons.
Vera Santos, José Manuel (2006). 'La influencia del constitucionalismo francés en la fase de reafirmación constitucional española (1837–1845)', *Revista de Derecho Político*, 67, 167–210.
Vilches, Jorge (2015). 'Entre el parlamentarismo y la insurrección. La minoría republicana en las Cortes Constituyentes de la revolución (1869–1871)', *Historia y Política*, 34, 239–67.
Weber, Max ([1922] 2019). *Economy and Society*, trans. Keith Tribe. Cambridge, MA & London: Harvard University Press.
Westler, Brendon (2015). 'Between Tradition and Revolution: The Curious Case of Francisco Martínez Marina, the Cadiz Constitution, and Spanish Liberalism', *Journal of the History of Ideas*, 76(3), 393–416.
Wiesner, Claudia, Taru Haapala & Kari Palonen (2017). *Debates, Rhetoric and Political Action: Practices of Textual Interpretation and Analysis*. London: Palgrave Macmillan.

Zugasti, Ricardo (2012). 'A Forge of Consensus: The Press During the Transition to Democracy in Spain', *Media History*, 18(2), 207–17.

Index

F. J. Bellido, *Constitutional Debates, Rhetoric, and Political Philosophy in Spain's Parliamentary History*, Rhetoric, Politics and Society,
https://doi.org/10.1007/978-3-031-56894-7

D

S

T

U

www.ingramcontent.com/pod-product-compliance
Ingram Content Group UK Ltd.
Pitfield, Milton Keynes, MK11 3LW, UK
UKHW020835290926
15470UKWH00004B/1368
9783031568930